The Laws of
the People's Republic
of China
1983–1986

The Laws of the People's Republic of China

1983–1986

Compiled by

the Legislative Affairs Commission of
the Standing Committee of
the National People's Congress of
the People's Republic of China

FOREIGN LANGUAGES PRESS   BEIJING

First Edition   1987

ISBN 0-8351-1999-8

ISBN 7-119-00289-9

Published by Foreign Languages Press
24 Baiwanzhuang Road, Beijing, China

Distributed by China International Book Trading Corporation
(Guoji Shudian), P.O. Box 399, Beijing, China

Printed in the People's Republic of China

Publication Note

Under the guidance of the policy of promoting socialist democracy and building a sound socialist legal system formulated at the Third Plenary Session of the Eleventh Central Committee of the Chinese Communist Party, the National People's Congress and its Standing Committee have, since 1979, enacted many important laws. Those adopted during the period 1979–86 have been compiled in three collections by the Legislative Affairs Commission of the NPC Standing Committee and have been published in Chinese.

In order to acquaint readers abroad with China's laws and with what China has achieved in building a new legal system, we are now publishing in two volumes an English translation of the Chinese edition of *The Laws of the People's Republic of China*, published by the People's Publishing House, Beijing. The publication note in the Chinese edition is not included

This volume (Vol. 2) includes all the laws, decisions amending or supplementing the laws and other decisions regarding the laws that were adopted by the National People's Congress and its Standing Committee during 1983-86.

This English edition represents a collective effort of many experts, under the aegis of the Legislative Affairs Commission. We wish to pay tribute to the following persons who took part in the revising and finalizing of the translations: Qiu Shaoheng, Li Haopei, Han Depei, Qian Weifan, Zheng Zhaohuang, Dong Shizhong, Chen Gongchuo, Zhang Hongzeng, Yan Zekui, Luo Liang, Zhao Yihe, Tang Bowen, Zhou Lifang, Li Boti, Tang Houzhi, Tang Zongshun, Lin Xiangting, Shao Xunyi, Gao Sunlai, Huang Shiqi, Wang Nongsheng, Jiang Guihua and Gao Yunxiang. We wish to express our sincere thanks to Lydia Chen and Denis Mair, two American experts of the Foreign Languages Press, Beijing, who edited the English translations.

We are also indebted to the many Chinese organizations that provided draft translations of relevant laws. Existing translations were consulted in the process of preparing our translations of some laws. Among them were three books published by the Foreign Languages Press, Beijing, namely *China's Foreign Economic Legislation*, Vols. I and II (1982 and 1986), and *Criminal Law and Criminal Procedure Law of the People's Republic of China* (1984).

All the experts have worked with great care and conscientiousness on

i

this book, endeavouring to produce an accurate translation. However, in a stupendous task like this, oversights are hardly avoidable. Readers are welcome to offer their criticisms.

In case of discrepancy between the English translation and the original Chinese text, the Chinese edition of *The Laws of the People's Republic of China* shall prevail.

The laws promulgated by the National People's Congress and its Standing Committee in 1987 and thereafter will be published in forthcoming volumes.

Legislative Affairs Commission of
the Standing Committee of
the National People's Congress

April 1987

Contents

1983

1984

1985

1986

1983

Maritime Traffic Safety Law of the People's Republic of China

(Adopted at the Second Meeting of the Standing Committee of the Sixth National People's Congress, promulgated by Order No. 7 of the President of the People's Republic of China on September 2, 1983, and effective as of January 1, 1984)

Contents

Chapter I

General Provisions

Article 1 This Law is formulated in order to strengthen the control of maritime traffic; ensure the safety of vessels, installations, human life and property; and safeguard the rights and interests of the state.

Article 2 This Law shall apply to all vessels, installations and personnel and to the owners and managers of such vessels and installations that navigate, berth or operate in the coastal waters of the People's Republic of China.

Article 3 The harbour superintendency agencies of the People's Republic of China shall be the competent authorities responsible for the unified supervision and administration of traffic safety in the coastal waters.

Chapter   II

Inspection and Registration of Vessels

Article 4   Vessels and their major equipment relating to navigation safety must have valid technical certificates issued by vessel inspection departments.

Article 5   A vessel must have a certificate showing its nationality, a vessel registry certificate or a vessel licence.

Chapter   III

Personnel on Vessels and Installations

Article 6   Vessels shall be manned with qualified   crew members according to a standard quota to ensure the vessels' safety.

Article 7   The captain, chief engineer, pilot, engineers, radio and telephone operators and similar personnel on board seaplanes or submersibles must hold valid job certificates.

All other crew members must undergo specialized technical training required for their work.

Article 8   In accordance with state provisions, all installations shall be provided with personnel who have mastered the techniques of collision avoidance, signalling, communications, fire control, life-saving and other operations.

Article 9   All personnel on vessels and installations must observe relevant rules and regulations concerning maritime traffic safety, follow the operating rules and ensure the safety of the vessels and installations in navigation, berthing and operations.

Chapter   IV

Navigation, Berthing and Operations

Article 10   While navigating, berthing or carrying out operations, vessels and installations must abide by the relevant laws, administrative statutes and rules and regulations of the People's Republic of China.

Article 11 Non-military vessels of foreign nationality may not enter the internal waters and harbours of the People's Republic of China without the approval of its competent authorities. However, under unexpected circumstances such as critical illness of personnel, engine breakdown or the vessels being in distress or seeking shelter from weather when they do not have the time to obtain approval, they may, while entering China's internal waters or harbours, make an emergency report to the competent authority and shall obey its directions.

Military vessels of foreign nationality may not enter the territorial waters of the People's Republic of China without the approval of the Government of the People's Republic of China.

Article 12 Vessels sailing on international routes that enter and leave the harbours of the People's Republic of China must accept inspection by the competent authorities. Vessels of Chinese nationality sailing on domestic routes that enter and leave such harbours must obtain port entry and departure visas.

Article 13 Vessels of foreign nationality entering and leaving a harbour of the People's Republic of China, navigating or shifting berths in the harbour area, or approaching or leaving mooring points or loading spots outside the harbour must be navigated by a pilot designated by the competent authority.

Article 14 When entering or leaving harbours or passing through controlled traffic areas, crowded navigable areas or areas where navigational conditions are restricted, vessels must observe the special regulations promulgated by the Government of the People's Republic of China or by the competent authority.

Article 15 Vessels shall be prohibited from entering or passing through restricted navigation zones unless specially permitted by the competent authority.

Article 16 Towing operations on the open sea involving large-sized installations and mobile platforms must undergo towing inspection conducted by vessel inspection departments and be reported to the competent authority for examination and approval.

Article 17 If the competent authority finds the actual condition of a vessel to be not in conformity with what is stated in the vessel's certificates, it shall have the right to require the vessel to apply for a new inspection or notify its owner or manager to adopt effective safety measures.

Article 18 If the competent authority believes that a vessel presents a menace to the safety of a harbour, it shall have the right to forbid the vessel from entering the harbour or to order it to leave the harbour.

Article 19 The competent authority shall have the right to forbid a vessel or an installation from leaving the harbour or order it to suspend its voyage, change its route or cease its operations under any one of the following circumstances:

(1) if it violates any law, administrative statute or other rule or regulation of the People's Republic of China;

(2) if it is in a condition unsuitable for navigation or towing;

(3) if it was involved in a traffic accident and has not completed the necessary formalities;

(4) if it has not paid the fees that are due or furnished appropriate security to the competent authority or the department concerned; or

(5) if the competent authority considers that there are other circumstances that will jeopardize or might jeopardize maritime traffic safety.

Chapter V

Safety Protection

Article 20 Construction operations to be carried out on the surface or underwater in coastal waters and the demarcation of corresponding safe operation zones must be reported to the competent authority for examination and approval and must be publicly announced. Vessels not involved in the construction project may not enter the safe operation zones. The construction unit may not enlarge such zones without authorization.

When shore lines are to be used in harbour areas or when construction work, including overhead operations, is to be carried out on the sea surface or underwater in such areas, the plan and a drawing thereof must be submitted to the competent authority for examination and approval.

Article 21 The designation of restricted navigation zones in coastal waters must be approved by the State Council or the competent authority. However, the designation of restricted navigation zones for military purposes shall be approved by the competent department of the state in charge of military affairs.

The restricted navigation zones shall be announced by the competent authority.

Article 22 Without the approval of the competent authority, no installations may be established or constructed, nor may any activities that hinder navigational safety be carried out in harbour areas, anchorages, navigation lanes, or crowded navigable areas, as well as in navigation routes announced by the competent authority.

With respect to any installations which have been established or constructed in the above-mentioned areas without authorization, the competent authority shall have the right to order their owners to remove or dismantle the installations within a given period.

Article 23 It shall be forbidden to damage navigation aids or navigational facilities. Whoever has damaged navigation aids or navigational facilities shall immediately report the damage to the competent authority and be liable for compensation.

Article 24 Vessels and installations shall promptly make a report to the competent authority if they discover any of the following situations:

(1) if navigation aids or navigational facilities malfunction or become abnormal;

(2) if an obstacle or drifting object jeopardizing the safety of navigation is discovered; or

(3) if there are other abnormal situations jeopardizing the safety of navigation.

Article 25 No obstacle affecting the efficacy of navigation aids may be erected or installed in areas surrounding the aids. Any lights in the vicinity of the navigation aids or navigational lanes that jeopardize navigation safety shall be properly screened.

Article 26 When removing or dismantling installations, salvaging or removing sunken ships or objects, and handling the finishing operations of underwater projects, no hidden dangers shall be left to menace navigational or operational safety. Before the aforesaid operations have been properly completed, their owners or managers must be responsible for erecting markers as required and making an accurate report to the competent authority on the type, shape, size and location of the obstacle and the depth of water over it.

Article 27 Safety administration must be strengthened with respect to harbour wharves, mooring points and loading spots outside of harbour areas as well as ship locks, so that they are always kept in good condition.

Article 28 To meet the requirements of maritime traffic safety, the competent authority shall fix and adjust traffic control areas and harbour anchorages. The designation of anchorages outside of harbour areas shall be announced by the competent authority after the report relative thereto has been submitted to and approved by higher authority.

Article 29 The competent authority shall, in accordance with relevant provisions of the state, be responsible for issuing navigational warnings and navigational notices.

Article 30 In order to ensure the safety of navigation, berthing and operations, the departments concerned shall maintain unimpeded communications facilities, ensure distinct and effective navigation aids and navigational facilities and, in a timely manner, provide offshore meteorological forecasts and necessary books and reference materials concerning maritime navigation.

Article 31 When vessels and installations are involved in accidents that jeopardize or may jeopardize traffic safety, the competent authority shall have the right to take necessary, compulsory measures to deal with the matter.

Chapter VI
Transport of Dangerous Goods

Article 32   When vessels or installations store, load, unload or transport dangerous goods, they must maintain safe and reliable equipment and conditions and observe the state provisions governing the control and transport of dangerous goods.

Article 33   When vessels load and transport dangerous goods, they must go through the procedures for declaration to the competent authority, and they may not enter or leave the harbour or load or unload until approval has been obtained.

Chapter VII
Rescue from Disasters at Sea

Article 34   When vessels, installations or aircraft are in distress, they shall, in addition to issuing distress signals calling for help, use the quickest method possible to report to the competent authority the time and place of the accident, the extent of damage, the assistance required and the cause of the accident.

Article 35   Vessels, installations or aircraft in distress and their owners or managers shall take all effective measures to organize their own rescue efforts.

Article 36   When vessels or installations in the vicinity of the scene of an accident receive a distress signal or discover that people's lives are endangered, they shall do their best to rescue the people in distress insofar as their own safety is not seriously endangered, and promptly report to the competent authority the situation at the scene, their own names, call numbers and positions.

Article 37   Vessels or installations involved in a collision shall exchange their names, nationalities and ports of registry and do their best to rescue personnel in distress. The vessels involved may not leave the scene of the accident without authorization, insofar as their own safety is not seriously endangered.

Article 38   Upon receiving a request for rescue, the competent authority shall immediately organize a rescue operation. All units concerned and vessels or installations in the vicinity of the scene must act under the orders of the competent authority.

Article 39   When a foreign country intends to dispatch vessels or aircraft into the territorial waters or the airspace over the territorial waters of the People's Republic of China to search for and rescue vessels or people in distress, it must obtain the approval of the competent [Chinese] authority.

Chapter VIII

Salvage and Removal of Sunken and Drifting Objects

Article 40   With respect to sunken or drifting objects that may affect the safety of navigation and the management of navigation lanes, as well as those constituting a threat of explosion, the owners or managers thereof shall salvage and remove such objects within a deadline set by the competent authority. Otherwise, the competent authority shall have the right to take measures to compel the salvage and removal of the objects, and their owners or managers shall bear all the expenses incurred thereby.

The provisions of this Article shall not prejudice the rights of the owners or managers of the sunken or drifting objects to demand compensation from third parties.

Article 41   No sunken vessels or sunken objects in the coastal waters may be salvaged or dismantled without the approval of the competent authority.

Chapter IX

Investigation and Handling of Traffic Accidents

Article 42   Any vessel or installation involved in a traffic accident shall submit a written accident report and relative materials to the competent authority and accept its investigation and handling of the accident.

While being investigated by the competent authority, the parties involved in the accident and relevant personnel must give a truthful account of circumstances at the scene of the accident and other relevant information.

Article 43   In the event of a traffic accident that involves a vessel or installation, the competent authority shall ascertain the cause of the accident and fix the responsibility for it.

Chapter   X
Legal Liability

Article 44   The competent authority shall, in the light of the circumstances, impose one or more of the following penalties on anyone who violates this Law:
(1) warnings;
(2) withholding or revoking work certificates; or
(3) fines.

Article 45   If a party does not accept the penalty of a fine or revocation of his work certificate imposed by the competent authority, he may bring suit in a people's court within 15 days after receiving notification of the penalty. If he neither brings suit nor complies with the penalty upon the expiration of that period, the competent authority shall request compulsory enforcement from the people's court.

Article 46   A civil dispute arising from a maritime traffic accident may be settled through mediation by the competent authority. If the parties are unwilling to have the case mediated or if the mediation is unsuccessful, the parties may bring suit in the people's court. Parties to a case involving foreign interests may also submit the case to an arbitration agency for mediation, in accordance with the written agreement concluded between them.

Article 47   Those whose violation of this Law constitutes a crime shall be investigated for their criminal responsibility by judicial organs in accordance with the Law.

Chapter   XI
Special Provisions

Article 48   Within the waters of fishing harbours, the state fisheries administration and fishing harbour superintendency agencies shall exercise the functions and powers of the competent authority as provided in this Law, being responsible for the supervision and administration of traffic safety and for the investigation and handling of traffic accidents between fishing vessels in coastal waters. Concrete measures for implementation shall be separately prescribed by the State Council.

Article 49   The internal administration of offshore military jurisdictional areas and military vessels and installations, the administration of surface and underwater operations carried out for military purposes, and the inspection and registration of public security vessels, the provision of their personnel and the issuing of their port entry and departure visas shall be separately prescribed by the relevant competent departments of the state in accordance with this Law.

Chapter XII

Supplementary Provisions

Article 50   For the purpose of this Law, the definitions of the following terms are:

"Coastal waters" means the harbours, inland waters, territorial waters and all other sea areas under the jurisdiction of the state along the seacoast of the People's Republic of China.

"Vessels" means all types of displacement or non-displacement ships, rafts, seaplanes, submersibles and mobile platforms.

"Installations" means all types of surface and underwater structures or installations, whether fixed or floating, and fixed platforms.

"Operations" means investigations, exploration, exploitation, survey, construction, dredging, demolition, rescue, salvage, towing, fishing, aquatic breeding, loading and unloading, scientific experimentation and other surface and underwater operations.

Article 51   The competent department of the State Council shall, on the basis of this Law, formulate rules for its implementation, which shall go into effect after being submitted to and approved by the State Council.

Article 52   In cases of conflict between laws and regulations pertaining to maritime traffic safety hitherto promulgated and this Law, this Law shall prevail.

Article 53   This Law shall go into effect on January 1, 1984.

Statistics Law of the People's Republic of China

(Adopted at the Third Meeting of the Standing Committee of the Sixth National People's Congress, promulgated by Order No. 9 of the President of the People's Republic of China on December 8, 1983, and effective as of January 1, 1984)

Contents

Chapter   I

General Provisions

Article 1   This Law is formulated in order to organize statistical work in an effective and scientific manner, to ensure accuracy and timeliness of statistical data, to bring into play the important role of statistics in comprehending the actual condition and strength of the country as well as in guiding national economic and social development, and to promote the smooth progress of the socialist modernization.

Article 2   The fundamental task of statistical work is to make statistical investigations and analyses of national economic and social development, to provide statistical data and to exercise statistical supervision.

Article 3   The state organs, public organizations, enterprises, institutions, and self-employed industrialists and businessmen, as well as all foreign-owned enterprises and institutions, all Chinese-foreign equity joint ventures and contractual joint ventures within the territory of China, shall, in accordance with the provisions of this Law and state provisions, provide statistical data. They may not make false entries or conceal statistical data, and they may not report statistical data belatedly or refuse to submit statistical reports. Falsification and tampering of statistical data shall be prohibited.

Autonomous mass organizations at the grass-roots level and citizens have the duty to provide truthful information needed for state statistical investigations.

Article 4   The state shall establish a centralized and unified statistical system, with a statistical administrative structure under unified leadership and with each level assuming responsibility for its own work.

A State Statistical Bureau shall be established under the State Council to be responsible for organizing, directing and coordinating the statistical work throughout the county.

People's governments at all levels and all departments, enterprises and institutions may, according to the needs of their statistical work, set up statistical organs and staff them with statistical personnel.

Article 5   The state shall introduce in a planned way modern techniques of statistical computing and data transmission.

Article 6   Leading members of all localities, departments and units shall direct and supervise statistical organs and personnel and other personnel concerned in enforcing this Law and the rules governing statistical work.

Leading members of all localities, departments and units may not revise the statistical data provided by statistical organs and personnel in accordance with the provisions of this Law and the rules governing statistical work; if they find any error in data computation or in data sources, they shall instruct the statistical organs and personnel and other personnel concerned to make verification and corrections.

Article 7   Statistical organs and personnel shall adopt the system of responsibility for work. They shall, in accordance with the provisions of this Law and the rules governing statistical work, truthfully provide statistical data, accurately and promptly accomplish the task of statistical work and protect state secrets.

In accordance with the provisions of this law, statistical organs and personnel shall exercise, independently and free from interference, their functions and powers with regard to statistical investigations, statistical reports and statistical supervision.

Chapter II

Plans for Statistical Investigations
and the Statistical System

Article 8   Statistical investigations shall be conducted in accordance with an approved plan. A statistical investigation plan shall be drawn up according to statistical investigation items.

State statistical investigation items shall be worked out by the State Statistical Bureau, or by the State Statistical Bureau jointly with the relevant department or departments of the State Council, and shall be submitted to the State Council for examination and approval.

Statistical investigation items of a department shall be worked out, if the units to be investigated lie within its jurisdiction, by the department itself and shall be reported to the State Statistical Bureau or to a statistical organ of a local people's government at the same level for the record; if the units to be investigated lie beyond its jurisdiction, the investigation items shall be worked out by the department and shall be reported to the State Statistical Bureau or to a statistical organ of a local people's government at the same level for examination and approval, but the important items shall be reported to the State Council or a local people's government at the same level for examination and approval.

Local statistical investigation items shall be worked out by statistical organs of local people's governments at or above the county level, or by statistical organs of local people's governments at or above the county level jointly with the relevant department or departments, and shall all be reported to local people's governments at the same level for examination and approval.

In the event of serious natural calamities or other unforeseeable situations, local people's governments at or above the county level may decide to make interim investigations beyond the original plan.

In drawing up a plan for statistical investigation items, it is necessary to draw up simultaneously appropriate statistical investigation forms, which shall be reported to the State Statistical Bureau or a statistical organ of a local people's government at the same level for examination or for the record.

State, departmental and local statistical investigations must be explicitly divided in their functions. They should be made to dovetail with each other and not overlap.

Article 9   For important general surveys of the condition and strength of the country where the joint efforts of different quarters are required, the State Council and local people's governments at various levels shall exercise unified leadership and organize joint execution by statistical organs and other departments concerned.

Article 10   The state shall formulate unified statistical standards to ensure standardization of definitions of statistical items, computing methods, classification catalogues, investigation forms and statistical coding employed in statistical investigations.

The state statistical standards shall be formulated by the State Statistical Bureau or by the State Statistical Bureau jointly with the State Bureau of Standards.

The various departments of the State Council may formulate supplementary departmental statistical standards. Departmental statistical standards may not conflict with the state statistical standards.

Article 11   Establishments concerned have the right to refuse to fill in statistical investigation forms drawn up and issued in violation of this Law and relevant state provisions.

Chapter   III

The Administration and Publication of Statistical Data

Article 12   Statistical data within the scope of state and local statistical investigations shall be separately placed under the unified administration of the State Statistical Bureau, the statistical organs of local people's governments at and above the county level or the statisticians of townships and towns.

Statistical data within the scope of departmental statistical investigations shall be placed under the unified administration of statistical organs or persons in charge of statistics of competent departments.

Statistical data of enterprises and institutions shall be placed under the unified administration of statistical organs or persons in charge of statistics of the enterprises and institutions.

Article 13   Statistical data shall, in accordance with state provisions, be published periodically by the State Statistical Bureau and statistical organs of the people's governments of provinces, autonomous regions and municipalities directly under the Central Government.

Statistical data to be published by various localities, departments and units shall be checked and ratified by the statistical organs or persons in charge of statistics as prescribed in Article 12 of this Law, and shall be submitted for examination and approval according to procedures stipulated by the state.

Article 14   Statistical data pertaining to state secrets must be kept confidential. Single item investigation data concerning any private individual or his/her family shall not be divulged without the consent of the said person.

Chapter   IV

Statistical Organs and Personnel

Article 15   Independent statistical organs shall be established in local people's governments at and above the county level, and people's governments of townships and towns shall be staffed with full-time or part-time statisticians, who shall be responsible for organizing, guiding and coordinating the statistical work in their respective administrative areas.

Article 16   The administrative structure with regard to statistical organs of local people's governments at and above the county level and statisticians of townships and towns shall be specifically prescribed by the State Council.

The sizes of the staff of statistical organs of local people's governments at various levels shall be prescribed by the state in a unified way.

Article 17   The departments of the State Council and local people's governments at various levels shall, according to the needs of their statistical work, establish statistical organs, or staff relevant organs with statistical personnel, and appoint persons in charge of statistics. These statistical organs and persons in charge of statistics are, in statistical work, under the direction of the State Statistical Bureau or statistical organs of local people's governments at the corresponding level.

Article 18   Enterprises and institutions shall, according to the needs of their statistical work, establish statistical organs or staff relevant organs with statistical personnel, and appoint persons in charge of statistics.

Enterprises and institutions shall fulfil state or local statistical investigation tasks and accept the direction of statistical organs of local people's governments.

Article 19   The main functions of the State Statistical Bureau and statistical organs of local people's governments at various levels are as follows:

(1) to draw up plans for statistical investigations and map out and inspect statistical work throughout the country or in their respective administrative areas;

(2) to organize state and local statistical investigations and to collect, compile and provide statistical data of the whole country or of their respective administrative areas;

(3) to make statistical analyses of national economic and social development and to exercise statistical supervision; and

(4) to administer and coordinate work concerning the statistical investigation forms and statistical standards worked out by the various departments.

Statisticians of townships and towns shall, together with personnel concerned, take charge of the statistical work in rural areas at the grass-roots level and accomplish the tasks of state and local statistical investigations.

Article 20   The main functions of statistical organs or persons in charge of statistics of departments of the State Council and local people's governments at various levels are as follows:

(1) to organize and coordinate the statistical work of various functional organs of such departments, to execute the tasks of state and local statistical investigations, to draw up and carry out statistical investigation plans of such departments and to collect, compile and provide statistical data;

(2) to make statistical analyses of and exercise statistical supervision over the implementation of plans of such departments and of the enterprises and institutions under their jurisdiction; and

(3) to organize and coordinate the statistical work of enterprises and institutions under the jurisdiction of such departments and handle statistical investigation forms of such departments.

Article 21 The main functions of statistical organs and persons in charge of statistics of enterprises and institutions are as follows:

(1) to organize and coordinate the statistical work of such units, to execute the tasks of state, departmental and local statistical investigations, and to collect, compile and provide statistical data;

(2) to make statistical analyses of and exercise statistical supervision over the implementation of plans of such units; and

(3) to handle statistical investigation forms of such units, to establish and improve statistical master-file systems and to establish and improve, jointly with organs or persons concerned, original record systems.

Article 22 Statistical personnel have the powers:

(1) to require units or persons concerned to provide data in accordance with state provisions;

(2) to check the accuracy of statistical data and to ask for correction of incorrect statistical data; and

(3) to expose and report any act done in statistical investigation work that contravenes the laws of the state and disrupts the state plan.

Article 23 Statistical personnel should possess the professional knowledge necessary for carrying out statistical tasks. Professional studies should be organized for statistical personnel lacking professional knowledge.

Article 24 Statistical organs of the State Council and of local people's governments at various levels, various departments, enterprises and institutions shall, in accordance with relevant state provisions, evaluate statistical personnel and confer on them appropriate professional titles in order to ensure a fixed number of statistical personnel holding professional titles.

Chapter V

Legal Responsibility

Article 25 Administrative sanctions may be imposed on leading members concerned or personnel bearing direct responsibility for any of the following unlawful practices when the circumstances are rather serious:

(1) making false entries in statistical data or concealing statistical data;

(2) falsifying or tampering with statistical data;

(3) refusing to submit statistical reports or repeated late reporting of statistical data;

(4) infringing upon the functions and powers exercised, as stipulated in this Law, by statistical organs or personnel;

(5) drawing up and distributing by themselves, without authorization and in violation of the provisions of this Law, statistical investigation forms;

(6) publishing by themselves, in violation of the provisions of this Law, unverified and unapproved statistical data; or

(7) violating the provisions of this Law for the protection of secrets.

Any self-employed industrialist or businessman who commits any one of the unlawful practices mentioned in (1), (2) and (3) above may, if the circumstances are serious, and with the approval of a people's government at or above the county level, be punished with suspension of business operations or revocation of his business licence by an administrative department for industry and commerce. If the party concerned does not agree with the decision, it may file suit in a people's court within 15 days from the date of receiving the notification of punishment.

Article 26   Anyone whose contravention of this Law constitutes a criminal offence shall be investigated for his criminal liability by judicial authorities in accordance with the law.

Chapter   VI

Supplementary Provisions

Article 27   The State Statistical Bureau shall, in accordance with this Law, formulate rules for its implementation and submit them to the State Council for approval before they are put into effect.

Article 28   This Law shall go into effect as of January 1, 1984. On that same day, the Regulations on Statistical Work for Trial Implementation promulgated by the State Council in 1963 shall be invalidated.

Decision of the Standing Committee of the National People's Congress on Authorizing the Ministry of Foreign Economic Relations and Trade to Exercise the Power of Ratification of the Former Foreign Investment Commission

(Adopted at the 26th Meeting of the Standing Committee of the Fifth National People's Congress on March 5, 1983)

The 22nd Meeting of the Standing Committee of the Fifth National People's Congress, in its Decision on the Question of Structural Reform of the State Council, decided to establish the Ministry of Foreign Economic Relations and Trade through a merger of the Import and Export Commission, the Ministry of Foreign Trade, the Ministry of Foreign Economic Relations and the Foreign Investment Commission. In view of this, the power of ratification formerly exercised by the Foreign Investment Commission pursuant to the Law of the People's Republic of China on Chinese-Foreign Equity Joint Ventures and other laws and regulations concerning foreign economic relations shall hereafter be exercised accordingly by the Ministry of Foreign Economic Relations and Trade.

Provisions of the Standing Committee of the National People's Congress for the Direct Election of Deputies to People's Congresses at or Below the County Level

(Adopted at the 26th Meeting of the Standing Committee of the Fifth National People's Congress on March 5, 1983)

To facilitate the implementation of the Electoral Law of the National People's Congress and Local People's Congresses of the People's Republic of China, the following provisions are made with respect to certain questions concerning the direct election of deputies to local people's congresses at or below the county level:

1. An election committee shall be established in every county, autonomous county, city not divided into districts, municipal district, township, nationality township and town. Members of the election committee in a county, an autonomous county, a city not divided into districts or a municipal district shall be appointed by the standing committee of the people's congress at the corresponding level. Members of the election committee in a township, a minority nationality township or a town shall be appointed by the standing committee of the people's congress of a county, an autonomous county, a city not divided into districts or a municipal district.

The election committee shall establish an office to handle specific matters related to the election.

2. The functions and powers of an election committee shall be:

(1) assume responsibility for the election of deputies to the people's congress at the corresponding level;

(2) conduct the registration of voters, examine the voters' qualifications and publish the name list of voters; handle and decide on petitions concerning the name list of voters;

(3) divide electoral districts for the election of deputies to the people's congress at the corresponding level and allocate the number of deputies to be elected in each electoral district;

(4) decide on and publish the official list of candidates for deputies on the basis of the opinions of the majority of voters;

(5) fix the date for the election;

(6) determine the validity or invalidity of the election results and publish the names of the deputies elected.

The election committee in a county, autonomous county, city not divided into districts or municipal district directs the work of the election committees of the townships, nationality townships and towns.

3. Mentally ill persons unable to exercise their voting rights shall not do so after confirmation of their cases by an election committee.

4. Upon decision by a people's procuratorate or a people's court, people who are held in custody for involvement in counterrevolutionary cases or in other serious criminal cases and who are subject to investigation, prosecution or trial shall be suspended from exercising their voting rights as long as they are in custody.

5. The following persons shall be allowed to exercise their voting rights:

(1) those who are sentenced to fixed-term imprisonment, who are undergoing criminal detention or who are under public surveillance without the additional penalty of deprivation of political rights;

(2) those who are being held in custody and who are subject to investigation, prosecution or trial without having been suspended from exercising their voting rights by decision of a people's procuratorate or a people's court;

(3) those who are awaiting trial on bail or are subject to residential surveillance;

(4) those who are undergoing rehabilitation through labour; and

(5) those who are being punished by detention.

The above-mentioned persons may participate in the elections at movable ballot boxes or entrust their relatives who have voting rights or other voters to vote on their behalf as may be decided jointly by the election committee and the institutions effecting the imprisonment, custody, detention or rehabilitation through labour. Those who are sentenced to criminal detention, who are being punished by detention or who are undergoing rehabilitation through labour may also go back to their original electoral districts to participate in the elections on the election day.

6. If the people's government of a county or an autonomous county is seated in a city, workers and staff members of its affiliated government agencies, people's organizations, enterprises and institutions may participate in the election of deputies to the people's congress of the county or autonomous county, and not in the election of deputies to the people's congress of a city or a municipal district.

7. The workers and staff members of enterprises and institutions which are located in a township, a nationality township or a town but are not affiliated to a government below the county level may participate only in the election of deputies to the people's congress at the county level, and not in the election of deputies to the people's congress of the township, the

nationality township or the town.

8. The size of an electoral district shall be determined according to the principle that one to three deputies may be elected from each electoral district.

9. With the permission of the election committee of their residential areas, voters who are temporarily doing manual or other work or are living in other places and who cannot go back to their electoral districts to vote may write a statement and entrust their relatives who have voting rights or other voters to vote on their behalf in their respective electoral districts.

Voters who have actually moved out to live in other places but who have not changed their permanent residence registration accordingly may take part in the election in the electoral districts of their present places of residence after obtaining a certificate of their qualifications as voters in their original electoral districts.

10. The number of candidates for deputies recommended by any voter (seconded by three or more voters) shall not exceed the number of deputies to be elected from the electoral district.

All candidates for deputies as recommended by voters or political parties or people's organizations shall be included in the list of candidates for deputies, and the election committees may not replace or delete any of the names or add more names.

Candidates for deputies determined through pre-elections shall be listed officially in order of the number of votes they have received.

Plan for the Allocation of the Number of Deputies to the Sixth National People's Congress Among the Minority Nationalities

(Approved at the 26th Meeting of the Standing Committee of the Fifth National People's Congress on March 5, 1983)

Introduction

The present draft plan has been worked out through consultation with the relevant central departments and provinces, autonomous regions, and municipalities directly under the Central Government, in line with the relevant stipulations of the Fifth Session of the Fifth National People's Congress on the number of deputies to the Sixth National People's Congress and their election and according to the population of the various minority nationalities and their geographical distribution.

1. China has 55 minority nationalities with a total population of more than 67.23 million, which accounts for 6.7 percent of the country's total. In accordance with the stipulation that "the number of deputies to the National People's Congress to be elected from among the minority nationalities shall be around 12 percent of the total number of deputies to the National People's Congress," about 360 deputies should be elected from among the minority nationalities.

2. This draft plan provides for an additional number of 45 deputies from the provinces or autonomous regions of Guangxi, Guizhou, Yunnan, Tibet and Xinjiang, which have a wider range of nationalities but a relatively small population. It allocates one deputy to each of the 30 minority nationalities that have a small population, ensuring at least one deputy from every minority nationality.

3. The draft allocation plan directly allocates 319 deputies of minority nationalities to the provinces, autonomous regions, and municipalities directly under the Central Government. This number and the 26 candidates for minority nationality deputies allocated to the central institutions make a total of 345, which comes to 11.5 percent of the total number of deputies to the National People's Congress. The election of deputies to previous National People's Congresses shows that the actual number of minority nationality deputies elected will be greater than this percentage, as more

23

minority nationality people will be elected than allocated according to a unified plan.

Nationality	Area(s) for allocation	Number of deputies
55 Nationalities	27 provinces, autonomous regions and municipalities	319 (total)
1. Mongol		24 (total)
	Inner Mongolia Autonomous Region	17
	Liaoning Province	3
	Jilin Province	1
	Heilongjiang Province	1
	Qinghai Province	1
	Xinjiang Uygur Autonomous Region	1
2. Hui		37 (total)
	Beijing Municipality	1
	Tianjin Municipality	1
	Hebei Province	3
	Liaoning Province	1
	Shanghai Municipality	1
	Jiangsu Province	1
	Anhui Province	2
	Shandong Province	3
	Henan Province	5
	Yunnan Province	2
	Shaanxi Province	1
	Gansu Province	4
	Qinghai Province	2
	Ningxia Hui Autonomous Region	8
	Xinjiang Uygur Autonomous Region	2
3. Tibetan		26 (total)
	Sichuan Province	6
	Yunnan Province	2
	Tibet Autonomous Region	12
	Gansu Province	2
	Qinghai Province	4
4. Uygur		22 (total)
	Xinjiang Uygur Autonomous Region	22
5. Miao		21 (total)
	Hubei Province	1
	Hunan Province	4
	Guangdong Province	1
	Guangxi Zhuang Autonomous Region	2
	Sichuan Province	2
	Guizhou Province	9

Nationality	Area(s) for allocation	Number of deputies
	Yunnan Province	2
6. Yi		20 (total)
	Sichuan Province	7
	Guizhou Province	3
	Yunnan Province	10
7. Zhuang		44 (total)
	Guangdong Province	1
	Guangxi Zhuang Autonomous Region	41
	Yunnan Province	2
8. Bouyei		8 (total)
	Guizhou Province	8
9. Korean		9 (total)
	Liaoning Province	1
	Jilin Province	6
	Heilongjiang Province	2
10. Manchu		20 (total)
	Beijing Municipality	1
	Hebei Province	2
	Inner Mongolia Autonomous Region	1
	Liaoning Province	10
	Jilin Province	2
	Heilongjiang Province	4
11. Dong		6 (total)
	Hunan Province	1
	Guangxi Zhuang Autonomous Region	1
	Guizhou Province	4
12. Yao		6 (total)
	Hunan Province	1
	Guangdong Province	1
	Guangxi Zhuang Autonomous Region	3
	Yunnan Province	1
13. Bai		4 (total)
	Yunnan Province	4
14. Tujia		14 (total)
	Hubei Province	8
	Hunan Province	4
	Sichuan Province	2
15. Hani		4 (total)
	Yunnan Province	4
16. Kazak		5 (total)
	Xinjiang Uygur Autonomous Region	5
17. Dai		5 (total)
	Yunnan Province	5

Nationality	Area(s) for allocation	Number of deputies
18. Li		5 (total)
	Guangdong Province	5
19. Lisu		2 (total)
	Yunnan Province	2
20. Va		1 (total)
	Yunnan Province	1
21. She		2 (total)
	Zhejiang Province	1
	Fujian Province	1
22. Gaoshan		1 (total)
	Fujian Province	1
23. Lahu		1 (total)
	Yunnan Province	1
24. Shui		1 (total)
	Guizhou Province	1
25. Dong-xiang		1 (total)
	Gansu Province	1
26. Naxi		1 (total)
	Yunnan Province	1
27. Jingpo		1 (total)
	Yunnan Province	1
28. Kirgiz		1 (total)
	Xinjiang Uygur Autonomous Region	1
29. Tu		1 (total)
	Qinghai Province	1
30. Daur		1 (total)
	Inner Mongolia Autonomous Region	1
31. Mulam		1 (total)
	Guangxi Zhuang Autonomous Region	1
32. Qiang		1 (total)
	Sichuan Province	1
33. Blang		1 (total)
	Yunnan Province	1
34. Salar		1 (total)
	Qinghai Province	1
35. Maonan		1 (total)
	Guangxi Zhuang Autonomous Region	1
36. Gelo		1 (total)
	Guizhou Province	1
37. Xibe		1 (total)
	Xinjiang Uygur Autonomous Region	1
38. Achang		1 (total)

Nationality	Area(s) for allocation	Number of deputies
	Yunnan Province	1
39. Pumi		1 (total)
	Yunnan Province	1
40. Tajik		1 (total)
	Xinjiang Uygur Autonomous Region	1
41. Nu		1 (total)
	Yunnan Province	1
42. Uzbek		1 (total)
	Xinjiang Uygur Autonomous Region	1
43. Russian		1 (total)
	Xinjiang Uygur Autonomous Region	1
44. Ewenki		1 (total)
	Inner Mongolia Autonomous Region	1
45. Beng- long		1 (total)
	Yunnan Province	1
46. Bonan		1 (total)
	Gansu Province	1
47. Yugur		1 (total)
	Gansu Province	1
48. Jing		1 (total)
	Guangxi Zhuang Autonomous Region	1
49. Tatar		1 (total)
	Xinjiang Uygur Autonomous Region	1
50. Drung		1 (total)
	Yunnan Province	1
51. Oroqen		1 (total)
	Inner Mongolia Autonomous Region	1
52. Hezhen		1 (total)
	Heilongjiang Province	1
53. Moinba		1 (total)
	Tibet Autonomous Region	1
54. Lhoba		1 (total)
	Tibet Autonomous Region	1
55. Jino		1 (total)
	Yunnan Province	1

Plan for the Consultative Election of Deputies of Taiwan Province to the Sixth National People's Congress

(Approved at the 26th Meeting of the Standing Committee of the Fifth National People's Congress on March 5, 1983)

In accordance with the Resolution of the Fifth Session of the Fifth National People's Congress on the Number of Deputies to the Sixth National People's Congress and the Election of the Deputies, and in light of the explanatory speech given by Yang Shangkun, Vice-Chairman of the Standing Committee of the National People's Congress, for the time being 13 deputies of Taiwan Province will be elected through consultation among people of Taiwan origin in the other provinces, the autonomous regions, and the municipalities directly under the Central Government and in the People's Liberation Army. The deputies will be elected in Beijing through consultation among representatives sent by Taiwan compatriots in these provinces, autonomous regions and municipalities and in the People's Liberation Army.

There are about 22,000 Taiwan compatriots on the mainland, who are residing in the 29 provinces, autonomous regions and municipalities or are in the central Party, government and army institutions. It is determined that about 100 representatives will participate in the consultation. The representatives will be chosen by the standing committees of the people's congresses of the provinces, autonomous regions, and municipalities directly under the Central Government on the basis of the distribution of Taiwan compatriots on the mainland, including those in the army units stationed in various localities. (See attached plan for allocation.)

The conference for consultative election will be convened in Beijing around April 10 and will last about one week.

The consultative election of deputies of Taiwan Province to the Sixth National People's Congress should be conducted in a spirit of democracy. In the discussions on the candidates, consideration should be given to exemplary and influential people in various fields and proper attention paid to the percentages of the young and middle-aged, women and minority nationalities.

In line with the relevant stipulations of the Electoral Law of the

National People's Congress and Local People's Congresses of the People's Republic of China, the deputies shall be elected by secret ballot from among a larger number of candidates.

The conference for consultative election will be called by Lin Liyun, a member of the National People's Congress Standing Committee, while specific affairs concerning the consultative election will be handled by the General Office of the Standing Committee.

Appendix:

Plan for the Allocation of the Number of Representatives Who Will Attend the Conference for the Consultative Election of Deputies of Taiwan Province to the Sixth National People's Congress (*Draft*)

Region or institution	Number of compatriots from Taiwan Province	Number of representatives to take part in the consultation in Beijing
Beijing Municipality	749	7
Tianjin Municipality	671	5
Hebei Province	391	2
Shanxi Province	113	1
Inner Mongolia Autonomous Region	134	1
Liaoning Province	730	5
Jilin Province	250	2
Heilongjiang Province	280	2
Shanghai Municipality	1,553	8
Jiangsu Province	1,256	7
Zhejiang Province	525	2
Anhui Province	517	2
Fujian Province	7,357	14
Jiangxi Province	812	7
Shandong Province	311	2
Henan Province	374	2
Hubei Province	454	2
Hunan Province	427	2
Guangdong Province	2,784	10
Guangxi Zhuang Autonomous Region	209	1

Region or institution	Number of compatriots from Taiwan Province	Number of representatives to take part in the consultation in Beijing
Sichuan Province	524	2
Guizhou Province	153	1
Yunnan Province	272	2
Tibet Autonomous Region	6	1
Shaanxi Province	110	1
Gansu Province	90	1
Qinghai Province	80	1
Ningxia Hui Autonomous Region	29	1
Xinjiang Uygur Autonomous Region	140	1
Institutions under the Central Committee of the Communist Party of China	139	5
State institutions	225	5
General Departments of the People's Liberation Army	160	3
Total	**21,825**	**108**

Decision of the Standing Committee of the National People's Congress on the Early Election of Municipal People's Congresses After the Merger of Prefectures and Cities

(Adopted at the 27th Meeting of the Standing Committee of the Fifth National People's Congress on May 9, 1983)

With a view to facilitating the important reform being carried out, in which prefectures are merged with cities in many provinces and autonomous regions, experimentally in some cases, it is hereby decided that where an early election of the municipal people's congress becomes necessary because of such a merger, it may be decided upon by the standing committee of the people's congress of a province or an autonomous region and reported to the Standing Committee of the National People's Congress for the record.

Decision of the Standing Committee of the National People's Congress Regarding the Severe Punishment of Criminals Who Seriously Endanger Public Security

(Adopted at the Second Meeting of the Standing Committee of the Sixth National People's Congress and promulgated for implementation by Order No. 3 of the President of the People's Republic of China on September 2, 1983)

In order to maintain public security, ensure the safety of the lives and property of the people and safeguard the smooth progress of the socialist construction, it is imperative to subject criminals who seriously endanger public security to severe punishment. To this end it is decided:

1. Punishment above the maximum punishment stipulated in the Criminal Law, up to and including death sentences, may be inflicted on the following criminals who seriously endanger public security:

(1) ringleaders of criminal hooligan groups or those who carry lethal weapons to engage in criminal hooligan activities, if the circumstances are serious, or those who engage in criminal hooligan activities leading to especially serious consequences;

(2) whoever intentionally inflicts serious bodily injury upon another person or causes the person's death, if the circumstances are flagrant, or whoever commits violence and injures a state functionary or citizen who has accused, exposed or arrested a criminal or stopped a criminal act;

(3) ringleaders of groups who abduct and traffic in human beings, or whoever abducts and traffics in human beings, when the circumstances are especially serious;

(4) whoever illegally manufactures, trades in, transports, steals or forcibly seizes guns, ammunition or explosives, when the circumstances are especially serious or when serious consequences are caused;

(5) whoever organizes reactionary secret societies or uses feudal superstition to carry on counterrevolutionary activities, thereby seriously endangering public security; or

(6) whoever lures or forces a woman into prostitution or shelters her in prostitution, when the circumstances are especially serious.

2. Whoever imparts criminal methods, when the circumstances are

relatively minor, shall be sentenced to fixed-term imprisonment of not more than five years; when the circumstances are serious, the offender shall be sentenced to fixed-term imprisonment of not less than five years; and when the circumstances are especially serious, he shall be sentenced to life imprisonment or death.

3. This Decision shall, upon its promulgation, be applicable to the adjudication of the criminal cases mentioned above.

Appendix:

The Relevant Articles in the Criminal Law

Article 160　Where an assembled crowd engages in affrays, creates disturbances, humiliates women or engages in other hooligan activities that undermine public order, if the circumstances are flagrant, the offenders shall be sentenced to fixed-term imprisonment of not more than seven years, criminal detention or public surveillance.

Ringleaders of hooligan groups shall be sentenced to fixed-term imprisonment of not less than seven years.

Article 134　Whoever intentionally inflicts bodily injury upon another person shall be sentenced to fixed-term imprisonment of not more than three years or criminal detention.

Whoever, by committing the crime mentioned in the preceding paragraph, causes severe injury to another person shall be sentenced to fixed-term imprisonment of not less than three years and not more than seven years; if he causes a person's death, he shall be sentenced to fixed-term imprisonment of not less than seven years or life imprisonment. Where this Law has other provisions, such provisions shall prevail.

Article 141　Whoever abducts and traffics in human beings shall be sentenced to fixed-term imprisonment of not more than five years; if the circumstances are serious, the offender shall be sentenced to fixed-term imprisonment of not less than five years.

Article 112　Whoever illegally manufactures, trades in or transports guns or ammunition or steals or forcibly seizes the guns or ammunition of state organs, members of the armed forces, the police or the people's militia shall be sentenced to fixed-term imprisonment of not more than seven years; if the circumstances are serious, the offender shall be sentenced to fixed-term imprisonment of not less than seven years or life imprisonment.

Article 99　Whoever organizes or uses feudal superstition, superstitious sects or secret societies to carry on counterrevolutionary activities shall be sentenced to fixed-term imprisonment of not less than five years; if the circumstances are relatively minor, the offender shall be sentenced to fixed-term imprisonment of not more than five years, criminal detention, public surveillance or deprivation of political rights.

Article 140   Whoever forces a woman to engage in prostitution shall be sentenced to fixed-term imprisonment of not less than three years and not more than ten years.

Article 169   Whoever, for the purpose of profit, lures women into prostitution or shelters them in prostitution shall be sentenced to fixed-term imprisonment of not more than five years, criminal detention or public surveillance; if the circumstances are serious, the offender shall be sentenced to fixed-term imprisonment of not less than five years and may concurrently be sentenced to a fine or confiscation of property.

Decision of the Standing Committee of the National People's Congress Regarding the Procedure for Prompt Adjudication of Cases Involving Criminals Who Seriously Endanger Public Security

(Adopted at the Second Meeting of the Standing Committee of the Sixth National People's Congress and promulgated for implementation by Order No. 4 of the President of the People's Republic of China on September 2, 1983)

In order to quickly and severely punish criminals who seriously endanger public security and to safeguard the interests of the state and the people, it is hereby decided:

1. In cases of criminals who cause explosions or commit murder, rape, robbery or other crimes seriously endangering public security and who are punishable by death, where the main facts of the crimes are clear, the evidence is conclusive and the popular indignation is exceedingly great, they shall be quickly brought to trial, and the restrictions provided in Article 110 of the Criminal Procedure Law regarding the time limit for the delivery to the defendant of a copy of the bill of prosecution and the time limit for the delivery of the summons and notices may be overstepped.

2. The time limit for appeal by the criminals listed in the preceding paragraph and the time limit for the people's procuratorates to present a protest shall be changed to three days from the ten days provided in Article 131 of the Criminal Procedure Law.

Appendix:

The Relevant Articles in the Criminal Procedure Law

Article 110   After a people's court has decided to open a court session, it shall proceed with the following work:

. . . .

(2) to deliver to the defendant a copy of the bill of prosecution of the people's procuratorate no later than seven days before the opening of the court session and inform the defendant that he may appoint a defender or, when necessary, designate a defender for him;

(3) to notify the people's procuratorate of the time and place of the court session three days before the opening of the session;

(4) to summon the parties and notify the defenders, witnesses, expert witnesses and interpreters, with the summons and notices to be delivered no later than three days before the opening of the court session;

. . . .

Article 131   The time limit for an appeal or a protest against a judgment shall be ten days and the time limit for an appeal or a protest against an order shall be five days; the time limit shall be counted from the day after the written judgment or order is received.

Decision of the Standing Committee of the National People's Congress Regarding the Revision of the Organic Law of the People's Courts of the People's Republic of China

(Adopted at the Second Meeting of the Standing Committee of the Sixth National People's Congress and promulgated for implementation by Order No. 5 of the President of the People's Republic of China on September 2, 1983)

The Second Meeting of the Standing Committee of the Sixth National People's Congress has decided to make the following amendments to the Organic Law of the People's Courts of the People's Republic of China:

1. Item (2), Paragraph 1 of Article 2, which reads "special people's courts; and" is amended as "military courts and other special people's courts; and."

Delete Paragraph 3 of Article 2, which reads, "The special people's courts shall include military courts, railway transport courts, water transport courts, forest affairs courts and other special courts."

2. Article 4, which reads, "The people's courts shall administer justice independently, subject only to the law," is amended as: "The people's courts shall exercise judicial power independently, in accordance with the provisions of the law, and shall not be subject to interference by any administrative organ, public organization or individual."

3. Delete Article 9, which reads, "The people's courts shall adopt a system of people's assessors in all cases of first instance, with the exception of simple civil cases, minor criminal cases and cases otherwise provided for by law."

Paragraph 2 of Article 10, which reads, "Cases of first instance in the people's courts shall be tried by a collegial panel of judges and people's assessors, with the exception of simple civil cases, minor criminal cases and cases otherwise provided for by law," is amended as: "Cases of first instance in the people's courts shall be tried by a collegial panel of judges or of judges and people's assessors; simple civil cases, minor criminal cases and cases otherwise provided for by law may be tried by a single judge."

4. Article 13, which reads, "Cases involving death sentences shall be tried or approved by the Supreme People's Court. The procedure for review

of death sentences shall comply with the provisions of Chapter IV, Part Three of the Criminal Procedure Law of the People's Republic of China," is amended as: "Cases involving sentences of death, except for those cases where the sentences are imposed by the Supreme People's Court, shall be submitted to the Supreme People's Court for approval. The Supreme People's Court may, when it deems it necessary, authorize higher people's courts of provinces, autonomous regions, and municipalities directly under the Central Government to exercise the power to approve cases involving the imposition of death sentences for homicide, rape, robbery, causing explosions and others gravely endangering public security and disrupting social order."

5. Delete Paragraph 3 of Article 17, which reads, "The judicial administrative work of the people's courts at various levels shall be directed by the judicial administrative organs."

6. Paragraph 2 of Article 19, which reads, "A basic people's court may set up a criminal division and a civil division, each with a chief judge and associate chief judges," is amended as: "A basic people's court may set up a criminal division, a civil division and an economic division, each with a chief judge and associate chief judges."

7. Item (2) of Article 22, which reads, "to direct the work of people's mediation committees and judicial assistants of people's communes, and," is amended as: "to direct the work of people's mediation committees."

Delete Item (3), which reads, "Control judicial administrative work within the scope of the functions and powers authorized by higher judicial administrative organs."

8. Paragraph 2 of Article 24, which reads, "Each intermediate people's court shall set up a criminal division and a civil division, and such other divisions as are deemed necessary," is amended as: "Each intermediate people's court shall set up a criminal division, a civil division and an economic division, and such other divisions as are deemed necessary."

Delete Paragraph 3, which reads, "Each intermediate people's court of a municipality directly under the Central Government and each intermediate people's court of a municipality under the jurisdiction of a province or autonomous region shall set up an economic division."

9. A second paragraph is added to Article 34, which reads, "Judicial personnel of people's courts must have an adequate knowledge of the law."

10. Paragraph 1 of Article 37, which reads, "People's courts at all levels may, according to their needs, be staffed with assistant judges, who shall be appointed or removed by the judicial administrative organs," is amended as: "People's courts at all levels may, according to their needs, be staffed with assistant judges, who shall be appointed or removed by the people's courts themselves."

11. Delete Article 42, which reads, "The establishment of people's

courts at all levels and their authorized number of personnel and administrative offices shall be separately stipulated by the judicial administrative organs."

Appendix:

Organic Law of the People's Courts of the People's Republic of China

(Adopted at the Second Session of the Fifth National People's Congress on July 1, 1979, and revised according to the Decision Concerning the Revision of the Organic Law of the People's Courts of the People's Republic of China adopted at the Second Meeting of the Sixth National People's Congress on September 2, 1983)

Contents

Chapter I   General Provisions
Chapter II   Organization, Functions and Powers of the People's Courts
Chapter III   Judicial and Other Personnel of People's Courts

Chapter I

General Provisions

Article 1   The people's courts of the People's Republic of China are the judicial organs of the state.

Article 2   The judicial authority of the People's Republic of China is exercised by the following people's courts:

(1) local people's courts at various levels;

(2) military courts and other special people's courts (*revised on September 2, 1983*); and

(3) the Supreme People's Courts.

The local people's courts at various levels are divided into: basic people's courts, intermediate people's courts and higher people's courts.

(*Paragraph 3 was deleted on September 2, 1983.*)

Article 3   The task of the people's courts is to try criminal and civil cases and, through judicial activities, to punish all criminals and settle civil disputes, so as to safeguard the system of dictatorship of the proletariat, maintain the socialist legal system and public order, protect socialist property owned by the whole people, collective property owned by working people and the legitimate private property of citizens, the citizens' right of the person and their democratic and other rights, and ensure the smooth progress of the socialist revolution and socialist construction in the country.

The people's courts, in all their activities, educate citizens in loyalty to their socialist motherland and voluntary observance of the Constitution and the law.

Article 4   The people's courts shall exercise judicial power independently, in accordance with the provisions of the law, and shall not be subject to interference by any administrative organ, public organization or individual. (*Revised on September 2, 1983.*)

Article 5   In judicial proceedings in the people's courts, the law is applied equally to all citizens, regardless of ethnic status, race, sex, occupation, family background, religious belief, education, property status or length of residence. No privilege whatsoever is allowed.

Article 6   Citizens of all nationalities have the right to use the spoken and written languages of their own nationalities in court proceedings. The people's courts shall provide translation for any party to the court proceedings who is not familiar with the spoken or written languages commonly used in the locality. In an area where people of a minority nationality live in concentrated communities or where a number of minority nationalities live together, the people's courts shall conduct hearings in the language or languages commonly used in the locality and issue judgments, notices and other documents in the language or languages commonly used in the locality.

Article 7   All cases in the people's courts shall be heard in public, except for those involving state secrets, private affairs of individuals and the commission of crimes by minors.

Article 8   The accused has the right to defence. Besides defending himself, the accused has the right to delegate a lawyer to defend him. He may also be defended by a citizen recommended by a people's organization or his place of employment, by a citizen approved by the people's court, or by a near relative or guardian. The people's court may also, when it deems it necessary, appoint a counsel to defend him.

Article 9   (*Deleted on September 2, 1983.*)

Article 10   The people's courts adopt the collegial system in the administration of justice.

Cases of first instance in the people's courts shall be tried by a collegial panel of judges or of judges and people's assessors; simple civil cases, minor criminal cases and cases otherwise provided for by law may be tried by a single judge. (*Revised on September 2, 1983.*)

Appealed or contested cases in the people's courts are handled by a collegial panel of judges.

The president of the court or the chief judge of a division appoints one of the judges to act as the presiding judge of the collegial panel. When the president of the court or the chief judge of a division participates in the judicial proceedings, he acts as the presiding judge.

Article 11   People's courts at all levels set up judicial committees which practise democratic centralism. The task of the judicial committees is to sum up judicial experience and to discuss important or difficult cases and other issues relating to the judicial work.

Members of judicial committees of local people's courts at various levels are appointed and removed by the standing committees of the people's congresses at the corresponding levels, upon the recommendation of the presidents of these courts. Members of the Judicial Committee of the Supreme People's Court are appointed and removed by the Standing Committee of the National People's Congress, upon the recommendation of the President of the Supreme People's Court.

The presidents of the people's courts preside over meetings of judicial committees of the people's courts at all levels; the chief procurators of the people's procuratorates at the corresponding levels may attend such meetings without voting rights.

Article 12   In the administration of justice, the people's courts adopt the system whereby the second instance is the last instance.

From a judgment or orders of first instance of a local people's court, a party may bring an appeal to the people's court at the next higher level in accordance with the procedure prescribed by law, and the people's procuratorate may present a protest to the people's court at the next higher level in accordance with the procedure prescribed by law.

Judgments and orders of first instance of the local people's courts at various levels become legally effective judgments and orders if, within the period for appeal, none of the parties has appealed and the procuratorate has not protested.

Judgments and orders of second instance of intermediate courts, higher people's courts and the Supreme People's Court and judgments and orders of first instance of the Supreme People's Court are all judgments and orders of last instance, that is, legally effective judgments and orders.

Article 13   Cases involving sentences of death, except for cases with sentences imposed by the Supreme People's Court, shall be submitted to the Supreme People's Court for approval. The Supreme People's Court may, when it deems it necessary, authorize higher people's courts of provinces, autonomous regions, and municipalities directly under the Central Government to exercise the power to approve cases involving the imposition of death sentences for homicide, rape, robbery, causing explosions and others gravely endangering public security and disrupting social order. (*Revised on September 2, 1983.*)

Article 14   If the president of a people's court finds, in a legally effective judgment or order of his court, some definite error in the determination of facts or application of law, he must submit the judgment or order to the judicial committee for disposal.

If the Supreme People's Court finds some definite error in a legally effective judgment or order of the people's court at a lower level or if the people's court at a higher level finds such error in a legally effective judgment or order of the people's court at a lower level, it has the authority to review the case itself or to direct the lower-level people's court to conduct a retrial.

If the Supreme People's Procuratorate finds some definite error in a legally effective judgment or order of a people's court at any level or if the people's procuratorate at a higher level finds such error in a legally effective judgment or order of any people's court at a lower level, it has the authority to lodge a protest in accordance with the procedure of judicial supervision.

The people's courts at all levels shall hold themselves responsible for seriously handling a petition lodged by a party to a case against a legally effective judgment or order.

Article 15   If a people's court considers that the principal facts of a case in which a people's procuratorate has initiated a public prosecution are not clear and the evidence is insufficient, or there are illegalities in the prosecution, the court may remand the case to the people's procuratorate for supplementary investigation or notify the people's procuratorate to rectify them.

Article 16   If a party to a case considers that a member of the judicial personnel has an interest in the case or, for any other reason, cannot administer justice impartially, he has the right to ask that member to withdraw. The president of the court shall decide whether the member should withdraw.

If a member of the judicial personnel considers that he should withdraw because he has an interest in the case or for any other reason, he should report the matter to the president of the court for decision.

Article 17   The Supreme People's Court is responsible to and reports on its work to the National People's Congress and its Standing Committee. Local people's courts are responsible to and report on their work to the local people's congresses at corresponding levels and their standing committees.

The judicial work of people's courts at lower levels is subject to supervision by people's courts at higher levels.

(*Paragraph 3 was deleted on September 2, 1983.*)

Chapter II

Organization, Functions and Powers of the People's Courts

Article 18　Basic people's courts are:

(1) county people's courts and municipal people's courts;

(2) people's courts of autonomous counties; and

(3) people's courts of municipal districts.

Article 19　A basic people's court is composed of a president, vice-presidents and judges.

A basic people's court may set up a criminal division, a civil division and an economic division, each with a chief judge and associate chief judges. (*Revised on September 2, 1983.*)

Article 20　A basic people's court may set up a number of people's tribunals according to the conditions of the locality, population and cases. A people's tribunal is a component part of the basic people's court, and its judgments and orders are judgments and orders of the basic people's courts.

Article 21　Except for cases otherwise provided for by laws or decrees, a basic people's court adjudicates criminal and civil cases of first instance.

When a basic people's court considers that a criminal or civil case it is handling is of major importance and requires trial by the people's court at a higher level, it may request that the case be transferred to that court for trial.

Article 22　Besides trying cases, a basic people's court undertakes the following tasks:

(1) settling civil disputes and handling minor criminal cases that do not need to be determined by trials;

(2) directing the work of people's mediation committees. (*Revised on September 2, 1983.*)

(*Item (3) was deleted on September 2, 1983.*)

Article 23　Intermediate people's courts are:

(1) intermediate people's courts established in prefectures of a province or autonomous region;

(2) intermediate people's courts established in municipalities directly under the Central Government;

(3) intermediate people's courts of municipalities directly under the jurisdiction of a province or autonomous region; and

(4) intermediate people's courts of autonomous prefectures.

Article 24　An intermediate people's court is composed of a president, vice-presidents, chief judges and associate chief judges of divisions, and judges.

Each intermediate people's court shall set up a criminal division, a civil division, an economic division, and such other divisions as are deemed necessary. (*Revised on September 2, 1983.*)

(*Paragraph 3 was deleted on September 2, 1983.*)

Article 25   An intermediate people's court handles the following cases:

(1) cases of first instance assigned by laws and decrees to their jurisdiction;

(2) cases of first instance transferred from the basic people's courts;

(3) cases of appeals and of protests lodged against judgments and orders of the basic people's courts; and

(4) cases of protests lodged by the people's procuratorates in accordance with the procedures of judicial supervision.

When an intermediate people's court considers that a criminal or civil case it is handling is of major importance and requires trial by the people's court at a higher level, it may request that the case be transferred to that court for trial.

Article 26   Higher people's courts are:

(1) higher people's courts of provinces;

(2) higher people's courts of autonomous regions; and

(3) higher people's courts of municipalities directly under the Central Government.

Article 27   A higher people's court is composed of a president, vice-presidents, chief judges and associate chief judges of divisions, and judges.

A higher people's court shall set up a criminal division, a civil division, an economic division, and such other divisions as are deemed necessary.

Article 28   A higher people's court handles the following cases:

(1) cases of first instance assigned by laws and decrees to their jurisdiction;

(2) cases of first instance transferred from people's courts at lower levels;

(3) cases of appeals and of protests lodged against judgments and orders of people's courts at lower levels; and

(4) cases of protests lodged by people's procuratorates in accordance with the procedures of judicial supervision.

Article 29   The organization, functions and powers of special people's courts shall be prescribed separately by the Standing Committee of the National People's Congress.

Article 30   The Supreme People's Court is the highest judicial organ of the state.

The Supreme People's Court supervises the administration of justice by the local people's courts at various levels and by the special people's courts.

Article 31   The Supreme People's Court is composed of a president, vice-presidents, chief judges and associate chief judges of divisions, and judges.

The Supreme People's Court shall set up a criminal division, a civil division, an economic division, and such other divisions as are deemed necessary.

Article 32 The Supreme People's Court handles the following cases:

(1) cases of first instance assigned by laws and decrees to its jurisdiction and which it considers should itself try;

(2) cases of appeals and of protests lodged against judgments and orders of higher people's courts and special people's courts; and

(3) cases of protests lodged by the Supreme People's Procuratorate in accordance with the procedures of judicial supervision.

Article 33 The Supreme People's Court gives interpretation on questions concerning specific application of laws and decrees in judicial proceedings.

Chapter III

Judicial and Other Personnel of People's Courts

Article 34 Citizens who have the right to vote and to stand for election and have reached the age of 23 are eligible to be elected presidents of people's courts or appointed vice-presidents of people's courts, chief judges or associate chief judges of divisions, judges or assistant judges; but persons who have ever been deprived of political rights are excluded.

Judicial personnel of people's courts must have an adequate knowledge of the law. (*This paragraph was added on September 2, 1983.*)

Article 35 Presidents of local people's courts at various levels are elected by the local people's congresses at corresponding levels, and their vice-presidents, chief judges and associate chief judges of divisions, and judges are appointed and removed by the standing committees of the local people's congresses at corresponding levels.

Presidents of intermediate people's courts established in prefectures of provinces or in municipalities directly under the Central Government are elected by the people's congresses of the provinces and municipalities directly under the Central Government, and their vice-presidents, chief judges and associate chief judges of divisions, and judges are appointed and removed by the standing committees of the people's congresses of the provinces and municipalities directly under the Central Government.

Presidents of local people's courts at various levels established in national autonomous areas are elected by local people's congresses at corresponding levels in these areas, and their vice-presidents, chief judges and associate chief judges of divisions, and judges are appointed or removed by the standing committees of local people's congresses at corresponding levels in these areas.

The President of the Supreme People's Court is elected by the National People's Congress, and its vice-presidents, chief judges and associate chief judges of divisions, and judges are appointed or removed by the Standing Committee of the National People's Congress.

Article 36   The term of office of presidents of people's courts at all levels is the same as that of people's congresses at corresponding levels.

People's congresses at all levels have the power to remove from office the presidents of people's courts elected by them. If the standing committee of a people's congress deems it necessary to replace the president of a local people's court at the corresponding level when the congress is not in session, it shall report the matter to the people's court at the next higher level for submission to the standing committee of the people's congress at the next higher level for approval.

Article 37   People's courts at all levels may, according to their needs, be staffed with assistant judges, who shall be appointed or removed by the people's courts themselves. (*Revised on September 2, 1983.*)

Assistant judges help the judges in their work. Upon the recommendation of the president of the court and with the approval of the judicial committee, an assistant judge may provisionally exercise the functions of a judge.

Article 38   Citizens who have the right to vote and to stand for election and have reached the age of 23 are eligible to be elected people's assessors, but persons who have ever been deprived of political rights are excluded.

During the period of the exercise of their functions in the people's courts, the people's assessors are members of the divisions of the courts in which they participate, and enjoy equal rights with the judges.

Article 39   During the period of the exercise of their functions, the people's assessors continue to receive wages as usual from their regular place of employment; people's assessors who are not wage-earners are given reasonable allowances by the people's courts.

Article 40   People's courts at all levels have clerks to keep records of the court proceedings and to take charge of other matters concerning the trials.

Article 41   Local people's courts at various levels have marshals to carry out the execution of judgments and orders in civil cases and the execution, in criminal cases, of the parts of judgments and orders concerned with property.

Local people's courts at various levels have forensic physicians.

People's courts at all levels have a certain number of judicial policemen.

Article 42   (*Deleted on September 2, 1983.*)

Decision of the Standing Committee of the National People's Congress on the Revision of the Organic Law of the People's Procuratorates of the People's Republic of China

(Adopted at the Second Meeting of the Sixth National People's Congress and promulgated for implementation by Order No. 6 of the President of the People's Republic of China on September 2, 1983)

The Second Meeting of the Standing Committee of the Sixth National People's Congress has decided to make the following revisions in the Organic Law of the People's Procuratorates of the People's Republic of China:

1. Paragraph 1 of Article 2, which reads, "The People's Republic of China shall establish the Supreme People's Procuratorate, people's procuratorates at various local levels and special people's procuratorates," is amended as: "The People's Republic of China shall establish the Supreme People's Procuratorate, people's procuratorates at various local levels, military procuratorates and other special people's procuratorates."

Paragraph 4, which reads, "Special people's procuratorates shall include: military procuratorates, railway transport procuratorates, waterway transport procuratorates and other special procuratorates," is deleted.

2. Paragraph 1 of Article 20, which reads, "The Supreme People's Procuratorate shall establish procuratorial departments in charge of criminal, legal and disciplinary, prison and reformatory, and economic affairs, and may also establish other professional agencies as needed," and Paragraph 2, which reads, "People's procuratorates at various local levels and special people's procuratorates may establish corresponding professional agencies," are amended as: "The Supreme People's Procuratorate shall establish a number of procuratorial departments and other professional agencies as needed. The people's procuratorates at various local levels may respectively establish corresponding procuratorial divisions, sections and other professional agencies."

3. Paragraph 2 of Article 22, which reads, "The appointment and removal of the chief procurators, deputy chief procurators and members of the procuratorial committees of the people's procuratorates of provinces, autonomous regions, and municipalities directly under the Central Government shall be reported to the Procurator-General of the Supreme People's Procuratorate for submission to the Standing Committee of the National

47

People's Congress for approval," is amended as: "The appointment and removal of the chief procurators of the people's procuratorates of provinces, autonomous regions, and municipalities directly under the Central Government shall be reported to the Procurator-General of the Supreme People's Procuratorate for submission to the Standing Committee of the National People's Congress for approval."

4. Paragraph 2 of Article 23, which reads, "The appointment and removal of the chief procurators, deputy chief procurators and members of the procuratorial committees of the people's procuratorates of autonomous prefectures, cities directly under the provincial governments, counties, cities and municipal districts shall be reported to the chief procurators of the people's procuratorates of provinces, autonomous regions, and municipalities directly under the Central Government for submission to the standing committee of the people's congress at the corresponding level for approval," is amended as: "The appointment and removal of the chief procurators of the people's procuratorates of autonomous prefectures, cities directly under the provincial governments, counties, cities and municipal districts shall be reported to the chief procurators of the people's procuratorates at the next higher level for submission to the standing committee of the people's congress at the corresponding level for approval."

Appendix:

Organic Law of the People's Procuratorates of the People's Republic of China

(Adopted at the Second Session of the Fifth National People's Congress on July 1, 1979, and amended according to the Decision on the Revision of the Organic Law of the People's Procuratorates of the People's Republic of China adopted at the Second Meeting of the Standing Committee of the Sixth National People's Congress on September 2, 1983)

Contents

Chapter I

General Provisions

Article 1 The people's procuratorates of the People's Republic of China are state organs for legal supervision.

Article 2 The People's Republic of China shall establish the Supreme People's Procuratorate, the people's procuratorates at various local levels, military procuratorates and other special people's procuratorates. (*Amended on September 2, 1983.*)

The people's procuratorates at various local levels shall be divided into:

(1) people's procuratorates of provinces, autonomous regions, and municipalities directly under the Central Government;

(2) branches of the people's procuratorates of provinces, autonomous regions, and municipalities directly under the Central Government, and people's procuratorates of autonomous prefectures and cities directly under the provincial governments; and

(3) people's procuratorates of counties, cities, autonomous counties and municipal districts.

People's procuratorates at the provincial or county level may, according to work requirements and upon the approval of the standing committee of the people's congress at the corresponding level, set up people's procuratorates as their agencies in industrial and mining areas, agricultural reclamation areas, forest zones, etc. (*A paragraph was deleted here on September 2, 1983.*)

The establishment, organization, functions and powers of special people's procuratorates shall be stipulated separately by the Standing Committee of the National People's Congress.

Article 3 People's procuratorates at all levels shall each have a chief procurator, a number of deputy chief procurators* and procurators. The chief procurator exercises unified leadership over the work of the procuratorates.

People's procuratorates at all levels shall each set up a procuratorial committee. The procuratorial committee shall apply the system of democratic centralism and, under the direction of the chief procurator, hold discussions and make decisions on important cases and other major issues. In the case of the chief procurator disagreeing with the majority's opinion over a decision on an important issue, the matter may be reported to the standing committee of the people's congress at the corresponding level for

---

* The leading officials of the Supreme People's Procuratorate are the Procurator-General and Deputy Procurators-General.—*Trans.*

final decision.

Article 4   The people's procuratorates shall, through exercising their procuratorial authority, suppress all treasonous activities, all activities to dismember the state and other counterrevolutionary activities, and strike at counterrevolutionaries and other criminals, so as to safeguard the unification of the country, the system of proletarian dictatorship and the socialist legal system; to maintain public order and order in production, education, scientific research and other work, and in the life of the people; to protect socialist property owned by the whole people and by the collectives of the working masses, and the private property lawfully owned by citizens; to protect the citizens' rights of the person and their democratic and other rights; and to ensure the smooth progress of socialist modernization.

The people's procuratorates, through procuratorial activities, educate the citizens to be loyal to their socialist motherland, to consciously observe the Constitution and the laws and to actively fight against illegal activities.

Article 5   People's procuratorates at all levels shall exercise the following functions and powers:

(1) exercise procuratorial authority over cases of treason, cases involving acts to dismember the state and other major criminal cases severely impeding the unified enforcement of state policies, laws, decrees and administrative orders;

(2) conduct investigations of criminal cases handled directly by themselves;

(3) review cases investigated by public security organs and determine whether to approve arrest, to prosecute or to exempt from prosecution; exercise supervision over the investigatory activities of public security organs to determine whether they conform to the law;

(4) initiate public prosecutions of criminal cases and support such prosecutions; exercise supervision over the judicial activities of people's courts to determine whether they conform to the law; and

(5) exercise supervision over the execution of judgments and orders in criminal cases and over the activities of prisons, detention houses and organs in charge of reform through labour to determine whether such execution and activities conform to the law.

Article 6   People's procuratorates shall, in accordance with the law, protect citizens' rights to lodge complaints against state functionaries who break the law and shall investigate the legal responsibility of those persons who infringe upon other citizens' rights of the person and their democratic and other rights.

Article 7   People's procuratorates must, in executing their work, persistently seek truth from facts, follow the mass line, heed the opinions of the masses and subject themselves to supervision by the masses; investigate and study, laying stress on evidence rather than readily giving credence to oral statements and strictly forbidding the obtainment of confessions by compulsion; and correctly differentiate and handle contradictions between the enemy and the people, and those among the people themselves.

The functionaries of the people's procuratorates at all levels must pay high regard to actual facts and the law, be faithful to the socialist cause and serve the people wholeheartedly.

Article 8   In the exercise of procuratorial authority by people's procuratorates at all levels, the law shall be applied equally to all citizens, and no privileges shall be allowed.

Article 9   The people's procuratorates shall exercise procuratorial authority independently, in accordance with the provisions of the law, and shall not be subject to interference by any administrative organ, public organization or individual.

Article 10   The Supreme People's Procuratorate shall be responsible to and report on its work to the National People's Congress and its Standing Committee. The people's procuratorates at various local levels shall be responsible to and report on their work to the people's congresses and their standing committees at corresponding levels.

The Supreme People's Procuratorate shall direct the work of the people's procuratorates at various local levels and of the special people's procuratorates; the people's procuratorates at higher levels shall direct the work of those at lower levels.

Chapter II

Procedures for People's Procuratorates in Exercising Their Functions and Powers

Article 11   If a people's procuratorate finds and confirms that a criminal act has been committed, it shall place the case on file for investigation in accordance with the procedure provided by law, or transfer it to a public security organ for investigation. If, upon conclusion of the investigation, the people's procuratorate deems it necessary to investigate criminal responsibility, it shall initiate a public prosecution in the people's court, or it shall rescind the case, if it deems it unnecessary to investigate criminal responsibility.

Article 12   The arrest of any citizen, unless decided on by a people's court, must be subject to the approval of a people's procuratorate.

Article 13   A people's procuratorate shall review the cases for which a public security organ requests prosecution and decide whether to initiate public prosecution, to exempt from prosecution or not to initiate prosecution. It may remand a case to the public security organ for supplementary investigation if the main facts of the crime are not clear or the evidence is insufficient.

If a people's procuratorate discovers violations of the law in the investigatory activities of a public security organ, it shall instruct that public security organ to rectify them.

Article 14   If a public security organ considers that there is an error in a decision of a people's procuratorate to disapprove arrest, not to initiate prosecution or to grant exemption from prosecution in the cases transferred by it to the people's procuratorate, it may request reconsideration by the people's procuratorate, and may also request review by the people's procuratorate at the next higher level. The higher-level people's procuratorate shall make a timely decision and instruct the lower-level people's procuratorate and the public security organ to execute it.

Article 15   In legal proceedings instituted by a people's procuratorate, the chief procurator or a procurator shall attend the court session, in the capacity of state prosecutor, to support the prosecution and exercise supervision over the court proceedings, and to determine whether they conform to the law.

Article 16   If a people's court considers that the main facts of a crime are not clear or the evidence is insufficient or there are violations of the law in a case in which the people's procuratorate has initiated prosecution, it may remand the case to the people's procuratorate for supplementary investigation or notify it to make corrections.

Article 17   If a local people's procuratorate discovers any error in a judgment or order of a people's court at the corresponding level in a case of first instance, it shall lodge a protest in accordance with the procedure of appeal.

Article 18   If the Supreme People's Procuratorate discovers some definite error in a legally effective judgment or order of a people's court at any level, or if a people's procuratorate at a higher level discovers some definite error in a legally effective judgment or order of a people's court at a lower level, it shall lodge a protest in accordance with procedures of judicial supervision.

People's procuratorates must send personnel to appear in court when cases are heard, in accordance with procedures of judicial supervision.

Article 19   If the people's procuratorates discover violations of the law in the execution of judgments or orders in criminal cases, they shall notify the executing organs to correct them.

If the people's procuratorates discover violations of the law in the activities of prisons, detention houses or organs in charge of reform through labour, they shall notify the organs responsible to correct them.

Chapter III

The Organizational Structure and the Appointment and Removal of Personnel of People's Procuratorates

Article 20   The Supreme People's Procuratorate shall establish a number of procuratorial departments and other professional agencies as needed. The people's procuratorates at various local levels may respectively establish corresponding procuratorial divisions, sections and other professional agencies. (*Amended on September 2, 1983.*)

Article 21   The Procurator-General of the Supreme People's Procuratorate shall be elected and removed by the National People's Congress.

The Deputy Procurators-General, members of the procuratorial committee and procurators of the Supreme People's Procuratorate shall be appointed and removed by the Standing Committee of the National People's Congress upon the recommendation of the Procurator-General of the Supreme People's Procuratorate.

Article 22   The chief procurators of the people's procuratorates of provinces, autonomous regions, and municipalities directly under the Central Government and their branches shall be elected and removed by the people's congresses of provinces, autonomous regions, and municipalities directly under the Central Government; the deputy chief procurators, members of procuratorial committees and procurators shall be appointed and removed by the standing committees of the people's congresses at corresponding levels upon the recommendation of the chief procurators of the provinces, autonomous regions, and municipalities directly under the Central Government.

The appointment and removal of the chief procurators of the people's procuratorates of provinces, autonomous regions, and municipalities directly under the Central Government shall be reported to the Procurator-General of the Supreme People's Procuratorate for submission to the Standing Committee of the National People's Congress for approval. (*Amended on September 2, 1983.*)

Article 23   The chief procurators of people's procuratorates of autonomous prefectures, cities directly under the provincial governments, counties, cities and municipal districts shall be elected and removed by the people's congresses at corresponding levels; the deputy chief procurators, members of procuratorial committees and procurators shall be appointed and removed by the standing committees of the people's congresses at corresponding levels upon the recommendation of the chief procurators.

The appointment and removal of the chief procurators of the people's procuratorates of autonomous prefectures, cities directly under the provincial governments, counties, cities and municipal districts shall be reported to the chief procurators of the people's procuratorates at the next higher level for submission to the standing committee of the people's congress at the corresponding level for approval. (*Amended on September 2, 1983.*)

Article 24   The chief procurators, deputy chief procurators, members of procuratorial committees and procurators of people's procuratorates set up in industrial and mining areas, agricultural reclamation areas and forest zones by people's procuratorates at the provincial or county level shall be appointed and removed by the standing committee of the people's congress at the corresponding level upon the recommendation of the chief procurators of the dispatching people's procuratorates.

Article 25   The term of office of the chief procurators of people's procuratorates at all levels shall be the same as that of the people's congresses at corresponding levels.

Article 26   The Standing Committee of the National People's Congress and the standing committees of the people's congresses of provinces, autonomous regions, and municipalities directly under the Central Government may, upon proposals put forward by the Procurator-General and chief procurators of people's procuratorates at the corresponding level, replace the chief procurators, deputy chief procurators and members of the procuratorial committees of people's procuratorates at lower levels.

Article 27   People's procuratorates at all levels shall have a number of assistant procurators and clerks. With the approval of the chief procurator, an assistant procurator may act in the function of a procurator. The clerks shall be responsible for keeping case records and other related matters.

The assistant procurators and clerks shall be appointed and removed by the chief procurators of people's procuratorates at all levels.

People's procuratorates at all levels may install judicial police as needed.

Article 28   The organizational structure and staff size of the people's procuratorates at all levels shall be stipulated separately by the Supreme People's Procuratorate.

Decision of the Standing Committee of the National People's Congress Regarding Revision of the Income Tax Law of the People's Republic of China Concerning Chinese-Foreign Equity Joint Ventures

(Adopted at the Second Meeting of the Standing Committee of the Sixth National People's Congress, promulgated by Order No. 8 of the President of the People's Republic of China on September 2, 1983, and effective as of the same date)

The Second Meeting of the Standing Committee of the Sixth National People's Congress has decided to revise the Income Tax Law of the People's Republic of China Concerning Chinese-Foreign Equity Joint Ventures as follows:

1. The first paragraph of Article 5, which reads: "A newly established joint venture scheduled to operate for a period of 10 years or more shall, upon approval by the tax authorities of an application filed by the venture, be exempted from income tax in the first profit-making year and allowed a 50% reduction in income tax in the second and third years," is revised to read: "A joint venture scheduled to operate for a period of 10 years or more shall, upon approval by the tax authorities of an application filed by the venture, be exempted from income tax in the first two years after it has begun to make a profit and allowed a 50% reduction in the third through the fifth years."

2. Article 8 reads: "Income tax on joint ventures shall be computed and levied on an annual basis and paid in advance in quarterly instalments. Such advance payments shall be made within 15 days after the end of each quarter, and the final settlement shall be made within three months after the end of each tax year, with a refund for any overpayment and a supplementary payment for any deficiency." The phrase "within three months after the end of each tax year" contained therein is revised to read: "within five months after the end of each tax year."

3. Article 9 reads: "Joint ventures shall file their income tax returns in respect of advance payments with the local tax authorities within the period prescribed for advance payments and shall file their annual income tax returns together with the statements of final accounts within three months

after the end of the tax year." The phrase "within three months after the end of the tax year" contained therein is revised to read: "within four months after the end of the tax year."

Appendix:

Income Tax Law of the People's Republic of China Concerning Chinese-Foreign Equity Joint Ventures

(Adopted at the Third Session of the Fifth National People's Congress, promulgated by Order No. 10 of the Chairman of the Standing Committee of the National People's Congress on September 10, 1980, and effective as of the same date)

Article 1   Income tax shall be paid in accordance with this Law by Chinese-foreign equity joint ventures (hereinafter referred to as "joint ventures") within the territory of the People's Republic of China on their income from production, business operations and other sources.

Income tax on the income derived from production, business operations and other sources by branches and subbranches of a joint venture that are within and outside the territory of China shall be paid by their head office on a consolidated basis.

Article 2   The taxable income of a joint venture shall be the amount remaining from its gross income in a tax year after the costs, expenses and losses have been deducted.

Article 3   The income tax rate on joint ventures shall be 30%. In addition, a local income tax of 10% of the assessed income tax shall be levied.

The income tax rates on joint ventures exploiting petroleum, natural gas and other resources shall be stipulated separately.

Article 4   In the case of a foreign joint venturer remitting out of China its share of profit obtained from the venture, an income tax of 10% shall be levied on the remitted amount.

Article 5   A joint venture scheduled to operate for a period of 10 years or more shall, upon approval by the tax authorities of an application filed by the venture, be exempted from income tax in the first two years after it has begun to make a profit and allowed a 50% reduction in the third through the fifth years.

With the approval of the Ministry of Finance of the People's Republic of China, joint ventures engaged in low-profit operations such as farming and forestry or joint ventures established in remote, economically under-developed areas may be allowed a 15-30% reduction in income tax for a period of another ten years following the expiration of the term for exemption and reductions prescribed in the preceding paragraph.

Article 6   A joint venturer which reinvests in China its share of profit obtained from the venture for a period of not less than five years shall, upon approval by the tax authorities of an application filed by the joint venturer, be refunded 40% of the income tax already paid on the reinvested amount. If it withdraws the reinvested funds before the end of the fifth year, it shall repay the refunded tax.

Article 7   Losses incurred by a joint venture in a tax year may be made up with a corresponding amount drawn from next year's income. Should the income in the subsequent tax year be insufficient to make up for the said losses, the balance may be made up with further deductions from its income year by year, but within a period not exceeding five years.

Article 8   Income tax on joint ventures shall be computed and levied on an annual basis and paid in advance in quarterly instalments. Such advance payments shall be made within 15 days after the end of each quarter, and the final settlement shall be made within five months after the end of each tax year, with a refund for any overpayment or a supplemental payment for any deficiency.

Article 9   Joint ventures shall file their income tax returns in respect of advance payments with the local tax authorities within the period prescribed for advance payments, and shall file their annual income tax returns together with the statements of final accounts within four months after the end of the tax year.

Article 10   Income tax on joint ventures shall be computed in terms of Renminbi (RMB). Income in foreign currency shall be taxed on the equivalent amount converted into Renminbi according to the exchange rate quoted by the State General Administration of Exchange Control of the People's Republic of China.

Article 11   When a joint venture starts operations, changes its line of production, moves to a new site, ceases to operate or changes or assigns its registered capital, it shall present the relevant certificates for tax registration with the local tax authorities within 30 days after registering with the General Administration for Industry and Commerce of the People's Republic of China.

Article 12   The tax authorities shall have the right to inspect the financial, accounting and tax affairs of joint ventures. The joint ventures must make reports according to the facts and provide all relevant information; they may not refuse to cooperate and may not conceal the facts.

Article 13   A joint venture must pay its tax within the prescribed time limit. In case of failure to do so, the tax authorities, in addition to setting a new time limit for tax payment, shall impose a surcharge for overdue payment equal to 0.5% of the overdue tax for every day in arrears, starting from the first day payment becomes overdue.

Article 14   The tax authorities may, in light of the circumstances, impose a fine on a joint venture which has violated the provisions of Articles 9, 11 or 12 of this Law.

In dealing with any joint venture which has evaded or refused to pay tax, the tax authorities may, in addition to pursuing the tax payment, impose a fine of not more than five times the amount of tax underpaid or not paid, in accordance with the seriousness of the case. Cases of gross violation shall be handled by the local people's courts in accordance with the law.

Article 15   In case of a dispute with the tax authorities over tax payment, a joint venture must pay tax according to the relevant regulations before applying to higher tax authorities for reconsideration. If it does not accept the decision made after such reconsideration, it may bring suit in the local people's court.

Article 16   Income tax paid abroad by a joint venture or its branches or subbranches may be credited against the assessed income tax of the head office.

When agreements on avoidance of double taxation have been concluded between the Government of the People's Republic of China and foreign governments, income tax credits shall be handled in accordance with the provisions of the respective agreements.

Article 17   Rules for the implementation of this Law shall be formulated by the Ministry of Finance of the People's Republic of China.

Article 18   This Law shall go into effect on the day of its promulgation.

Decision of the Standing Committee of the National People's Congress Regarding the Exercise by the State Security Organs of the Public Security Organs' Powers of Investigation, Detention, Preparatory Examination and Arrest

(Adopted at the Second Meeting of the Standing Committee of the Sixth National People's Congress on September 2, 1983)

The state security organs established by decision of the First Session of the Sixth National People's Congress shall undertake investigatory work concerning cases of espionage and special agents of which the public security organs have hitherto been in charge. Being of the nature of state public security organs, the state security organs may exercise the public security organs' powers of investigation, detention, preparatory examination and arrest as provided by the Constitution and the law.

Appendix:

(1) The Relevant Articles in the Constitution
Article 37 ...
No citizen may be arrested except with the approval or by decision of a people's procuratorate or by decision of a people's court, and arrests must be made by a public security organ.
Article 40 Freedom and privacy of correspondence of citizens of the People's Republic of China are protected by law. No organization or individual may, on any ground, infringe upon citizens' freedom and privacy of correspondence, except in cases where, to meet the needs of state security or of criminal investigation, public security or procuratorial organs are permitted to censor correspondence in accordance with procedures prescribed by law.
(2) The Relevant Articles in the Criminal Procedure Law
Article 3 The public security organs shall be responsible for investigation, detention and preliminary examination in criminal cases. The people's procuratorates shall be responsible for approving arrests, conducting

procuratorial work (including investigation) and initiating public prosecution. The people's courts shall be responsible for adjudication. No other organ, organization or individual has the right to exercise such powers.

. . . .

Article 38   The people's courts, people's procuratorates and public security organs may, according to the circumstances of a case, issue a warrant to compel the appearance of the defendant, order him to obtain a guarantor pending trial or subject him to residential surveillance.

. . . .

Article 39   Arrests must be approved by a people's procuratorate or decided by a people's court and must be carried out by a public security organ.

Article 41   The public security organs may initially detain an active criminal deserving arrest or a major suspect under any of the following circumstances:

. . . .

Article 58   For the purpose of this Law, the definitions of the following terms are:

(1) "Investigation" means the specialized investigatory work and related compulsory measures carried out according to law by public security organs and people's procuratorates in the process of handling cases;

. . . .

Article 73   Investigatory personnel must carry a certificate issued by a public security organ while conducting an inquest or examination.

Article 86   If the investigatory personnel deem it necessary to seize the mail or telegrams of a defendant, they may, upon approval of a public security organ or a people's procuratorate, notify the post and telecommunications offices to hand over the relevant mail and telegrams for seizure.

. . . .

Article 91   If a defendant who should be arrested is a fugitive, a public security organ may issue a wanted order and take effective measures to pursue him for arrest and bring him to justice.

. . . .

Decision of the Standing Committee of the National People's Congress on the Time for the Election of Deputies to the People's Congresses at County and Township Levels

(Adopted on September 2, 1983)

The Second Meeting of the Standing Committee of the Sixth National People's Congress has decided that the election of deputies to the people's congresses at county and township levels may be postponed until the end of the year 1984 upon decision by the standing committees of the people's congresses of the relevant provinces, autonomous regions, and municipalities directly under the Central Government, provided they cannot be held by the end of 1983 because of the structural reform of the government and the separation of government administration from commune management.

Decision of the Standing Committee of the National People's Congress on Authorizing the State Council to Make Partial Amendments and Supplements to the Measures Concerning the Retirement and Resignation of Staff Members and Workers

(Adopted on September 2, 1983)

The Second Meeting of the Standing Committee of the Sixth National People's Congress has decided to authorize the State Council to make necessary amendments and supplements to certain provisions of the State Council's Provisional Measures for Taking Care of the Aged, Physically Weak, Sick and Disabled Cadres and the State Council's Provisional Measures Concerning the Retirement and Resignation of Workers, both approved in principle at the Second Meeting of the Standing Committee of the Fifth National People's Congress on May 24, 1978.

1984

Patent Law of the People's Republic of China

(Adopted at the Fourth Meeting of the Standing Committee of the Sixth National People's Congress, promulgated by Order No. 11 of the President of the People's Republic of China on March 12, 1984, and effective as of April 1, 1985)

Contents

Chapter I

General Provisions

Article 1   This Law is formulated in order to protect patent rights for invention-creations, encourage invention-creations and facilitate their popularization and application, promote the development of science and technology and meet the needs of socialist modernization.

Article 2   For the purpose of this Law, "invention-creation" means inventions, utility models and designs.

Article 3   The Patent Office of the People's Republic of China shall accept and examine patent applications and grant patent rights for invention-creations that conform to the provisions of this Law.

Article 4   If an invention-creation for which a patent is applied for involves national security or other vital interests of the state that require secrecy, the matter shall be treated in accordance with the relevant provisions of the state.

Article 5   No patent right shall be granted for any invention-creation that violates the laws of the state, goes against social morals or is detrimental to the public interest.

Article 6   For a job-related invention-creation made by any person in execution of the tasks of the unit to which he belongs or by primarily using the material resources of the unit, the right to apply for a patent shall belong to the unit. For an invention-creation that is not job-related, the right to apply for a patent shall belong to the inventor or designer. After an application is approved, if it was filed by a unit owned by the whole people, the patent right shall be held by such unit; if it was filed by a collectively owned unit or an individual, the patent right shall be owned by such unit or individual.

For a job-related invention-creation made by any staff member or worker of a foreign-owned enterprise or a Chinese-foreign equity joint venture within the territory of China, the right to apply for a patent shall belong to the enterprise or joint venture. For an invention-creation that is not job-related, the right to apply for a patent shall belong to the inventor or designer. After the application is approved, the patent right shall be owned by the enterprise, joint venture or individual that applied for it.

The owners and holders of patent rights are uniformly referred to herein as "patentees."

Article 7   No unit or individual may suppress the application of an inventor or designer for a patent in respect of an invention-creation that is not job-related.

Article 8   For an invention-creation made jointly by two or more units, or made by a unit in execution of a commission for research or design given to it by another unit, the right to apply for a patent shall belong, unless otherwise agreed upon, to the unit which made or the units which jointly made the invention-creation. After the application is approved, the patent right shall be owned or held by the unit or units that applied for it.

Article 9   If two or more applicants apply separately for a patent on the same invention-creation, the patent right shall be granted to the person who applied first.

Article 10   The right of patent application and the patent right itself may be assigned.

If a unit owned by the whole people wishes to assign a right of patent application or a patent right, it must obtain the approval of the competent authority at the next higher level.

If a Chinese unit or individual wishes to assign a right of patent application or a patent right to a foreigner, it or he must obtain the approval of the relevant competent department of the State Council.

In cases where a right of patent application or a patent right is assigned, the parties must conclude a written contract, which shall come into force after it is registered with and publicly announced by the Patent Office.

Article 11   After the grant of the patent right for an invention or utility model, no unit or individual may, except as provided for in Article 14 of this Law, exploit the patent without the authorization of the patentee, that is, no unit or individual may manufacture, use or sell the patented product or use the patented process for production or business purposes.

After the grant of the patent right for a design, no unit or individual may exploit the patent without the authorization of the patentee, that is, no entity or individual may manufacture or sell products incorporating the patented design for production or business purposes.

Article 12   Except as provided for in Article 14 of this Law, any unit or individual exploiting the patent of another must conclude a written licensing contract with the patentee and pay the patentee a fee for the exploitation of its patent. The licensee shall not have the right to authorize any unit or individual other than that referred to in the contract to exploit the patent.

Article 13   After the application for an invention patent has been publicly announced, the applicant may require the units or individuals exploiting the invention to pay an appropriate fee.

Article 14   The relevant competent departments of the State Council and the people's governments of provinces, autonomous regions, and municipalities directly under the Central Government shall, in accordance with the state plan, have the power to permit designated units to exploit important invention-creation patents held by units owned by the whole people under the organizational system or jurisdiction of these departments and governments. The units exploiting such patents shall, in accordance with state provisions, pay an exploitation fee to the unit holding the patent right.

If patents held by Chinese individuals or collectively owned units are of great significance to the interests of the state or the public and need to be applied on an extended scale, the matter shall be handled by the relevant competent department of the State Council according to the provisions of the preceding paragraph, after reporting to the State Council and obtaining its approval.

Article 15   The patentee shall have the right to affix a patent marking and indicate the patent number on the patented product or on the packaging of that product.

Article 16   The unit owning or holding the patent right on a job-related invention-creation shall reward the inventor or designer and shall, upon exploitation of the patented invention-creation, reward the inventor or designer in accordance with the scope of its application and the economic benefits derived from it.

Article 17   An inventor or designer shall have the right to name himself as such in the patent document.

Article 18   If a foreigner, foreign enterprise or other foreign organization having no regular residence or place of business in China files an application for a patent in China, the application shall be handled under this Law in accordance with any agreement concluded between the country to which the applicant belongs and China, or any international treaty to which both countries are parties, or on the basis of the principle of reciprocity.

Article 19   If a foreigner, foreign enterprise or other foreign organization having no regular residence or place of business in China applies for a patent or has other patent matters to attend to in China, he or it shall entrust a patent agency designated by the State Council of the People's Republic of China to act on his or its behalf.

If any Chinese unit or individual applies for a patent or has other patent matters to attend to in the country, it or he may entrust a patent agency to act on its or his behalf.

Article 20   If a Chinese unit or individual intends to file an application in a foreign country for a patent on an invention-creation completed in China, it or he shall first file an application for patent with the Patent Office and shall, with the sanction of the relevant competent department of the State Council, entrust a patent agency designated by the State Council to act on its or his behalf.

Article 21   Until the publication or public announcement of a patent application, staff members of the Patent Office and persons involved shall have the duty to keep the contents of the patent application confidential.

Chapter   II

Conditions for the Grant of Patent Rights

Article 22   Any invention or utility model for which a patent right may be granted must possess the characteristics of novelty, inventiveness and usefulness.

"Novelty" means that, before the filing date of the application, no identical invention or utility model has been publicly disclosed in domestic or foreign publications or has been publicly used or made known to the public by any other means in the country, nor has any other person previously filed with the Patent Office an application describing an identical invention or utility model which was recorded in patent application documents published after the said date of filing.

"Inventiveness" means that, compared with the technology existing before the filing date of the application, the invention has prominent and substantive distinguishing features and represents a marked improvement, or the utility model possesses substantive distinguishing features and represents an improvement.

"Usefulness" means that the invention or utility model is manufacturable or usable and can produce positive results.

Article 23 Any design for which a patent right may be granted must not be identical with or similar to any design which, before the filing date of the application, has been publicly disclosed in domestic or foreign publications or has been publicly used within the country.

Article 24 Any invention-creation for which a patent is applied for shall not lose its novelty if, within six months before the filing date of the application, one of the following events has occurred:

(1) it was exhibited for the first time at an international exhibition sponsored or recognized by the Chinese Government;

(2) it was made public for the first time at a prescribed academic or technical conference; or

(3) it was disclosed by any person without the consent of the applicant.

Article 25 No patent right shall be granted for any of the following:

(1) scientific discoveries;

(2) rules and methods for mental activities;

(3) methods for the diagnosis or treatment of diseases;

(4) foods, beverages and condiments;

(5) pharmaceutical products and substances obtained by means of a chemical process;

(6) animal and plant varieties; and

(7) substances obtained by means of nuclear fission.

For the processes used in the manufacture of the products listed in items (4) to (6) of the preceding paragraph, a patent right may be granted in accordance with the provisions of this Law.

Chapter III

Application for Patents

Article 26 When a patent application is filed for an invention or a utility model, relevant documents shall be submitted, including a written request, a specification and an abstract thereof, and a patent claim.

The written request shall state the title of the invention or utility model, the name of the inventor or designer, the name and address of the applicant and other related matters.

The specification shall describe the invention or utility model in a manner sufficiently clear and complete so that a person skilled in the relevant field of technology can accurately produce it; where necessary, drawings shall be appended. The abstract shall describe briefly the technical essentials of the invention or utility model.

The patent claim shall, on the basis of the specification, state the scope of the patent protection requested.

Article 27   When a patent application is filed for a design, relevant documents shall be submitted, including a written request and drawings or photographs of the design; the product on which the design is to be used and the category of that product shall also be indicated.

Article 28   The date on which the Patent Office receives the patent application documents shall be the filing date of the application. If the application documents are sent by mail, the postmark date shall be the filing date of the application.

Article 29   If a foreign applicant applies for a patent in China within 12 months from the date on which it first filed an application in a foreign country for a patent on the same invention or utility model, or within six months from the date on which it first filed an application in a foreign country for a patent on the same design, it may enjoy a right of priority in accordance with any agreement concluded between the country to which it belongs and China, or any international treaty to which both countries are parties, or on the basis of the principle of mutual recognition of the right of priority, that is, the date on which the application was first filed in the foreign country shall be regarded as the filing date of the application.

If one of the events listed in Article 24 of this Law has occurred before an applicant claims a right of priority, the period of the right of priority shall be counted from the date on which that event occurred.

Article 30   An applicant who claims a right of priority shall make a written declaration at the time of application, indicating the date of filing of the earlier application in a foreign country and the specific country in which that application was accepted, and it shall submit within three months copies of the application documents certified by the agency that accepted the application in the foreign country; if the applicant fails to make the written declaration or meet the time limit for submitting the documents, the claim to the right of priority shall be deemed not to have been made.

Article 31   Each patent application for an invention or a utility model should be limited to a single invention or utility model. Two or more inventions or utility models belonging to a single inventive concept may be submitted together in one application.

Each patent application for a design should limited to a single design used on one type of product. Two or more designs used on products belonging to a single category and sold or used in sets may be submitted together in one application.

Article 32   An applicant may withdraw its patent application at any time before the patent right is granted.

Article 33   An applicant may amend its patent application documents, but the amendments may not go beyond the scope of what was recorded in the original specifications.

Chapter IV

Examination and Approval of Patent Applications

Article 34 If, after receiving an application for an invention patent, the Patent Office finds upon preliminary examination that the application conforms with the requirements of this Law, it shall publish the application within 18 months from its filing date. Upon the request of the applicant, the Patent Office may publish the application at an earlier date.

Article 35 Upon the applicant's request for an invention patent made at any time within three years from the filing date of an application, the Patent Office may carry out substantive examination of that application. If, without any justified reason, the applicant fails to meet the time limit for requesting such substantive examination, the application shall be deemed to have been withdrawn.

The Patent Office may of its own accord carry out substantive examination of an application for an invention patent when it deems it necessary.

Article 36 When requesting substantive examination of an invention patent application, the applicant shall furnish reference materials concerning the invention that were available prior to the filing date of the application.

When an applicant requests substantive examination of his application for an invention patent after he has applied in a foreign country for a patent on the same invention, he shall furnish documents from any investigations made in the foreign country for the purpose of examining that application, or documents stating the results of that examination. If, without any justified reason, the said documents are not furnished, the application shall be deemed to have been withdrawn.

Article 37 If, after completing the substantive examination of an invention patent application, the Patent Office finds that the application does not conform with the provisions of this Law, it shall notify the applicant and ask it to state its observations or amend the application within a specified time limit. If, without any justified reason, the applicant fails to respond within the time limit, the application shall be deemed to have been withdrawn.

Article 38 If, after the applicant has stated its observations or made amendments, the Patent Office still finds that the invention patent application does not conform with the provisions of this Law, it shall reject the application.

Article 39 If, after completing the substantive examination of an invention patent application, the Patent Office finds no cause for rejection, it shall make a decision, publicly announce it and notify the applicant.

Article 40 If, after receiving an application for a utility model patent or a design patent, the Patent Office finds upon preliminary examination that the application conforms with the requirements of this Law, it shall not carry out substantive examination of the application but shall immediately make a public announcement and notify the applicant.

Article 41   Within three months from the date of the public announcement of a patent application, any person may, in accordance with the provisions of this Law, file with the Patent Office an opposition to that application. The Patent Office shall send a copy of the opposition to the applicant, and the applicant shall respond in writing within three months from the date of receiving the copy. If, without any justified reason, the applicant fails to submit a written response within the time limit, the application shall be deemed to have been withdrawn.

Article 42   If after examination the Patent Office finds that the opposition is justified, it shall make a decision to reject the application and shall notify the opponent and the applicant.

Article 43   The Patent Office shall set up a Patent Reexamination Board. If an applicant disagrees with the Patent Office's decision to reject its application, it may, within three months from the date of receiving notification of the decision, request the Patent Reexamination Board to make a reexamination. The Patent Reexamination Board shall, after reexamination, make a decision and notify the applicant.

If the applicant for an invention patent disagrees with the decision of the Patent Reexamination Board to reject its request for reexamination, it may, within three months from the date of receiving notification of the decision, file suit in a people's court.

The decision of the Patent Reexamination Board on any reexamination requested by the applicant concerning a utility model or design shall be final.

Article 44   If there is no opposition to a patent application or if after examination the opposition is found unjustified, the Patent Office shall make a decision to grant the patent right, issue the patent certificate and register and publicly announce the relevant matters.

Chapter   V

Term, Termination and Invalidation
of Patent Rights

Article 45   The term of the patent right for inventions shall be 15 years, counted from the filing date of the application.

The term of the patent right for utility models or designs shall be five years, counted from the filing date of the application. Before the expiration of the said term, the patentee may apply for an extension of three years.

Where a patentee enjoys a right of priority, the term of the patent right shall be counted from the date on which the application was filed in China.

Article 46   The patentee shall pay an annual fee beginning with the year in which its patent right is granted.

Article 47   In either of the following cases, the patent right shall be terminated prior to the expiration of its term:

(1) if the annual fee is not paid as prescribed; or

(2) if the patentee renounces its patent right by a written declaration.

The termination of a patent right shall be registered and publicly announced by the Patent Office.

Article 48   After the grant of a patent right, any unit or individual that considers the grant of the said patent right not in conformity with the provisions of this Law may request the Patent Reexamination Board to declare the patent right invalid.

Article 49   The Patent Reexamination Board shall examine the request for invalidation of a patent right, make a decision and notify the party who made the request and the patentee. Any decision declaring a patent right invalid shall be registered and publicly announced by the Patent Office.

If any party disagrees with a decision of the Patent Reexamination Board either invalidating or upholding the patent right for an invention, it may, within three months after receiving notification of the decision, file suit in a people's court.

The decision of the Patent Reexamination Board on a request to invalidate the patent right for a utility model or design shall be final.

Article 50   A patent right that has been invalidated shall be deemed to have been nonexistent from the outset.

Chapter   VI

Compulsory Licence for
Exploitation of a Patent

Article 51   The patentee itself shall have the obligation to manufacture the patented product or use the patented process in China, or it shall authorize other persons to manufacture the patented product or use the patented process in China.

Article 52   If, three years after the date of the grant of a patent right, the patentee of an invention or utility model has failed, without any justified reason, to fulfil the obligation set forth in Article 51 of this Law, the Patent Office may, upon the request of a unit possessing the means to exploit the invention or utility model, grant a compulsory licence to exploit the patent.

Article 53   If a patented invention or utility model is technically more advanced than another invention or utility model that was patented earlier and the exploitation of the later invention or utility model is dependent on the exploitation of the earlier invention or utility model, the Patent Office may, upon the application of the later patentee, grant a compulsory licence to exploit the earlier invention or utility model.

If a compulsory licence has been granted in accordance with the provisions of the preceding paragraph, the Patent Office may, upon the application of the earlier patentee, also grant a compulsory licence to exploit the later invention or utility model.

Article 54   Any unit or individual applying for a compulsory licence in accordance with the provisions of this Law shall furnish proof that it or he has not been able to conclude a licensing contract on reasonable terms with the patentee.

Article 55   Any decision made by the Patent Office granting a compulsory licence shall be registered and publicly announced.

Article 56   Any unit or individual that is granted a compulsory licence shall not have an exclusive right to exploit the patent in question, nor shall it or he have the right to authorize exploitation of the patent by others.

Article 57   Any unit or individual that is granted a compulsory licence shall pay the patentee a reasonable exploitation fee. The amount of the fee shall be decided by both parties through consultation. If the parties fail to reach an agreement, the Patent Office shall make a ruling.

Article 58   If a patentee disagrees with the decision of the Patent Office granting a compulsory licence or with its ruling regarding the exploitation fee, it may, within three months from receiving notification of the decision, file suit in a people's court.

Chapter   VII

Protection of Patent rights

Article 59   The scope of protection in the patent right for an invention or a utility model shall be determined by the contents of the patent claim. The specification and appended drawings may be used to interpret the patent claim.

The scope of protection in the patent right for a design shall be determined by the product incorporating the patented design as shown in the drawings or photographs.

Article 60   If any acts of infringement arise from the exploitation of a patent without the authorization of the patentee, the patentee or interested parties may request the patent administrative authorities to handle the matter or may directly file suit in a people's court. In handling the matter, the patent administrative authorities shall have the power to order the infringer to stop the acts of infringement and compensate for losses. Any party dissatisfied with the order may, within three months from receiving notification of it, file suit in a people's court. If, at the expiration of such period, the party has neither filed suit nor complied with the order, the patent administrative authorities may approach the people's court for compulsory enforcement of the order.

When an infringement dispute arises, if the patented invention is a manufacturing process for a product, the unit or individual manufacturing the similar product shall furnish proof of its manufacturing process.

Article 61 The period of limitation for filing suit concerning the infringement of a patent right shall be two years, counted from the day on which the patentee or the interested parties became aware or should have become aware of the act of infringement.

Article 62 None of the following shall be deemed an infringement of a patent right:

(1) use or sale of a patented product after it has been manufactured by the patentee or with the authorization of the patentee and subsequently sold;

(2) use or sale of a patented product without knowledge of its having been manufactured and sold without the authorization of the patentee;

(3) continued manufacture or use of a similar product, only within its original scope, by a party that, prior to the date of application for the patent in question, had already manufactured that similar product, used the same process or made the necessary preparations for such manufacture or use;

(4) use of the patent in question by a foreign means of transport which temporarily passes through the territorial land, water or airspace of China for its own needs, in its devices and installations, in accordance with any agreement concluded between China and the country to which the foreign means of transport belongs, or any international treaty to which both countries are parties, or on the basis of the principle of reciprocity; or

(5) use of the patent in question solely for the purposes of scientific research and experimentation.

Article 63 Whoever counterfeits the patent of another person shall be dealt with in accordance with Article 60 of this Law. If the circumstances are serious, the criminal liability of the person directly responsible shall be investigated by applying mutatis mutandis Article 127 of the Criminal Law.

Article 64 Whoever, in violation of the provisions of Article 20 of this Law, files in a foreign country without authorization an application for a patent divulging an important state secret shall be given administrative sanctions by the unit to which he belongs or by the competent authority at the next higher level. If the circumstances of the case are serious, his criminal liability shall be investigated in accordance with the law.

Article 65   Whoever usurps the right of an inventor or designer to apply for a patent on an invention-creation that is not job-related, or usurps any other right or interest of an inventor or designer prescribed by this Law, shall be given administrative sanctions by the unit to which he belongs or by the competent authority at the next higher level.

Article 66   If any staff member of the Patent Office or any of the relevant state functionaries engages in malpractices for the benefit of friends, he shall be given administrative sanctions by the Patent Office or the competent authority concerned. If the circumstances are serious, criminal liability shall be investigated by applying mutatis mutandis Article 188 of the Criminal Law.

Chapter   VIII

Supplementary Provisions

Article 67   For patent applications filed with the Patent Office and other procedures carried out there, fees shall be paid as prescribed.

Article 68   Rules for the implementation of this Law shall be formulated by the Patent Office and shall be submitted to the State Council for approval before they are put into effect.

Article 69   This Law shall go into effect on April 1, 1985.

Law of the People's Republic of China on the Prevention and Control of Water Pollution

(Adopted at the Fifth Meeting of the Standing Committee of the Sixth National People's Congress, promulgated by Order No. 12 of the President of the People's Republic of China on May 11, 1984, and effective as of November 1, 1984)

Contents

Chapter I

General Provisions

Article 1 This Law is formulated for the purpose of preventing and controlling water pollution, protecting and improving the environment, safeguarding human health, ensuring the effective use of water resources and facilitating the development of socialist modernization.

Article 2 This Law shall apply to the prevention and control of pollution of rivers, lakes, canals, irrigation channels, reservoirs and other surface water bodies and of groundwater within the territory of the People's Republic of China.

This Law is not applicable to the prevention and control of marine pollution, which is provided for by a separate law.

Article 3 Competent departments under the State Council and local people's governments at various levels shall incorporate the protection of the water environment into their plans and adopt ways and measures to prevent and control water pollution.

Article 4 The environmental protection departments of the people's governments at all levels shall be the organs exercising unified supervision and management of the prevention and control of water pollution.

Navigation administrative offices of transportation departments at various levels shall be the organs exercising supervision and management of pollution from ships.

Water conservancy administration departments, public health administration departments, geological and mining departments, municipal administration departments, and water sources protection agencies on major rivers of people's governments at various levels shall, through performing their respective functions and in conjunction with environmental protection departments, implement supervision and management of the prevention and control of water pollution.

Article 5 All units and individuals shall have the duty to protect the water environment and the right to supervise any act that pollutes or damages the water environment and to inform against the polluter.

Any unit or individual that has suffered losses directly from a water pollution hazard shall have the right to claim damages from and demand the elimination of the hazard by the polluter.

Chapter   II

Establishment of Water Environment Quality Standards and Pollutant Discharge Standards

Article 6 The environmental protection department of the State Council shall establish national water environment quality standards.

The people's governments of provinces, autonomous regions, and municipalities directly under the Central Government may establish their own local, supplementary standards for those items not specified in the national water environment quality standards and report the same to the environmental protection department of the State Council for the record.

Article 7 The environmental protection department of the State Council shall, in accordance with the national water environment quality standards and the country's economic and technological conditions, establish national pollutant discharge standards.

Where the implementation of the national pollutant discharge standards cannot ensure the attainment of the water environment quality standards for local water bodies, the people's governments of provinces, autonomous regions, and municipalities directly under the Central Government may establish local pollutant discharge standards which are more stringent than the national standards and report the same to the environmental protection department of the State Council for the record.

Those who discharge pollutants into any water body where local pollutant discharge standards have been established shall observe such local standards.

Article 8   The environmental protection department of the State Council and the people's governments of provinces, autonomous regions,and municipalities directly under the Central Government shall amend in due time their respective water environment quality standards and pollutant discharge standards in accordance with the requirements of water pollution prevention and control and with the country's economic and technological conditions.

Chapter III

Supervision and Management of the Prevention and Control of Water Pollution

Article 9   Competent departments under the State Council and local people's governments at various levels shall, in the process of developing, utilizing, regulating and allocating water resources, make integrated plans for maintaining proper river flows, proper water levels of lakes and reservoirs and proper groundwater tables, in order to sustain the natural purification capacity of water bodies.

Article 10   Competent departments under the State Council and local people's governments at various levels shall incorporate into their plans of municipal construction the protection of urban water sources and the prevention and control of urban water pollution by constructing and perfecting municipal drainage systems and sewage treatment facilities.

Article 11   Competent departments under the State Council and local people's governments at various levels shall make rational plans for the placement of industry, and see to it that enterprises causing water pollution are modified and technically renovated, adopting comprehensive prevention and control measures, raising the frequency of water reuse, utilizing resources rationally and reducing the quantity of waste water and pollutants discharged.

Article 12   For domestic and drinking water sources, water bodies at scenic or historic sites, important fishery water bodies and other water bodies of special economic or cultural value, people's governments at or above the county level may delineate protected zones and take measures to ensure that the water quality in those protected zones complies with the standards for their designated uses.

Article 13   New construction projects, extensions, or reconstruction projects which discharge pollutants into water bodies directly or indirectly and installations on water shall be subject to the state provisions concerning environmental protection for such projects.

The environmental impact statement of a construction project shall assess the water pollution hazards the project is likely to produce and its impact on the ecosystem, with prevention and control measures provided therein; the statement shall be submitted, according to the specified procedure, to the environmental protection department concerned for review and approval. The setting up of sewage outfalls within any water conservancy projects such as canals, irrigation channels and reservoirs shall be approved by the relevant department in charge of water conservancy.

Whwn a construction project is to be put into operation or to use, its water pollution prevention and control facilities must be inspected by the environmental protection department; if the facilities do not conform to the specified requirements, the said project shall not be permitted to be put into operation or to use.

Article 14   Enterprises and institutions that discharge pollutants directly or indirectly into a water body shall, pursuant to the provisions of the environmental protection department of the State Council, report to and register with their local environmental protection department their existing treatment and discharge facilities for pollutants and the categories, quantities and concentrations of pollutants discharged under their normal operating conditions and also submit to the same department the relevant technical information concerning the prevention and control of water pollution.

Enterprises and institutions shall report in time if any substantial change occurs in the categories, quantities or concentrations of the pollutants discharged. When pollutant treatment facilities are to be dismantled or left idle, permission from the local environmental protection department must be obtained.

Article 15   Enterprises and institutions discharging pollutants into a water body shall pay a discharge fee as provided for by the state. If the discharge of pollutants exceeds the limits set by national or local standards, they shall pay a fee for excess discharge according to state provisions and shall assume responsibility to eliminate and control the pollution.

Article 16   If a unit discharging pollutants has caused severe pollution of a water body, it shall be ordered to eliminate and control the pollution within a certain period.

For enterprises and institutions directly under the jurisdiction of the

Central Government or the people's government of a province, autonomous region, or municipality directly under the Central Government, the determination of a deadline for elimination or control of pollution shall be recommended by the environmental protection department of the people's government of the province, autonomous region or municipality, and be reported to the people's government at the corresponding level for decision. For enterprises and institutions under the jurisdiction of a people's government at or below the city or county level, such recommendation shall be made by the environmental protection department of the people's government at the corresponding level for decision. The pollutant discharging units shall accomplish the elimination or control of pollution within the specified period.

Article 17   In case of emergency, such as the severe pollution of a domestic and drinking water source which threatens safe water supply, the relevant environmental protection department shall, with the approval of the people's government at the corresponding level, take compulsory emergency measures, including ordering the enterprises or institutions concerned to reduce or stop the discharge of pollutants.

Article 18   Environmental protection departments and relevant supervisory and management departments of people's governments at various levels shall be empowered to make on-site inspections of units under their jurisdiction that discharge pollutants. The units being inspected shall report the situation truthfully and provide the necessary information. The inspecting authorities shall have the obligation to keep the technological and trade secrets of the units inspected.

Chapter IV

Prevention of Surface Water Pollution

Article 19   No new sewage outfalls shall be set up in the protected zones for domestic and drinking water sources, water bodies at scenic or historic sites, important fishery water bodies and other water bodies of special economic or cultural value. When new sewage outfalls are set up in the vicinity of such protected zones, the water bodies within those zones must be ensured against pollution.

Measures for the elimination or control of pollution shall be taken for any sewage outfall which was established before the promulgation of this Law and which discharges pollutants in excess of the limits set by national or local standards. Outfalls endangering drinking water sources shall be relocated.

Article 20   Where any pollutant discharging unit, as a result of an accident or other exigency, discharges pollutants in excess of normal quantities, thereby causing or threatening to cause a water pollution accident, it shall immediately take emergency measures, inform such units as are likely to be endangered or damaged by the water pollution and report the case to the local environmental protection department. Ships that have caused any pollution accident shall report the case to the nearest navigation administration office for its investigation and disposal.

Article 21   The discharge of any oil, acid or alkaline solutions or deadly toxic liquid waste into any water body shall be prohibited.

Article 22   The washing in any water body of vehicles or containers which have been used for storing oil or toxic pollutant shall be prohibited.

Article 23   The discharge or dumping into any water body, or the direct underground burying of deadly toxic soluble slag, tailings, etc., containing such substances as mercury, cadmium, arsenic, chromium, lead, cyanide and yellow phosphorus, is prohibited.

Sites for depositing deadly toxic soluble slag, tailings, etc., shall be made waterproof and protected against seepage and leaking.

Article 24   The discharge or dumping of industrial waste residues, urban refuse or other wastes into any water body shall be prohibited.

Article 25   The piling or depositing of solid wastes and other pollutants on beaches and bank slopes below the highest water level of rivers, lakes, canals, irrigation channels and reservoirs shall be prohibited.

Article 26   The discharge or dumping of radioactive solid wastes or of waste water containing any high- or medium- level radioactive substances into any water body shall be prohibited.

The discharge of waste water containing low-level radioactive substances shall comply with the relevant national provisions and standards for radioactive protection.

Article 27   Where discharge of heated waste water into any water body is to be made, measures shall be taken to ensure that the temperature of the water body conforms to the water environment quality standards, so as to prevent any heat pollution hazard.

Article 28   Pathogen-contaminated sewage can be discharged only after it is disinfected to meet the relevant national standards.

Article 29   The discharge of industrial waste water or urban sewage into agricultural irrigation channels shall be made only with the assurance that the water quality at the nearest irrigation intake downstream conforms to the agricultural irrigation water quality standards.

When industrial waste water or urban sewage is used for irrigation, attention shall be paid to guarding against pollution of the soil, groundwater or agricultural products.

Article 30   The application of pesticides shall comply with the state provisions and standards for their safe use.

Transportation and storage of pesticides and disposal of expired or ineffective pesticides shall be strictly controlled to prevent water pollution.

Article 31 The discharge of oil-bearing waste water or domestic sewage from ships shall comply with ship pollutant discharge standards. Ocean navigating ships, on entering inland rivers or harbours, shall observe ship pollutant discharge standards for inland rivers.

Residual oil or waste oil of ships must be recovered, and its discharge into any water body shall be prohibited.

The dumping of ship refuse into any water body shall be prohibited.

In the process of loading and transporting oils or toxic cargoes, ships must be safeguarded against spillage and leakage and against such cargoes falling into the water, so as to prevent water pollution therefrom.

Chapter V

Prevention of Groundwater Pollution

Article 32 Enterprises and institutions shall be prohibited from discharging waste water containing toxic pollutants or pathogens or dumping other wastes into seepage wells, cesspools, crevices or karst caves.

Article 33 At places where no satisfactory impervious strata exist, enterprises and institutions shall be prohibited from using ditches, pits or ponds which are without safeguards against seepage for conveyance or storage of waste water containing toxic pollutants or pathogens, or of other wastes.

Article 34 In exploiting groundwater from multiple aquifers, layered exploitation shall be resorted to if water quality differs greatly from one aquifer to another. Combined exploitation of artesian water and polluted phreatic water shall not be permitted.

Article 35 While constructing underground engineering facilities or carrying out prospecting, mining or other underground activities, protective measures shall be taken for prevention of groundwater pollution.

Article 36 Artificial recharge of groundwater shall not be deleterious to groundwater quality.

Chapter VI

Legal Liability

Article 37 Any violator of this Law shall, according to the circumstances of the case, be warned or fined by the competent environmental protection department or the navigation office of the competent transportations department for any of the following:

(1) refusing to report or submitting a false report on items for which registration is required by the environmental protection department of the State Council for the discharge of pollutants;

(2) putting into operation or to use a construction project whose water pollution control facilities either have not been completed or fail to meet the requirements specified in state provisions for environmental protection management for construction projects;

(3) refusing an on-site inspection by the competent environmental protection department or supervisory and management department, or resorting to deception;

(4) storing, piling, abandoning, dumping or discharging any pollutant or waste in violation of Chapters IV and V of this Law; or

(5) failing to pay, as provided for by the state, the fee for pollutant discharge or for excess discharge.

The amount of the fine and the procedure for its imposition shall be stipulated in the rules for the implementation of this Law.

Article 38 An enterprise or institution which has caused severe pollution to water bodies but has failed to accomplish its elimination by the deadline as required shall, as provided for by the state, pay twice or more the fee for excess discharge; in addition, a fine may be imposed in accordance with the consequent damage and loss, or the said enterprise or institution may be ordered to suspend operations or close down.

The fine shall be decided by the competent environmental protection department. Orders for the suspension of operations or the shutdown of enterprises and institutions shall be issued by the local people's government which set the deadline for the elimination of pollution. Orders for the suspension of operations or shutdown of enterprises and institutions under the jurisdiction of the Central Government shall be submitted to and approved by the State Council.

Article 39 An enterprise or institution which violates this Law, thereby causing a water pollution accident, shall be fined by the competent environmental protection department or the navigation office of the competent transportation department in accordance with the consequent damage and loss. In a serious case, the persons responsible shall be subject to administrative sanction by the unit to which they belong or by a higher competent authority.

Article 40 A party refusing to accept the decision of administrative sanction may bring suit before a people's court within 15 days from the date of receiving the notification. If upon the expiration of the period the party neither brings suit nor complies with the decision, the organ which imposed the sanction may apply to the people's court for compulsory enforcement.

Article 41   The unit which has caused a water pollution hazard has the responsibility to eliminate it and make compensation to the unit or individual that suffered direct losses.

A dispute over liability to make compensation or the amount of compensation may, at the request of the parties, be settled by the competent environmental protection department or by the navigation office of the competent communications department. If a party refuses to accept the decision, he may bring suit before a people's court. The party may also bring suit before the people's court directly.

If the water pollution losses are caused by a third party intentionally or negligently, the third party shall be liable to make compensation.

The unit discharging pollutants shall bear no liability for water pollution losses occasioned by the victim's own fault.

Article 42   If water pollution losses result entirely from irresistible natural disasters which cannot be averted even after reasonable measures have been promptly taken, the party concerned shall be exempted from liability.

Article 43   Should any violation of this Law give rise to a serious water pollution accident leading to any grave consequence of heavy public or private property losses or serious personal injury or death, the person responsible for such violation may be investigated for criminal liability by application of Article 115 or 187 of the Criminal Law.

Chapter   VII

Supplementary Provisions

Article 44   For the purpose of this Law, the definitions of the following terms are:

(1) "Water pollution" means the introduction into a water body of any substance which alters the chemical, physical, biological or radioactive properties of the water in such a way as to affect its effective use, endanger human health, damage the ecosystem or be deleterious to water quality.

(2) "Pollutant" means a substance that is capable of causing water pollution.

(3) "Toxic pollutant" means a pollutant that, when ingested by organisms directly or indirectly, leads to diseases, abnormal behaviour, genetic mutation, physiological functional disturbance, organism deformity or death of the organisms themselves or their offspring.

(4) "Oil" means any kind of oil or its refined products.

(5) "Fishery water bodies" means those parts of water bodies designated for the spawning, feeding, wintering or migratory passage of fish or

shrimp, and for breeding fish, shrimp or shellfish or growing algae.

Article 45   The environmental protection department of the State Council shall, on the basis of this Law, formulate rules for its implementation, which shall be put into effect after being submitted to and approved by the State Council.

Article 46   This Law shall come into force on November 1, 1984.

Law of the People's Republic of China on Regional National Autonomy

(Adopted at the Second Session of the Sixth National People's Congress, promulgated by Order No. 13 of the President of the People's Republic of China on May 31, 1984, and effective as of October 1, 1984)

Contents

Preface

The People's Republic of China is a unitary multinational state created jointly by the people of all its nationalities. Regional national autonomy is the basic policy adopted by the Communist Party of China for the solution of the national question in China through its application of Marxism-Leninism; it is an important political system of the state.

Regional national autonomy means that the minority nationalities, under unified state leadership, practise regional autonomy in areas where they live in concentrated communities and set up organs of self-government for the exercise of the power of autonomy. Regional national autonomy embodies the state's full respect for and guarantee of the right of the minority nationalities to administer their internal affairs and its adherence to the principle of equality, unity and common prosperity for all its nationalities.

Regional national autonomy has played an enormous role in giving full play to the initiative of all nationalities as masters of the country, in developing among them a socialist relationship of equality, unity and mutual assistance, in consolidating the unification of the country and in promoting socialist construction in the national autonomous areas and the rest of the country. The system of regional national autonomy will have a still greater role to play in the country's socialist modernization in the years to come.

It has been proven by practice that adherence to regional national autonomy requires that the national autonomous areas be given effective guarantees for implementing state laws and policies in the light of existing local conditions; that large numbers of cadres at various levels and specialized personnel and skilled workers of various professions and trades be trained from among the minority nationalities; that the national autonomous areas strive to promote local socialist construction in the spirit of self-reliance and hard work and contribute to the nation's construction as a whole; and that the state strive to help the national autonomous areas speed up their economic and cultural development in accordance with the plans for national economic and social development. In the effort to maintain the unity of the nationalities, both big-nation chauvinism, mainly Han chauvinism, and local national chauvinism must be opposed.

Under the leadership of the Communist Party of China and the guidance of Marxism-Leninism and Mao Zedong Thought, the people of various nationalities in the autonomous areas shall, together with the people of the whole country, adhere to the people's democratic dictatorship and to the socialist road, concentrate their efforts on socialist modernization, speed up the economic and cultural development of the national autonomous areas, work towards their unity and prosperity and strive for the common prosperity of all nationalities and for the transformation of China into a socialist country with a high level of culture and democracy.

The Law of the People's Republic of China on Regional National Autonomy is the basic law for the implementation of the system of regional national autonomy prescribed in the Constitution.

Chapter I

General Principles

Article 1   The Law of the People's Republic of China on Regional

National Autonomy is formulated in accordance with the Constitution of the People's Republic of China.

Article 2   Regional autonomy shall be practised in areas where minority nationalities live in concentrated communities.

National autonomous areas shall be classified into autonomous regions, autonomous prefectures and autonomous counties.

All national autonomous areas are integral parts of the People's Republic of China.

Article 3   Organs of self-government shall be established in national autonomous areas as local organs of state power at a particular level.

The organs of self-government of national autonomous areas shall apply the principle of democratic centralism.

Article 4   The organs of self-government of national autonomous areas shall exercise the functions and powers of local organs of state as specified in Section 5 of Chapter III of the Constitution. At the same time, they shall exercise the power of autonomy within the limits of their authority as prescribed by the Constitution, by this Law and other laws, and implement the laws and policies of the state in the light of existing local conditions.

The organs of self-government of autonomous prefectures shall exercise the functions and powers of local state organs over cities divided into districts and cities with counties under their jurisdiction and, at the same time, exercise the power of autonomy.

Article 5   The organs of self-government of national autonomous areas must uphold the unity of the country and guarantee that the Constitution and other laws are observed and implemented in these areas.

Article 6   The organs of self-government of national autonomous areas shall lead the people of the various nationalities in a concentrated effort to promote socialist modernization.

On the principle of not contravening the Constitution and the laws, the organs of self-government of national autonomous areas shall have the power to adopt special policies and flexible measures in the light of local conditions to speed up the economic and cultural development of these areas.

Under the guidance of state plans and on the basis of actual conditions, the organs of self-government of national autonomous areas shall steadily increase labour productivity and economic results, develop social productive forces and gradually raise the material living standards of the people of the various nationalities.

The organs of self-government of national autonomous areas shall inherit and carry forward the fine traditions of national cultures, build a socialist society with an advanced culture and ideology and with national characteristics, and steadily raise the socialist consciousness and scientific and cultural levels of the people of the various nationalities.

Article 7   The organs of self-government of national autonomous areas shall place the interests of the state as a whole above anything else and make positive efforts to fulfil the tasks assigned by state organs at higher levels.

Article 8   State organs at higher levels shall guarantee the exercise of the power of autonomy by the organs of self-government of national autonomous areas and shall, in accordance with the characteristics and needs of these areas, strive to help them speed up their socialist construction.

Article 9   State organs at higher levels and the organs of self-government of national autonomous areas shall uphold and develop the socialist relationship of equality, unity and mutual assistance among all of China's nationalities. Discrimination against and oppression of any nationality shall be prohibited; any act which undermines the unity of the nationalities or instigates national division shall also be prohibited.

Article 10   The organs of self-government of national autonomous areas shall guarantee the freedom of the nationalities in these areas to use and develop their own spoken and written languages and their freedom to preserve or reform their own folkways and customs.

Article 11   The organs of self-government of national autonomous areas shall guarantee the freedom of religious belief to citizens of the various nationalities.

No state organ, public organization or individual may compel citizens to believe in, or not to believe in, any religion, nor may they discriminate against citizens who believe in, or do not believe in, any religion.

The state shall protect normal religious activities. No one may make use of religion to engage in activities that disrupt public order, impair the health of citizens or interfere with the educational system of the state.

Religious bodies and religious affairs shall not be subject to any foreign domination.

Chapter II

Establishment of National Autonomous Areas and the Structure of the Organs of Self-Government

Article 12   Autonomous areas may be established where one or more minority nationalities live in concentrated communities, in the light of local conditions such as the relationship among the various nationalities and the level of economic development, and with due consideration for historical background.

Within a national autonomous area, appropriate autonomous areas or nationality townships may be established where other minority nationalities live in concentrated communities.

Some residential areas and towns of the Han nationality or other nationalities may be included in a national autonomous area in consideration of actual local conditions.

Article 13 With the exception of special cases, the name of a national autonomous area shall be composed of the name of the locality and the name of the nationality and the administrative status, in that order.

Article 14 The establishment of a national autonomous area, the delineation of its boundaries and the elements of its name shall be proposed by the state organ at the next higher level jointly with the state organ in the relevant locality, after full consultation with representatives of the relevant nationalities, before they are submitted for approval according to the procedures prescribed by law.

Once defined, the boundaries of a national autonomous area may not be altered without authorization. When an alteration is found necessary, it shall be proposed by the relevant department of the state organ at the next higher level after full consultation with the organ of self-government of the national autonomous area before it is submitted to the State Council for approval.

Article 15 The organs of self-government of national autonomous areas shall be the people's congresses and people's governments of autonomous regions, autonomous prefectures and autonomous counties.

The people's governments of national autonomous areas shall be responsible to and report on their work to the people's congresses at corresponding levels and to the administrative organs of the state at the next higher level. When the people's congresses at corresponding levels are not in session, they shall be responsible to and report on their work to the standing committees of these people's congresses. The people's governments of all national autonomous areas shall be administrative organs of the state under the unified leadership of the State Council and shall be subordinate to it.

The organization and work of the organs of self-government of national autonomous areas shall be specified in these areas' regulations on the exercise of autonomy or separate regulations, in accordance with the Constitution and other laws.

Article 16 In the people's congress of a national autonomous area, in addition to the deputies from the nationality exercising regional autonomy in the administrative area, the other nationalities inhabiting the area are also entitled to appropriate representation.

The number and proportion of deputies to the people's congress of a national autonomous area from the nationality exercising regional autonomy and from the other minority nationalities shall be decided upon by the standing committee of the people's congress of a province or an autonomous region, in accordance with the principles prescribed by law, and shall be reported to the Standing Committee of the National People's Congress for the record.

Among the chairman and vice-chairmen of the standing committee of the people's congress of a national autonomous area shall be one or more citizens of the nationality exercising regional autonomy in the area.

Article 17   The chairman of an autonomous region, the prefect of an autonomous prefecture or the head of an autonomous county shall be a citizen of the nationality exercising regional autonomy in the area concerned. Other posts in the people's government of an autonomous region, an autonomous prefecture or an autonomous county should, whenever possible, be assumed by people of the nationality exercising regional autonomy and of other minority nationalities in the area concerned.

The people's governments of national autonomous areas shall apply the system of giving overall responsibility to the chairman of an autonomous region, the prefect of an autonomous prefecture or the head of an autonomous county, who shall direct the work of the people's governments at their respective levels.

Article 18   The cadres in the departments under the organs of self-government of a national autonomous area should, whenever possible, be chosen from among citizens of the nationality exercising regional autonomy and of the other minority nationalities in the area.

Chapter   III

The Power of Autonomy of the Organs of Self-Government

Article 19   The people's congresses of national autonomous areas shall have the power to enact regulations on the exercise of autonomy and separate regulations in the light of the political, economic and cultural characteristics of the nationality or nationalities in the areas concerned. The regulations on the exercise of autonomy and separate regulations of autonomous regions shall be submitted to the Standing Committee of the National People's Congress for approval before they go into effect. The regulations on the exercise of autonomy and separate regulations of autonomous prefectures and autonomous counties shall be submitted to the standing committees of the people's congresses of provinces or autonomous regions for approval before they go into effect, and they shall be reported to the

Standing Committee of the National People's Congress for the record.

Article 20   If a resolution, decision, order or instruction of a state organ at a higher level does not suit the conditions in a national autonomous area, the organ of self-government of the area may either implement it with certain alterations or cease implementing it after reporting to and receiving the approval of the state organ at a higher level.

Article 21   While performing its functions, the organ of self-government of a national autonomous area shall, in accordance with the regulations on the exercise of autonomy of the area, use one or several languages commonly used in the locality; where several commonly used languages are used for the performance of such functions, the language of the nationality exercising regional autonomy may be used as the main language.

Article 22   In accordance with the needs of socialist construction, the organs of self-government of national autonomous areas shall take various measures to train large numbers of cadres at different levels and various kinds of specialized personnel, including scientists, technicians and managerial executives, as well as skilled workers from among the local nationalities, giving full play to their roles, and shall pay attention to the training of cadres at various levels and specialized and technical personnel of various kinds from among the women of minority nationalities.

The organs of self-government of national autonomous areas may adopt special measures to provide preferential treatment and encouragement to specialized personnel joining in the various kinds of construction in these areas.

Article 23   When recruiting personnel, enterprises and institutions in national autonomous areas shall give priority to minority nationalities and may enlist them from the population of minority nationalities in rural and pastoral areas. When recruiting personnel from the population of minority nationalities in rural and pastoral areas, autonomous prefectures and autonomous counties must report to and secure the approval of the people's governments of the provinces or autonomous regions.

Article 24   The organs of self-government of national autonomous areas may, in accordance with the military system of the state and practical local need and with the approval of the State Council, organize local public security forces for the maintenance of public order.

Article 25   Under the guidance of state plans, the organs of self-government of national autonomous areas shall independently arrange for and administer local economic development.

Article 26   Under the guidance of state plans, the organs of self-government of national autonomous areas shall work out the guidelines, policies and plans for economic development in the light of local characteristics and needs.

Article 27   Given the prerequisite of adherence to the principles of socialism, the organs of self-government of national autonomous areas shall, in accordance with legal stipulations and in the light of the characteristics of local economic development, rationally readjust the relations of production and reform the structure of economic administration.

In accordance with legal stipulations, the organs of self-government of national autonomous areas shall define the ownership of, and the right to use, the pastures and forests within these areas.

Article 28   In accordance with legal stipulations, the organs of self-government of national autonomous areas shall manage and protect the natural resources of these areas.

The organs of self-government of national autonomous areas shall protect and develop grasslands and forests and organize and encourage the planting of trees and grass. Destruction of grasslands and forests by any organization or individual by whatever means shall be prohibited.

In accordance with legal stipulations and unified state plans, the organs of self-government of national autonomous areas may give priority to the rational exploitation and utilization of the natural resources that the local authorities are entitled to develop.

Article 29   Under the guidance of state plans, the organs of self-government of national autonomous areas shall independently arrange local capital construction projects according to their financial and material resources and other specific local conditions.

Article 30   The organs of self-government of national autonomous areas shall independently administer the enterprises and institutions under local jurisdiction.

Article 31   The organs of self-government of national autonomous areas shall independently arrange for the use of industrial, agricultural and other local and special products after fulfilling the quotas for state purchase and for state distribution at a higher level.

Article 32   In accordance with state provisions, the organs of self-government of national autonomous areas may pursue foreign economic and trade activities and may, with the approval of the State Council, open foreign trade ports.

National autonomous areas adjoining foreign countries may develop border trade with the approval of the State Council.

While conducting foreign economic and trade activities, the organs of self-government of the national autonomous areas shall enjoy preferential treatment by the state with regard to the proportion of foreign exchange retained by them and in other respects.

Article 33   The finance of a national autonomous area constitutes a particular level of finance and is a component of state finance.

The organs of self-government of national autonomous areas shall have the power of autonomy in administering the finances of their areas. All revenues accruing to the national autonomous areas under the financial system of the state shall be managed and used by the organs of self-government of these areas on their own.

The revenues and expenditures of national autonomous areas shall be specified by the State Council on the principle of giving preferential treatment to such areas.

In accordance with stipulations concerning the state financial system, if the revenues of a national autonomous area exceed its expenditures, a fixed amount of the surplus shall be delivered to the financial department at a higher level. Once fixed, the amount to be delivered may remain unchanged for several years. If the expenditures of a national autonomous area exceed its revenues, a subsidy shall be granted by the financial department at a higher level.

A national autonomous area shall, in accordance with state stipulations, lay aside a reserve fund for expenditure in its budget. The proportion of the reserve fund in its budget shall be higher than that in the budgets of other areas.

While implementing its fiscal budget, the organ of self-government of a national autonomous area shall arrange for the use of extra income and savings from expenditures at its own discretion.

Article 34 In accordance with the principles set by the state and in the light of local conditions, the organs of self-government of national autonomous areas may work out supplementary provisions and concrete procedures with regard to the standards of expenditure, the sizes of the staff and the quotas of work for their respective areas. The supplementary provisions and concrete procedures worked out by autonomous regions shall be reported to the State Council for the record; those worked out by autonomous prefectures and autonomous counties shall be reported to the people's governments of the relevant provinces or autonomous regions for approval.

Article 35 While implementing the tax laws of the state, the organs of self-government of national autonomous areas may grant tax exemptions or reductions for certain items of local financial income which should be encouraged or given preferential consideration in taxation, in addition to items on which tax reduction or exemption requires unified examination and approval by the state. The decisions of autonomous prefectures and autonomous counties on tax reduction and exemption shall be reported to the people's governments of the relevant provinces or autonomous regions for approval.

Article 36 In accordance with the guidelines of the state on education and with the relevant stipulations of the law, the organs of self-government of national autonomous areas shall decide on plans for the development of education in these areas, on the establishment of various kinds of schools at different levels, and on their educational system, forms, curricula, the language used in instruction and enrollment procedures.

Article 37   The organs of self-government of national autonomous areas shall independently develop education for the nationalities by eliminating illiteracy, setting up various kinds of schools, spreading compulsory primary education, developing secondary education and establishing specialized schools for the nationalities, such as teachers' schools, secondary technical schools, vocational schools and institutes of nationalities to train specialized personnel from among the minority nationalities.

The organs of self-government of national autonomous areas may set up public primary schools and secondary schools, mainly boarding schools and schools providing subsidies, in pastoral areas and economically underdeveloped, sparsely populated mountain areas inhabited by minority nationalities.

Schools where most of the students come from minority nationalities should, whenever possible, use textbooks in their own languages and use these languages as the media of instruction. Classes for the teaching of Chinese (the Han language) shall be opened for senior grades of primary schools or for secondary schools to popularize *putonghua*, the common speech based on Beijing pronunciation.

Article 38   The organs of self-government of national autonomous areas shall independently develop literature, art, the press, publishing, radio broadcasting, the film industry, television and other cultural undertakings in forms and with characteristics unique to the nationalities.

The organs of self-government of national autonomous areas shall collect, sort out, translate and publish books of the nationalities and protect the scenic spots and historical sites in their areas, their precious cultural relics and their other important historical and cultural legacies.

Article 39   The organs of self-government of national autonomous areas shall make independent decisions on local plans for developing science and technology and spreading knowledge of science and technology.

Article 40   The organs of self-government of national autonomous areas shall make independent decisions on plans for developing local medical and health services and for advancing both modern medicine and the traditional medicine of the nationalities.

The organs of self-government of national autonomous areas shall see to a more effective prevention and treatment of endemic diseases, provide better protection for the health of women and children, and improve sanitary conditions.

Article 41   The organs of self-government of national autonomous areas shall independently develop sports, promote the traditional sports of the nationalities and improve the physical fitness of the people of the various nationalities.

Article 42   The organs of self-government of the national autonomous areas shall strive to develop exchanges and cooperation with other areas in education, science and technology, culture and art, public health, sports, etc.

In accordance with relevant state provisions, the organs of self-government of autonomous regions and autonomous prefectures may conduct exchanges with foreign countries in education, science and technology, culture and art, public health, sports, etc.

Article 43   In accordance with legal stipulations, the organs of self-government of national autonomous areas shall work out measures for control of the transient population.

Article 44   In accordance with legal stipulations, the organs of self-government of national autonomous areas shall, in the light of local conditions, work out measures for family planning.

Article 45   The organs of self-government of national autonomous areas shall protect and improve the living environment and the ecological environment and shall prevent and control pollution and other public hazards.

Chapter   IV

The People's Courts and People's Procuratorates of National Autonomous Areas

Article 46   The people's courts and people's procuratorates of national autonomous areas shall be responsible to the people's congresses at corresponding levels and their standing committees. The people's procuratorates of national autonomous areas shall also be responsible to the people's procuratorates at higher levels.

The administration of justice by the people's courts of national autonomous areas shall be supervised by the Supreme People's Court and by people's courts at higher levels. The work of the people's procuratorates of national autonomous areas shall be directed by the Supreme People's Procuratorate and by people's procuratorates at higher levels.

Members of the leadership and of the staff of the people's court and of the people's procuratorate of a national autonomous area shall include people from the nationality exercising regional autonomy in that area.

Article 47   In the prosecution and trial of cases, the people's courts and people's procuratorates of national autonomous areas shall use the language commonly used in the locality. They shall guarantee that citizens of the various nationalities enjoy the right to use the spoken and written languages of their own nationalities in court proceedings. The people's courts and people's procuratorates should provide translation for any party to the court proceedings who is not familiar with the spoken or written languages commonly used in the locality. Legal documents should be written, according to actual needs, in the language or languages commonly used in the locality.

Chapter   V

Relations Among Nationalities Within a National Autonomous Area

Article 48   The organ of self-government of a national autonomous area shall guarantee equal rights for the various nationalities in the area.

The organ of self-government of a national autonomous area shall unite the cadres and masses of the various nationalities and give full play to their initiative in a joint effort to develop the area.

Article 49   The organ of self-government of a national autonomous area shall persuade and encourage cadres of the various nationalities to learn each other's spoken and written languages. Cadres of Han nationality should learn the spoken and written languages of the local minority nationalities. While learning and using the spoken and written languages of their own nationalities, cadres of minority nationalities should also learn *putonghua* and the written Chinese (Han) language commonly used throughout the country.

Awards should be given to state functionaries in national autonomous areas who can use skillfully two or more spoken or written languages that are commonly used in the locality.

Article 50   The organ of self-government of a national autonomous area shall help other minority nationalities living in concentrated communities in the area establish appropriate autonomous areas or nationality townships.

The organ of self-government of a national autonomous area shall help the various nationalities in the area develop their economic, educational, scientific, cultural, public health and physical culture affairs.

The organ of self-government of a national autonomous area shall give consideration to the characteristics and needs of nationalities living in settlements scattered over the area.

Article 51   In dealing with special issues concerning the various nationalities within its area, the organ of self-government of a national autonomous area must conduct full consultation with their representatives and respect their opinions.

Article 52   The organ of self-government of a national autonomous area shall guarantee that citizens of the various nationalities in the area enjoy the rights of citizens prescribed in the Constitution and shall educate them in the need to perform their duties as citizens.

Article 53   The organ of self-government of a national autonomous area shall promote the civic virtues of love of the motherland, of the people, of labour, of science and of socialism and conduct education among the citizens of the various nationalities in the area in patriotism, communism and state policies concerning the nationalities. The cadres and masses of the various nationalities must be educated to trust, learn from and help one another and to respect the spoken and written languages, folkways and customs and religious beliefs of one another in a joint effort to safeguard the unification of the country and the unity of all the nationalities.

Chapter   VI

Leadership and Assistance
from State Organs at Higher Levels

Article 54   The resolutions, decisions, orders and instructions concerning national autonomous areas adopted by state organs at higher levels should suit the conditions in these areas.

Article 55   State organs at higher levels shall provide financial, material and technical assistance to national autonomous areas to accelerate their economic and cultural development.

In making plans for national economic and social development, state organs at higher levels should take into consideration the characteristics and needs of national autonomous areas.

Article 56   The state shall set aside special funds to help national autonomous areas develop their economy and culture.

The special funds set aside by the state and its provisional grants to the nationalities may not be deducted, withheld or misappropriated by any state agency, nor may they be used to substitute for the normal budgetary revenues of national autonomous areas.

Article 57   In accordance with the state policy for trade with the minority nationalities, state organs at higher levels shall give consideration to the commercial, supply and marketing, and medical and pharmaceutical enterprises in national autonomous areas.

Article 58   State organs at higher levels shall rationally review or readjust the base figures for the financial revenues and expenditures of national autonomous areas.

Article 59   While distributing the means of production and means of subsistence, state organs at higher levels shall give consideration to the needs of national autonomous areas.

While making plans for the state purchase of industrial and agricultural products and other local and special products of national autonomous areas and for state distribution of such products at a higher level, state organs at higher levels shall give consideration to the interests of the national autonomous areas and the producers, and set reasonable base figures for state distribution at a higher level or a reasonable ratio between the amount to be purchased and the amount to be kept.

Article 60   In matters of investment, loans and taxation and in production, supply, transportation and sales, state organs at higher levels shall help national autonomous areas in the rational exploitation of local resources to develop local industry, transportation and energy and to advance and improve the production of goods specially needed by minority nationalities and of traditional handicrafts.

Article 61   State organs at higher levels shall enlist and support economically developed areas in pursuing economic and technological cooperation with national autonomous areas to help the latter areas raise their level of operation and management and their level of production technology.

Article 62   While exploiting resources and undertaking construction in national autonomous areas, the state shall give consideration to the interests of these areas, make arrangements favourable to the economic construction there and pay proper attention to the productive pursuits and the life of the minority nationalities there.

Enterprises and institutions affiliated to state organs at higher levels but located in national autonomous areas shall give priority to local minority nationalities when recruiting personnel.

Enterprises and institutions affiliated to state organs at higher levels but located in national autonomous areas shall respect the power of autonomy of the local organs of self-government and accept their supervision.

Article 63   Without the consent of the organ of self-government of a national autonomous area, no state agency at a higher level may change the affiliation of an enterprise under the administration of the local government.

Article 64   State organs at higher levels shall help national autonomous areas train, from among local nationalities, large numbers of cadres at various levels and specialised personnel and skilled workers of different professions and trades; in accordance with local needs and in various forms, they shall send appropriate numbers of teachers, doctors, scientists and technicians as well as managerial executives to work in national autonomous areas and provide them with proper benefits.

Article 65   State organs at higher levels shall help national autonomous areas speed up the development of education and raise the scientific and cultural levels of the people of local nationalities.

The state shall set up institutes of nationalities and, in other institutions of higher education, nationality-oriented classes and preparatory classes that enroll only students from minority nationalities. Preferred enrollment and preferred assignment of jobs may also be introduced. In enrollment, institutions of higher education and secondary technical schools shall appropriately set lower standards and requirements for the admission of students from minority nationalities.

Article 66 State organs at higher levels shall intensify education among cadres and masses of the various nationalities in the government's policies concerning nationalities and frequently review the observance and implementation of these policies and relevant laws.

Chapter VII

Supplementary Provisions

Article 67 This Law has been adopted by the National People's Congress and shall go into effect on October 1, 1984.

Military Service Law of the People's Republic of China

(Adopted at the Second Session of the Sixth National People's Congress, promulgated by Order No. 14 of the President of the People's Republic of China on May 31, 1984, and effective as of October 1, 1984)

Contents

Chapter I

General Provisions

Article 1 This Law is formulated pursuant to Article 55 of the Constitution of the People's Republic of China, which stipulates, "It is the sacred duty of every citizen of the People's Republic of China to defend the motherland and resist aggression. It is the honourable duty of citizens of the People's Republic of China to perform military service and join the militia in accordance with the law," and in accordance with other relevant provisions of the Constitution.

Article 2   The People's Republic of China shall practise a military service system which is based mainly on conscription and which combines conscripts with volunteers and a militia with a reserve service.

Article 3   All citizens of the People's Republic of China, regardless of ethnic status, race, occupation, family background, religious belief and education, have the obligation to perform military service according to the provisions of this Law.

Exemptions from military service shall be granted to persons unfit for it owing to serious physical defects or serious deformities.

Persons deprived of political rights by law may not perform military service.

Article 4   The armed forces of the People's Republic of China shall be composed of the Chinese People's Liberation Army, the Chinese People's Armed Police Force and the Militia.

Article 5   The military service shall comprise an active service and a reserve service. Those serving in the Chinese People's Liberation Army are active servicemen while those regimented into militia organizations or registered in the reserve service are reservists.

Article 6   The active servicemen and reservists must abide by the Constitution and the law, and shall perform their duties and at the same time enjoy their rights as citizens; their rights and duties resulting from their joining the military service shall be specified separately in military regulations in addition to the provisions of this Law.

Article 7   Active servicemen must abide by the rules and regulations of the army, faithfully discharge their duties and always be ready to fight for the defence of the motherland.

Reservists must participate in military training according to the regulations and always be ready to join the army and take part in war for the defence of the motherland.

Article 8   Medals, decorations or titles of honour shall be given to active servicemen and reservists who perform meritorious deeds.

Article 9   The People's Liberation Army shall practise a system of military ranks.

Article 10   Responsibility for military service work throughout the country shall be assumed by the Ministry of National Defence under the leadership of the State Council and the Central Military Commission.

The military commands shall be responsible for military service work within their respective areas as assigned by the Ministry of National Defence.

The provincial commands (garrison commands), sub-commands (garrison commands) and the departments of people's armed forces of counties, autonomous counties, cities and municipal districts shall concurrently act as the military service organs of the people's governments at corresponding levels and shall be responsible for military service work in their respective areas under the leadership of military organs at higher levels and the people's governments at corresponding levels.

Government organs, public organizations, enterprises and institutions and the people's governments of townships, nationality townships, and towns shall carry out military service work according to the provisions of this Law. Professional work concerning military service shall be handled by the department of people's armed forces or by a designated department where there is no such department.

Chapter   II

Enlistment in Peacetime

Article 11   The number of citizens to be enlisted for active service each year, the requirements for them to be enlisted and the time schedule for enlistment shall be prescribed by order of the State Council and the Central Military Commission.

Article 12   Each year, male citizens who have reached 18 years of age by December 31 shall be enlisted for active service. Those who are not enlisted during the year shall remain eligible for active service until they are 22.

To meet the needs of the armed forces, female citizens may be enlisted for active service according to the provision of the preceding paragraph.

To meet the needs of the armed forces and on the principle of voluntary participation, male and female citizens who have not yet reached 18 years of age by December 31 of a certain year may be enlisted for active service.

Article 13   Each year, male citizens who will be 18 years old by December 31 shall be registered for military service by September 30 according to the arrangements of the military service organs of counties, autonomous counties, cities or municipal districts. Those who have registered and have passed the preliminary examination are called citizens eligible for enlistment.

Article 14   During the period of enlistment, citizens eligible for enlistment shall, upon notification by the military service organs of counties, autonomous counties, cities or municipal districts, go to the designated health centres in time for physical examination.

Citizens eligible for enlistment who are qualified for active service shall be enlisted for such service upon approval by the military service organs of counties, autonomous counties, cities or municipal districts.

Article 15   The enlistment of a citizen eligible for enlistment may be deferred if he is the only worker in his family providing its means of subsistence or if he is a student in a full-time school.

Article 16   A citizen eligible for enlistment shall not be enlisted if he is detained for investigation, prosecution or trial, or if he has been sentenced to imprisonment, criminal detention or public surveillance and is serving his sentence.

Chapter III

The Active Service and Reserve Service of Soldiers

Article 17   There shall be two types of soldiers: conscripts and volunteers.

Article 18   The term of service for conscripts shall be three years in the army and four years in the navy and the air force.

Upon the expiration of his active service, a conscript may, according to the need of the armed forces and on a voluntary basis, extend his service. The extended period of service shall be one to two years in the army and one year in the navy and the air force.

Article 19   A conscript on extended active duty who has completed five years of active service and who has become professionally or technically skilled may, by his application and upon approval by a division headquarters or a higher organ, change to a volunteer.

The term of active service for a volunteer shall be no less than eight years and no more than twelve years, counting from the day he changes to a volunteer, up to a maximum age of 35; the term may be extended appropriately upon approval by an army headquarters or a higher organ if the volunteer is specially needed in the armed forces and if he desires the extension.

Article 20   A soldier shall be discharged from active service upon the expiration of his term of active service. Those who have to be discharged from active service because of a reduction in the personnel of the armed forces, a condition of health unfit for continued service as diagnosed and certified by a hospital of the armed forces, or other special reasons may be discharged before the expiration of the terms of their active service upon approval by a division headquarters or a higher organ.

Article 21   A soldier who is discharged from active service but is qualified for reserve service shall be assigned by his army unit to serve in the soldiers' reserve; a soldier who is considered after assessment to be fit for the post of an officer shall serve in the officers' reserve.

A soldier who is discharged from active service and assigned by his army unit to serve in the reserve shall, within thirty days of returning to his place of residence, register for reserve service with the military service organ of his county, autonomous county, city or municipal district.

Article 22   Citizens eligible for enlistment who have registered for military service according to the provisions of Article 13 of this Law but who have not been enlisted for active service shall serve in the soldiers' reserve.

Article 23   Persons serving in the soldiers' reserve shall be between the ages of 18 and 35.

Article 24   Persons in the soldiers' reserve shall be divided into two categories:

Category One of persons in the soldiers' reserve shall include:

(1) persons regimented into primary militia organizations pursuant to the provisions of Article 38 of this Law;

(2) soldiers under the age of 28 who have been discharged from active service and have registered for reserve service in work units where no militia organizations are to be established; and

(3) professional and technical personnel under the age of 28 who have registered for reserve service.

Category Two of persons in the soldiers' reserve shall include:

(1) persons regimented into ordinary militia organizations pursuant to the provisions of Article 38 of this Law; and

(2) soldiers aged between 29 and 35 who have been discharged from active service and have registered for reserve service as well as other male citizens qualified for reserve service in work units where no militia organizations are to be established.

Reserve soldiers in Category One shall be transferred to Category Two upon attaining the age of 29; those in Category Two shall be discharged from the reserve service at the age of 35.

Chapter   IV

The Active Service and
Reserve Service of Officers

Article 25   Officers in active service shall be replenished with the following personnel:

(1) graduates of military institutes and academies;

(2) soldiers who have been trained at officers' training centres established with the approval of the Central Military Commission and who are considered after assessment to be fit for the post of officer;

(3) graduates of institutions of higher learning and secondary technical schools who are fit for officers' posts; and

(4) civilian cadres of the armed forces and professional and technical personnel recruited individually from non-military departments.

In wartime, officers in active service shall also be replenished with the following personnel:

(1) soldiers who can be appointed directly as officers; and

(2) reserve officers called into active service and cadres of non-military departments fit for active service.

Article 26   Officers in reserve service shall consist of the following:

(1) officers who have been discharged from active service and transferred to reserve service;

(2) soldiers who have been discharged from active service and assigned to serve in the officers' reserve;

(3) graduates of institutions of higher learning assigned to serve in the officers' reserve;

(4) full-time cadres of the departments of people's armed forces and cadres of the militia assigned to serve in the officers' reserve; and

(5) cadres and professional and technical personnel of non-military departments assigned to serve in the officers' reserve.

Article 27   The maximum age for officers in active and reserve services shall be stipulated in the Regulations of the Chinese People's Liberation Army on the Military Service of Officers.

Article 28   Officers in active service who have attained the maximum age stipulated for such service shall be discharged from such service; those who have not attained the maximum age but have to be discharged from active service for special reasons may be discharged from such service with approval.

Officers discharged from active service may be transferred to the officers' reserve if they are qualified to serve in it.

Article 29   Officers who have been discharged from active service and transferred to reserve service, soldiers who have been discharged from active service and assigned to serve in the officers' reserve and graduates of institutions of higher learning assigned to serve in the officers' reserve shall, within 30 days of their arrival at their places of work or residence, register for reserve service with the military service organs of their counties, autonomous counties, cities or municipal districts.

Full-time cadres of the departments of people's armed forces, cadres of the militia, and cadres and professional and technical personnel of non-military departments fit for officers' posts shall serve in the officers' reserve through registration with the military service organs of counties, autonomous counties, cities or municipal districts and upon approval by military organs at a higher level.

Reserve officers who have attained the maximum age stipulated for reserve service shall be discharged from such service.

Chapter   V

Cadets Enrolled by Military Institutes and Academies from Among Young Students

Article 30   Military institutes and academies may, according to needs in building up the armed forces, enroll cadets from among young students. The age limit for the cadets to be enrolled need not be the same as that for the active servicemen to be enlisted.

Article 31   Cadets who have completed their studies and passed their examinations shall be given a diploma by the institutes or academies and shall be appointed officers in active service or civilian cadres according to relevant regulations.

Article 32   Cadets who have completed the required courses but have failed in the examinations shall be given a certificate of their completion of the courses by the institutes or academies and return to their places of residence before they enrolled in such military institutes or academies, and shall be placed by the people's governments of their respective counties, autonomous counties, cities or municipal districts according to state regulations on the placement for those who have completed their studies at other colleges and schools of similar status.

Article 33   Cadets who suffer from chronic diseases or are otherwise unfit for continuing their studies at military institutes or academies and who thus leave school upon approval shall be given a certificate by the institutes or academies of the amount of academic work they have done and shall be accepted for placement by the people's governments of the counties, autonomous counties, cities or municipal districts at their places of residence before they enrolled in such institutes or academies.

Article 34   Cadets dismissed from school shall be accepted by the people's governments of the counties, autonomous counties, cities or municipal districts at their places of residence before enrollment, which shall treat them according to the state regulations on the treatment of students dismissed from other colleges and schools of similar status.

Article 35   The provisions of Articles 31, 32, 33 and 34 of this Law shall also apply to cadets enrolled from among soldiers in active service.

Chapter   VI

The Militia

Article 36   The militia is an armed organization of the masses not divorced from production and is an assisting and reserve force for the

Chinese People's Liberation Army.

The tasks of the militia shall be:

(1) take an active part in the socialist modernization and be exemplary in completing the tasks in production and other fields;

(2) undertake the duties related to preparations against war, defend the frontiers and maintain public order; and

(3) be always ready to join the armed forces to take part in war, resist aggression and defend the motherland.

Article 37 Militia organizations shall be set up in townships, nationality townships, towns, enterprises and institutions. Male citizens who belong to the 18-35 age group and are fit for military service, excluding those enlisted for active service, shall be regimented into militia units to perform reserve service. The age limit for militia cadres may be handled flexibly.

In units where no militia organizations are to be established, male citizens qualified for military service shall be registered for reserve service in accordance with the regulations.

Article 38 The militia shall consist of a primary militia and an ordinary militia. A selected group of militiamen under 28 years of age, including soldiers discharged from active service and other persons who have received or are selected for military training, shall be regimented into the primary militia; other male citizens belonging to the age group of 18 to 35 who are qualified for military service shall be regimented into the ordinary militia.

The primary militia may recruit female citizens when necessary.

The age limit for primary militiamen may be extended appropriately in frontier areas on land or sea, areas inhabited by minority nationalities as well as urban units in special circumstances.

Chapter VII

Military Training for Reservists

Article 39 Military training for soldiers in reserve service shall be conducted either in militia organizations or separately.

Primary militiamen belonging to the age group of 18-20 who have not been in active service shall receive military training for 30 to 40 days; the period of training for professional and technical militiamen may be extended appropriately according to actual needs.

The retraining of primary militiamen who have performed active service or have received military training and the military training for ordinary militiamen and for soldiers in reserve service who are not regimented into militia organizations shall be conducted as provided for by the Central Military Commission.

Article 40   Officers in reserve service shall receive military training for three to six months during the period of their reserve service.

Article 41   The State Council and the Central Military Commission may, when necessary, decide that the reservists shall participate in emergency training.

Article 42   During the period of military training, reservists in government organs, public organizations, enterprises and institutions shall receive their wages and bonuses from their respective units as usual, and their welfare benefits shall not be affected either.

Reservists in rural areas shall, during the period of military training, be subsidized for the loss of work time according to the income of similar workers through an equal sharing of the burden effected by the people's governments of townships, nationality townships, and towns.

Chapter VIII

Military Training for Students of Institutions of Higher Learning and Students of Senior Middle Schools

Article 43   Students of institutions of higher learning must receive basic military training during the period of their schooling.

To meet the needs of national defence, additional short-term, concentrated training shall be given to students fit for the posts of officers, and those who are considered as qualified after assessment shall serve in the officers' reserve upon approval by military organs.

Article 44   Offices in charge of military training shall be set up and military instructors provided in institutions of higher learning to organize and conduct the military training of the students.

The short-term, concentrated training for promoting people as reserve officers prescribed in paragraph 2 of Article 43 shall be organized and conducted jointly by officers in active service sent from military organs and the offices of the institutions of higher learning in charge of military training.

Article 45   Senior middle schools and schools equivalent to them shall be provided with military instructors to conduct military training for the students.

Article 46   The military training of students of institutions of higher learning and students of senior middle schools shall be under the charge of the Ministry of Education and the Ministry of National Defence. Educational departments and military departments shall set up agencies or appoint full-time personnel to handle matters concerning the military training of students.

Chapter IX
Mobilization of Troops in Wartime

Article 47   In order to cope with an enemy's surprise attack and resist aggression, people's governments and military organs at all levels must, in peacetime, make preparations for the mobilization of troops in wartime.

Article 48   Upon the issuance of a mobilization order by the state, people's governments and military organs at all levels must promptly carry out the mobilization:

(1) Active servicemen must not be discharged from active service, and those on vacation or on home leave must immediately return to their respective units.

(2) Reservists must be ready to be called into active service at any time and, as soon as they are notified, must punctually report at the designated places.

(3) Responsible persons of government organs, public organizations, enterprises and institutions and of the people's governments of townships, nationality townships, and towns must see to it that the reservists in their respective units who have been called up report at the designated places on time.

(4) Transportation departments must provide priority transportation for reservists who have been called up and for active servicemen returning to their units in the armed forces.

Article 49   The State Council and the Central Military Commission may decide to call into active service male citizens of the age of 36-45 in special wartime circumstances.

Article 50   When the war is over, active servicemen to be demobilized shall be discharged from active service in staggered groups in accordance with the demobilization order issued by the State Council and the Central Military Commission, and shall be properly placed by the people's governments at various levels.

Chapter X
Preferential Treatment for Active Servicemen and Placement of Ex-servicemen

Article 51   Active servicemen, disabled revolutionary armymen, ex-servicemen, and family members of revolutionary martyrs, of armymen who were killed in action or died of diseases, and of active servicemen shall be esteemed by the general public and given preferential treatment by the state and the masses of people.

Article 52 Disabled revolutionary armymen shall enjoy priority in buying tickets at favourable discount prices according to relevant regulations when travelling by train, ship, airplane or long-distance bus.

Ordinary mail sent by conscripts from their units shall be free of charge.

Article 53 Active servicemen who are wounded or disabled while taking part in military operations or performing military duties shall be graded for their disability by their army units and be given pension certificates for disabled revolutionary armymen. Disabled revolutionary armymen of Special Grade and First Grade discharged from active service shall be provided for by the state throughout their lives. Disabled revolutionary armymen of Second and Third Grades who are residents of cities or towns shall be given jobs suited to their abilities by the people's governments of their counties, autonomous counties, cities or municipal districts; those who are residents of rural areas may be given suitable jobs in enterprises or institutions if this can be done locally, or they may get an increase in the pension for the disabled in accordance with relevant regulations as a guarantee for their livelihood.

Article 54 Families of conscripts which reside in rural areas shall be given favourable treatment through an equal sharing of the burden to be effected by the people's governments of townships, nationality townships or towns. The specific measures and standards for such favourable treatment shall be formulated by the people's governments of provinces, autonomous regions, and municipalities directly under the Central Government.

Families of conscripts which reside in cities and towns and which face financial difficulties shall be given appropriate subsidies by the people's governments of counties, autonomous counties, cities or municipal districts.

Article 55 A pension in a lump sum shall be given by the state to the family of an active serviceman who was killed in action or died of a disease. If the family cannot provide for itself because it has no one who can work or because it has no regular income, it shall be given a periodical pension by the state.

Article 56 Conscripts discharged from active service shall, on the principle of returning to the place where they came from, be accepted and placed by the people's governments of the counties, autonomous counties, cities or municipal districts where they were enlisted:

(1) Conscripts who are residents of rural areas, when discharged from active service, shall be provided with proper arrangements for their work and livelihood by the people's governments of townships, nationality townships and towns. Government organs, public organizations, enterprises and institutions shall give appropriate preference to them when recruiting staff and workers from rural areas.

(2) Conscripts who are residents of cities and towns, when discharged from active service, shall be given jobs by the people's governments of counties, autonomous counties, cities or municipal districts. Those who, prior to enlistment, had been regular staff members or workers of government organs, public organizations, enterprises or institutions shall be allowed to resume their original work or positions.

(3) When conscripts discharged from active service take entrance examinations for institutions of higher learning or secondary vocational schools, they shall enjoy enrollment priority over contenders who are equally qualified in other respects.

Article 57 Conscripts discharged from active service because of mental disorder acquired during the period of their active service shall, depending on the seriousness of their cases, be sent to a civilian hospital for medical treatment or sent home for recuperation. Their medical and living expenses shall be borne by the people's governments of their respective counties, autonomous counties, cities or municipal districts.

Conscripts discharged from active service who contracted chronic diseases during the period of their active service and who need medical treatment because of a recurrence of such diseases shall be treated by a civilian medical institution. If they have financial difficulties and cannot meet the necessary medical and living expenses, the people's governments of their counties, autonomous counties, cities or municipal districts shall give them a subsidy.

Article 58 Volunteers discharged from active service shall be given jobs by the people's governments of their counties, autonomous counties, cities or municipal districts where they were enlisted; in special cases they may also be placed through an overall arrangement by the people's governments at the next higher level or of provinces, autonomous regions, or municipalities directly under the Central Government. Those who wish to return to the rural areas to take part in agricultural production shall be encouraged to do so and given extra subsidies for setting up a home there.

Volunteers who have basically lost their ability to work because they were disabled while taking part in military operations or performing military duties or because their health broke down as a result of constant overwork during the period of their active service shall go through the procedures of retirement and shall be accepted and taken care of by the people's governments of the counties, autonomous counties, cities or municipal districts where they were enlisted or where their lineal relatives reside.

Article 59 Officers discharged from active service shall be properly placed by the state.

Article 60 In cases where militiamen died or were disabled while taking part in military operations or performing military duties, or where reservists or students died or were disabled while taking part in military training, pensions and preferential treatment shall be granted by the local people's governments in accordance with the Regulations on Pensions and Preferential Treatment Concerning Militiamen.

Chapter   XI

Punishments

Article 61   If any citizen who, pursuant to the provisions of this Law, has the duty to perform military service refuses to register for military service or evades such registration, if any citizen who is eligible for enlistment refuses to be enlisted or evades enlistment, or if a reservist refuses to undergo military training or evades such training, and if any such person refuses to mend his ways in spite of persuasion, the people's government at the grassroots level shall compel him to fulfil his duty of performing military service.

In wartime, if a reservist refuses to be called into active service or evades such service, or if he refuses to undergo military training or evades such training, and if the case is a serious one, he shall be punished with reference to the first paragraph of Article 6 of the Interim Regulations of the People's Republic of China on Punishment of Servicemen Who Commit Crimes Contrary to Their Duties.

Article 62   State functionaries who take bribes or engage in malpractices for selfish purposes while conducting military service work or who cause serious losses to such work by their dereliction of duty shall be punished, as the circumstances may require, according to the provisions of Articles 185 and 187 of the Criminal Law of the People's Republic of China. Administrative sanctions may be given where the circumstances are less serious.

Chapter   XII

Supplementary Provisions

Article 63   This Law shall apply to the Chinese People's Armed Police Force.

Article 64   The Chinese People's Liberation Army shall, when necessary, provide itself with civilian cadres. The regulations on civilian cadres shall be formulated separately.

Article 65   This Law shall come into force on October 1, 1984.

Forestry Law of the
People's Republic of China

*(Adopted at the Seventh Meeting of the Standing Committee of
the Sixth National People's Congress, promulgated by Order
No.17 of the President of the People's Republic of
China on September 20,1984, and effective
as of January 1, 1985)*

Contents

Chapter   I

General Provisions

Article 1 This Law is formulated for the purpose of protecting, cultivating and rationally utilizing forest resources, speeding up afforestation of our land, giving full play to the forests' role of conserving water and soil, moderating the climate, improving the environment and providing forest products, so as to meet the needs of socialist construction and the people's life.

Article 2 This Law must be observed in all activities relating to afforestation and tree felling as well as forest utilization, cultivation, management and administration within the territory of the People's Republic of China.

Article 3 Forest resources, with the exception of those owned by collectives as provided for by law, shall be owned by the whole people.

The forests, trees and forest land owned by the whole people and by collectives, as well as the trees owned and forest land used by individuals, shall be registered by the local people's governments at the county level and above, which shall, upon verification, issue certificates to confirm such ownership or right of use.

The lawful rights and interests of the owners and users of forests, trees and forest land shall be protected by law and shall not be infringed upon by any unit or individual.

Article 4 Forests are classified into the following five categories:

(1) Protective forests: forests, trees and shrubberies that mainly serve the purpose of protection. They consist of forests for water supply conservation, checking soil erosion, for windbreak and sand-fixation, farmland and pasture protection, embankment protection and road protection.

(2) Timber forests: forests and trees that are used mainly for producing timber, including bamboo forests that are used mainly for producing bamboo timber.

(3) Economic forests: forest trees that are used mainly for producing fruit, edible oil, beverage ingredients, condiments, industrial raw material and medicinal materials.

(4) Firewood forests: forest trees that are used mainly for producing fuel wood.

(5) Forests for special uses: forests and forest trees that are used mainly for national defence, environmental protection and scientific experiment purposes. These include forests for national defence, experimental forests, seed forests, environmental protection forests, aesthetic forests, forest trees at scenic spots, historical sites and places with historic significance in the Chinese revolution and forests in nature reserves.

Article 5 The guiding policy for forestry development shall be: put the emphasis on forest management, universalize forest protection, vigorously promote afforestation, coordinate cutting with cultivation and ensure the sustained utilization of forest resources.

The state shall encourage research in forest science so as to raise the level of forest science and technology.

Article 6 The state shall adopt the following measures to protect forest resources:

(1) Quotas shall be imposed on tree felling, and efforts to plant trees and close hillsides to facilitate afforestation shall be encouraged, in order to enlarge the forest-covered area.

(2) Financial assistance or long-term loans shall be provided for collectives and individuals engaged in tree planting and forest cultivation in accordance with the relevant regulations of the state and local people's

governments.

(3) Forest culture fees shall be collected for the exclusive use of tree planting and forest cultivation.

(4) Departments of coal and paper manufacturing industries shall set aside a certain amount of funds commensurate to the output of coal, wood pulp and paper for the exclusive use of cultivating timber forests that will be used for mine timber and paper-making.

(5) A forestry funding system shall be established.

Article 7 With regard to the forestry production and development in autonomous areas of minority nationalities, the state and people's governments of the provinces and autonomous regions shall, in accordance with the power of autonomy the state has provided for national autonomous areas, grant these areas greater decision-making power and more economic benefits than other areas in forestry development, timber distribution and use of the forest fund.

Article 8 The forestry department under the State Council shall be responsible for forestry work throughout the country. The forestry departments of the people's governments at the county level and above shall be responsible for forestry work in their respective areas. Full-time or part-time posts shall be set up in people's governments at the township level to take charge of forestry work.

Article 9 Planting trees and protecting forests are the bounden duty of every citizen. People's governments at all levels shall launch afforestation activities and organize tree planting on a voluntary and nationwide basis.

Article 10 The people's governments at various levels shall give commendation or material awards to units and individuals with outstanding achievements in tree planting, afforestation and forest protection and administration.

Chapter II

Forest Management and Administration

Article 11 Forestry departments at all levels shall, in accordance with the provisions of this Law, administer and supervise the protection, utilization and regeneration of forest resources.

Article 12 Competent forestry departments at all levels shall be responsible for organizing surveys and keeping files of records of forest resources so as to have a good grasp of the changes in forest resources.

Article 13 The people's governments at all levels shall each work out a long-term forestry development plan. State-owned forestry enterprises and institutions as well as nature reserves shall, in accordance with the long-term forestry development plan, formulate their own forest management plans and submit them to the competent departments at the next higher level for approval before putting them into effect.

The competent forestry departments shall direct the rural collective economic organizations, state-owned agricultural and pastoral farms, industrial enterprises and mines in drawing up their forest management plans.

Article 14 Disputes over ownership and right of use of trees and forest land arising between units owned by the whole people, between units owned by collectives or between units owned by the whole people and units owned by collectives shall be handled by people's governments at the county level or above.

Disputes over ownership and right of use of trees and forest land arising between individuals and between individuals and units owned by the whole people or collectives shall be handled by local people's governments at the county or township level.

A party to a dispute who refuses to accept the decision of the people's government may bring suit in a people's court within one month after receiving notification of the decision.

Pending a settlement of the dispute over the ownership or right of use of trees and forest land, neither of the parties may cut down the trees under dispute.

Article 15 No forest land or only a small amount of forest land should be used in carrying out prospecting and designing, building engineering facilities or mining. When it is necessary to use or requisition forest land, the matter shall be dealt with in accordance with the relevant legal provisions. If 2,000 *mu* or more of forest land need to be used or requisitioned, an application shall be submitted to the State Council for approval.

Chapter III

Forest Protection

Article 16 Local people's governments at various levels shall enjoin the relevant departments to set up agencies to be responsible for forest protection. They shall, in light of the actual needs, increase facilities in large forest areas to strengthen forest protection, urge grass-roots units which own forests or which are located in forest areas to formulate forest protection pledges, mobilize the masses to protect the forests, delimit areas of responsibility for forest protection and appoint full-time or part-time forest guards.

Forest guards may be appointed by people's governments at the county or township level. The main duties of forest guards shall be: patrol the forests and prevent acts of destroying forest resources. Forest guards shall have the right to request local departments concerned to deal with those who have caused damage to forest resources.

Article 17   Local people's governments at various levels shall adopt practical measures to prevent and fight forest fires:

(1) fix fire prevention periods. During such periods, it shall be forbidden to use fire in the open in a forest area. Where the use of fire is necessary under special circumstances, prior approval must be secured from a people's government at the county level or its authorized agency;

(2) install fire prevention facilities in the forest areas;

(3) immediately mobilize the local military and civilians as well as departments concerned to fight forest fire the moment it breaks out; and

(4) in case people are wounded, disabled or killed in fighting forest fires, those who are state employees shall be given medical treatment and pensions by their own units, which shall also grant pensions to families of the deceased. If the persons wounded, disabled or killed are not state employees, the medical treatment and pensions shall be provided by the units where the fire occurred, in accordance with the provisions laid down by the relevant competent departments under the State Council; if the units where the fire occurred are not responsible for causing the fire or are really incapable of bearing such expenses, the medical treatment and pensions shall be provided by the local people's government.

Article 18   The competent forestry departments at various levels shall be responsible for organizing prevention and control of plant diseases and insect pests in the forests.

The competent forestry departments shall be responsible for determining the categories of forest tree seeds and seedlings that should be quarantined, setting up quarantine zones and protection zones and instituting quarantine on tree seeds and seedlings.

Article 19   It shall be forbidden to cut down trees for the purpose of opening up farmland, quarrying and digging sand or earth as well as other activities of deforestation.

It shall be forbidden to cut firewood and graze in young growth areas and in forests for special uses.

People entering a forest or its fringe areas shall be forbidden to move or damage any markers set up in the service of forestry.

Article 20   The competent forestry department under the State

Council as well as people's governments of provinces, autonomous regions, and municipalities directly under the Central Government shall, for the purpose of better protection and administration, set up nature reserves in forest areas calling for special protection, such as areas with typical forest ecology in different natural regions, forest areas where rare plants and animals propagate, and natural tropical rain forests.

The administrative measures for nature reserves shall be formulated by the competent forestry department under the State Council and shall be implemented after being submitted to and approved by the State Council.

Rare trees growing outside the nature reserves as well as plant species of special value in the forest areas shall be well protected; they shall not be cut or collected unless approved by the competent forestry department of a province, autonomous region, or municipality directly under the Central Government.

Article 21   It shall be forbidden to hunt wild animals that have been put under state protection in the forest areas. Where hunting of such animals is desired for special needs, the matter shall be dealt with in accordance with the relevant laws and regulations of the state.

Chapter   IV

Tree Planting and Afforestation

Article 22   The people's governments at various levels shall work out afforestation plans and, in light of the specific local conditions, set forth targets for increasing the forest coverage of their respective areas.

People's governments at various levels shall organize people of all walks of life and urban and rural inhabitants to accomplish the tasks provided for in the afforestation plans.

Afforestation on barren hills and wastelands owned by the whole people that are suitable for afforestation shall be organized by the competent forestry departments and other competent departments; afforestation on collectively owned barren hills and wastelands shall be organized by collective economic organizations.

Afforestation of areas on both sides of railways, highways and rivers and around lakes and reservoirs shall be organized by the competent departments concerned in light of the actual local conditions; afforestation in industrial and mining areas, on grounds occupied by government departments and schools, around army barracks as well as in areas managed by agricultural, pastoral and fish farms shall be carried out by those units respectively.

The barren hills and wastelands owned by the whole people and by collectives that are suitable for afforestation may be contracted by collectives or individuals for afforestation.

Article 23 The forest trees planted by units owned by the whole people shall be managed by such units, and they shall distribute the proceeds from those trees as provided for by the state.

Forest trees planted and managed by units under collective ownership shall be owned by them.

Trees planted by rural inhabitants around their houses and on privately farmed plots of cropland and hilly land shall be individually owned by themselves. Trees planted by urban inhabitants and staff and workers in the courtyards of their privately owned houses shall be individually owned by themselves.

In cases where a collective or an individual contracts to afforest barren hills and wastelands owned by the whole people or by collectives that are suitable for afforestation, the forest trees planted pursuant to the contract shall be owned by the contracting collective or individual; if there are other provisions in the contract, such provisions of the contract shall be followed.

Article 24 Local people's governments shall be responsible for closing the newly cultivated young growth land and hillsides that must be closed to facilitate afforestation.

Chapter V

Forest Tree Cutting

Article 25 The state shall, acting on the principle that the consumption of a timber forest should be lower than its growth, impose strict control on the annual forest cut. Annual quotas for cutting down forests and forest trees owned by the whole people shall be worked out, taking a state enterprise, institution, farm, factory or mine as a unit, and annual quotas for cutting down forests and forest trees owned by the collective shall be worked out, taking the county as a unit. These quotas shall then be aggregated by the competent forestry departments of provinces, autonomous regions, or municipalities directly under the Central Government and examined by the people's governments at the corresponding level, before they are submitted to the State Council for approval.

Article 26 The state shall draw up a unified annual timber production plan, which shall not exceed the approved annual cutting quota. The scope of planning management shall be stipulated by the State Council.

Article 27 The following provisions must be observed in cutting down a forest and forest trees:

(1) Selection cutting, clear cutting and gradual cutting may be carried out for mature timber forests in light of their different conditions. Clear cutting shall be strictly controlled and regenerative reforestation must be completed during the same year or the following year after such cutting has been carried out.

(2) Only cultivation cutting and regeneration cutting may be allowed in protective forests and in such forests for special uses as forests for national defence, seed forests, environmental protection forests and scenic forests.

(3) It shall be strictly forbidden to cut down forest trees in such forests for special uses as forest trees at scenic and historical spots and places with historic significance in the Chinese revolution as well as the forest trees in nature reserves.

Article 28 Anyone who wants to cut down forest trees must apply for a cutting licence and carry out cutting operations according to the provisions of the cutting licence, but exceptions shall be made for rural inhabitants who want to cut down scattered trees belonging to themselves and growing on their private plots and around their houses.

Cutting licences required for state-owned forestry enterprises and institutions, government agencies, people's organizations, army units, schools as well as other state-owned enterprises and institutions to cut down forest trees shall be issued, after examination, by the competent forestry departments at or above the county level in the areas where they are located.

Cutting licences required for regeneration cutting of protective belts along railways and highways as well as forest trees in cities and towns shall be issued, after examination, by the competent departments concerned.

Cutting licences required for cutting down forest trees by rural collective economic organizations shall be issued, after examination, by the competent forestry departments at the county level.

Cutting licences required for rural inhabitants to cut down forest trees on hills allocated for their private use and forest trees of the collective that individuals have contracted for cultivation shall be issued, after examination, by the competent forestry department at the county level or the people's government at the township or town level authorized by it.

Provisions of the preceding paragraphs shall apply to cutting bamboo in bamboo forests cultivated mainly for producing bamboo timber.

Article 29 The departments in charge of examining tree cutting applications and issuing cutting licences shall not issue cutting licences in excess of the approved annual cutting quotas.

Article 30 When applying for cutting licences, state-owned forestry enterprises and institutions must submit documents of survey and design of the cutting area. When applying for cutting licences, other units must submit documents stating the purpose, location, area, types and existing state of the forest, the growing stock involved, the method of cutting, as well as regeneration measures.

In case a unit carries out timber felling operations in a cutting area in violation of the pertinent rules, the cutting licence issuing departments shall have the right to revoke its licence and order it to suspend its cutting operations until such violations are rectified.

Article 31 Units or individuals engaged in timber felling must complete regenerative reforestation within the specified time limit and according to the requirements in terms of area, number of trees and types of trees provided for in the cutting licence. The area of reforestation and the number of trees to be planted must be larger than the cutting area and the number of trees already cut.

Article 32 Measures for the management, supervision and administration of timber in forest areas shall be separately formulated by the State Council.

Article 33 A transport licence issued by the competent forestry department shall be required for transporting timber out of a forest area, except for timber under unified distribution by the state.

With the approval of people's governments at the level of the province, autonomous region or municipality directly under the Central Government, timber checkpoints may be set up in forest areas to supervise timber transportation. The timber checkpoints shall have the right to stop anyone who transports timber without a transport licence or allocation notice issued by the competent department in charge of goods and material.

Chapter VI
Legal Liability

Article 34 Whoever illegally cuts down trees, bamboo, etc., if the circumstances are minor, shall be ordered by the competent forestry department to compensate for the losses incurred and to plant several dozen times the number of trees cut down and pay a fine equal to three to ten times the unlawful income. Whoever denudes forests or other woodlands, if the circumstances are minor, shall be ordered by the competent forestry department to plant five times the number of trees denuded and pay a fine equal to two to five times the unlawful income.

Whoever illegally cuts down or denudes forest and other woodlands, if the circumstances are serious, shall be investigated for criminal responsibility in accordance with Article 128 of the Criminal Law.

Whoever illegally cuts down and appropriates a huge number of forest trees shall be investigated for criminal responsibility in accordance with

Article 152 of the Criminal Law.

Article 35   In cases where forest tree cutting licences are issued in excess of the approved annual cutting quotas or by overstepping authority in violation of this Law, the personnel directly responsible shall be given administrative sanctions; in cases where serious damage is caused to the forest, the personnel directly responsible shall be investigated for criminal responsibility in accordance with Article 187 of the Criminal Law.

Article 36   Whoever counterfeits or resells forest tree cutting licences shall have his unlawful income confiscated and be fined by the competent forestry department; if the circumstances are serious, criminal responsibility shall be investigated by analogy to Article 120 of the Criminal Law.

Article 37   Whoever reclaims land, quarries stones, digs sand or earth, gathers seeds or resin, cuts firewood or engages in other activities in violation of this Law and thereby causes damage to forests and forest trees shall be ordered by the competent forestry department to compensate for the losses incurred and to plant one to three trees for each one damaged.

Article 38   The departments issuing cutting licences shall have the right to stop issuing licences to lumbering units or individuals that fail to accomplish their regeneration tasks as required; licences may be reissued to them only after they have completed the regeneration tasks. If the circumstances are serious, they may be fined by the competent forestry department, and those directly responsible shall be given administrative sanctions by the units to which they belong or by the competent department at the next higher level.

Article 39   If a party refuses to accept the decision of the competent forestry department to impose a fine, it may file suit with a people's court within one month after receiving notification of the decision. If, upon the expiration of this period, the party has neither filed suit nor paid the fine, the competent forestry department may request the people's court for compulsory execution.

Chapter VII

Supplementary Provisions

Article 40   The competent forestry department under the State Council shall, in accordance with this Law, formulate measures for its implementation, which shall go into effect after being submitted to and approved by the State Council.

Article 41   In national autonomous areas in which the provisions of this Law cannot be applied in toto, the organs of self-government may, in light of the principle of this Law and the characteristics of the autonomous areas, formulate adoptive or supplementary provisions, which shall be submitted according to the legally prescribed procedure to the standing committee of the provincial or autonomous regional people's congress or to the Standing Committee of the National People's Congress for approval before they are implemented.

Article 42   This Law shall go into effect on January 1, 1985.

Appendix:

The Relevant Articles of the Criminal Law

Article 128   Whoever illegally cuts down trees or denudes forests or other woodlands, in violation of the laws and regulations on forestry protection, if the circumstances are serious, shall be sentenced to fixed-term imprisonment of not more than three years or criminal detention and may concurrently or exclusively be sentenced to a fine.

Article 152   A habitual thief or habitual swindler or anyone who steals, swindles or forcibly seizes a huge amount of public or private property shall be sentenced to fixed-term imprisonment of not less than five years and not more than ten years; if the circumstances are especially serious, he shall be sentenced to fixed-term imprisonment of not less than ten years or life imprisonment, and may concurrently be sentenced to confiscation of property.

Article 187   Any state functionary who, because of neglect of duty, causes public property or the interests of the state and the people to suffer heavy losses shall be sentenced to fix-term imprisonment of not more than five years or criminal detention.

Article 120   Whoever, for the purpose of profit, counterfeits or resells ration coupons, if the circumstances are serious, shall be sentenced to fixed-term imprisonment of not more than three years or criminal detention, and may concurrently or exclusively be sentenced to a fine or confiscation of property.

Ringleaders of a crime mentioned in the preceding paragraph and perpetrators of particularly serious cases of such crime shall be sentenced to fixed-term imprisonment of not less than three years and not more than seven years, and may concurrently be sentenced to confiscation of property.

Pharmaceutical Administration Law of the People's Republic of China

(Adopted at the Seventh Meeting of the Standing Committee of the Sixth National People's Congress, promulgated by Order No. 18 of the President of the People's Republic of China on September 20, 1984, and effective as of July 1, 1985)

Contents

Chapter I

General Provisions

Article 1 This Law is formulated with a view to enhancing the supervision and control of pharmaceuticals, ensuring their quality, improving their curative effects, guaranteeing safety in medication and safeguarding the health of the people.

Article 2 The administrative department of health under the State Council shall be responsible for the supervision and control of pharmaceuticals throughout the country.

Article 3 The state shall develop both modern and traditional medicines and give full play to their role in the prevention and treatment of diseases and in health care.

The state shall protect the resources of wild medicinal materials and encourage the domestic cultivation of Chinese traditional medicinal crops.

Chapter II

Administration of Pharmaceutical Producing Enterprises

Article 4   The establishment of a pharmaceutical producing enterprise must be sanctioned by the competent authorities for the production and trading of pharmaceuticals of the province, autonomous region, or municipality directly under the Central Government in which the enterprise is located, and approved by the administrative department of health of the same province, autonomous region or municipality, which will issue a Pharmaceuticals Producer Licence. The administrative authorities for industry and commerce shall not issue business licences to any enterprises producing pharmaceuticals without the Pharmaceutical Producer Licence.

The Pharmaceutical Producer Licence shall have a period of validity, upon expiration of which a new licence shall be issued after an examination for its renewal. Detailed measures for the renewal of such licences shall be stipulated by the administrative department of health under the State Council.

Article 5   To establish a pharmaceutical producing enterprise, the following requirements must be met:

(1) It shall be staffed with the necessary personnel required for producing the medicines concerned, that is, pharmacists or technical personnel with a qualification equivalent to or higher than assistant engineer as well as skilled workers.

If an enterprise processing Chinese traditional medicines into ready-to-use mixture and powder forms does not have pharmacists or technical personnel with a qualification equivalent to or higher than assistant engineer, it shall be staffed instead with skilled pharmaceutical workers who are familiar with the properties of the medicines processed and are registered with the administrative department of health at or above the county level.

(2) It shall have factory premises, facilities and a sanitary environment suitable for the medicines produced.

(3) It shall have a unit or competent personnel capable of inspecting the quality of the medicines produced, as well as necessary instruments and equipment.

Article 6   Pharmaceuticals must be produced in accordance with the technological procedure, and the record of production must be complete and accurate.

The process for preparing traditional Chinese medicines in ready-to-use forms must conform to the Pharmacopoeia of the People's Republic of China or the Processing Norms stipulated by the administrative departments of health of the provinces, autonomous regions, or municipalities directly under the Central Government.

Article 7   The raw and supplementary materials used for the production of pharmaceuticals and containers and packaging materials in direct contact with pharmaceuticals must conform to the requirements for medicinal use.

Article 8   Pharmaceuticals must go through quality inspection before they leave the factory; products which do not meet the standards shall not leave the factory.

Article 9   Pharmaceutical producing enterprises must draw up and carry out rules and regulations and sanitary requirements for ensuring the quality of pharmaceuticals in accordance with the Standards for Quality Control of Pharmaceutical Production stipulated by the administrative department of health under the State Council.

Chapter   III

Administration of Pharmaceutical Trading Enterprises

Article 10   The establishment of a pharmaceutical trading enterprise must be sanctioned by the local competent authorities for the production and trading of pharmaceuticals and approved by the administrative department of health at or above the county level, which will issue a Pharmaceutical Trading Enterprise Licence. The administrative authorities for industry and commerce shall not issue business licences to any enterprises without the Pharmaceutical Trading Enterprise Licence.

The Pharmaceutical Trading Enterprise Licence shall have a period of validity, upon expiration of which a new licence shall be issued after an examination for its renewal. Detailed measures for the renewal of such licences shall be stipulated by the administrative department of health under the State Council.

Article 11   To establish a pharmaceutical trading enterprise, the following requirements must be met:

(1) It shall be staffed with pharmaceutical technicians qualified for the handling of the pharmaceuticals.

If an enterprise trading in Chinese traditional medicines or an enterprise concurrently trading in medicines does not have pharmaceutical technicians, it shall be staffed instead with pharmaceutical workers who are familiar with the properties of the medicines it trades in and are registered with the administrative department of health at or above the county level.

(2) It shall have business premises, equipment, storage facilities and a sanitary environment suitable for the pharmaceuticals in which it trades.

Article 12 The quality of pharmaceuticals must be inspected on purchasing. Pharmaceuticals that do not meet the required standards must not be purchased.

Article 13 It is imperative, in the sale of pharmaceuticals, to be accurate and free of mistakes, and to provide correct directions for use, dosage and precautions. Prescriptions being dispensed must be checked. Pharmaceuticals listed in prescriptions must not be presumptuously changed or substituted. Prescriptions containing incompatible substances or excessive dosages shall be rejected by the dispensary. If necessary, such prescriptions can be dispensed after they have been corrected or re-signed by the doctors who wrote them out.

When famous traditional Chinese medicinal materials are offered for sale, their origin must be indicated.

Article 14 Rules for storage of pharmaceuticals shall be formulated and implemented by pharmaceutical warehouses, which must adopt necessary measures to facilitate cold storage and protection against moisture, insects and rodents.

An inspection system shall be carried out for pharmaceuticals entering or leaving warehouses.

Article 15 Unless otherwise stipulated by the state, traditional Chinese medicinal materials may be marketed at urban or rural fairs.

Pharmaceuticals other than traditional Chinese medicinal materials may not be sold at urban or rural fairs, except by those who have Pharmaceuticals Trading Enterprise Licences.

Chapter IV

Administration of Pharmaceuticals at Medical Units

Article 16 Medical units must be staffed with pharmaceutical technical personnel commensurate with their medical functions. Non-pharmaceutical technical personnel may not engage directly in pharmaceutical technical work.

Article 17 To make medicinal preparations, a medical unit must be examined, approved and issued a Dispensing Permit by the administrative department of health of the province, autonomous region, or municipality directly under the Central Government in which the unit is located.

The Dispensing Permit shall have a period of validity, upon expiration of which a new permit shall be issued after an examination for its renewal. Detailed measures for the renewal of such permits shall be stipulated by the administrative department of health under the State Council.

Article 18   Medical units making medicinal preparations must be equipped with facilities, inspection instruments and sanitary conditions capable of ensuring the quality of the preparations.

Article 19   The quality of the medicinal preparations made by medical units must be inspected in accordance with relevant regulations and clinical needs. Those up to standard can be used as the doctor prescribes.

Medicinal preparations made by medical units may not be sold on the market.

Article 20   Medical units must implement a system of quality inspection when purchasing pharmaceuticals.

Chapter V

Pharmaceutical Administration

Article 21   The state encourages research on and development of new medicines.

When working on a new medicine, it is necessary to submit, as required, the methods of production, quality indices, pharmacological and toxicological testing results, and other related materials and samples to the administrative department of health under the State Council or to the administrative department of health of the relevant province, autonomous region, or municipality directly under the Central Government. Clinical tests or clinical verifications can be carried out only after approval.

A new medicine which has completed its clinical tests or clinical verification and been approved after appraisal shall be issued a certificate by the administrative department of health under the State Council.

Article 22   A new medicine can be put into production only after the administrative department of health under the State Council has approved it and issued a registered document of approval. However, this does not apply to the production of traditional Chinese medicines prepared in ready-to-use forms.

A medicine standardized by the state or by a province, an autonomous region, or a municipality directly under the Central Government shall be put into production only after the administrative department of health of the relevant province, autonomous region, or municipality directly under the Central Government has made an examination of the medicine, given it approval and issued a registered document of approval, seeking beforehand the opinions of the authorities at the same level in charge of the production and trading of medicines. However, this does not apply to the production of traditional Chinese medicines prepared in ready-to-use forms.

Article 23   Pharmaceuticals must meet the pharmaceutical standards of the state or those of the relevant province, autonomous region, or municipality directly under the Central Government.

The Pharmacopoeia of the People's Republic of China and the pharmaceutical standards promulgated by the administrative department of health under the State Council shall be the state pharmaceutical standards.

The Pharmacopoeia Committee of the administrative department of health under the State Council shall be responsible for organizing the formulation and revision of the state pharmaceutical standards.

Article 24   The administrative department of health under the State Council and administrative departments of health of provinces, autonomous regions, and municipalities directly under the Central Government may establish pharmaceutical examination and evaluation committees to carry out examination and evaluation of new medicines and re-evaluate medicines already put into production.

Article 25   The administrative department of health under the State Council shall organize investigations of medicines which have been approved for production. It shall revoke the registered documents of approval if it discovers that the medicines' curative effects are uncertain or poor, or that they produce serious adverse reactions or for other reasons are harmful to people's health.

Production and sale of medicines whose registered documents of approval have been revoked shall not be allowed to continue; those which have already been produced shall be destroyed or disposed of under the supervision of the local administrative department of health.

Article 26   Import of medicines whose curative effects are uncertain or poor, or which produce adverse reactions or have other harmful effects on people's health shall be prohibited.

Article 27   For any medicine which is to be imported for the first time, the importer must submit the manuals, quality standards, methods of inspection and other related information and samples, as well as the exporting country's (region's) certification documents approving its production, to the administrative department of health under the State Council, and import contracts may be signed only with the prior approval of the said department.

Article 28   Imported medicines must be inspected by the pharmaceutical inspection institutions authorized by the administrative department of public health under the State Council; those having passed the inspection shall be allowed to be imported.

Medicines to be imported in small quantities for urgent clinical needs by medical units or for personal use shall be handled according to customs regulations.

Article 29   The administrative department of health under the State Council shall have the power to restrict or prohibit the export of traditional Chinese medicinal materials and prepared Chinese medicines which are in short supply in the domestic market.

Article 30   Import Licences or Export Licences issued by the administrative department of health under the State Council are required for the import or export of narcotics and psychotropic substances falling within the restricted scope prescribed by the administrative department of health under the State Council.

Article 31   Newly discovered domestic medicinal plants or medicinal plants introduced from abroad may be sold only after they have been examined and approved by the administrative department of health of the relevant province, autonomous region, or municipality directly under the Central Government.

Article 32   Measures for controlling medicinal materials traditionally used by local people in certain regions shall be formulated by the administrative department of health under the State Council.

Article 33   The production and sale of fake medicines are prohibited. A fake medicine has either of the following characteristics:

(1) The names of its components are different from those prescribed for it by state pharmaceutical standards or pharmaceutical standards of the relevant province, autonomous region, or municipality directly under the Central Government;

(2) A non-medical substance is passed off as a medicine, or one medicine is passed off as another.

A medicine shall be handled as fake medicine in any of the following cases:

(1) Where the use of the medicine has been prohibited by the administrative department of health under the State Council;

(2) Where the medicine has been produced without being assigned a registration number;

(3) Where the medicine has deteriorated and cannot be used as such; or

(4) Where the medicine has been contaminated and cannot be used

as such.

Article 34   The production and sale of medicines of inferior quality shall be prohibited. A medicine of inferior quality has any of the following characteristics:

(1) The components of the medicine do not conform in quantity to that required by state pharmaceutical standards or pharmaceutical standards of the relevant province, autonomous region, or municipality directly under the Central Government;

(2) The medicine has passed its expiry date; or

(3) The medicine fails to meet the prescribed standards in other respects.

Article 35   Personnel in pharmaceutical producing or trading enterprises and in medical units who have direct contact with medicines must undergo an annual medical examination. Persons who have contracted contagious diseases or any other disease which may contaminate the medicines shall not be allowed to engage in any work which has direct contact with pharmaceuticals.

Chapter VI
Packaging and Repackaging of Pharmaceuticals

Article 36   Packaging must meet the specific quality requirements of the pharmaceuticals and facilitate their storage, transportation and medical use. If a medicine has a period of validity, it must be clearly indicated on the package.

Traditional Chinese medicinal materials must be packaged before transportation. There must appear on the package the name of the medicine, place of production, date, name of the consignor, and an indication that the quality of the medicine is up to standard.

Article 37   Packages of pharmaceuticals must, in accordance with the regulations, be labeled and include directions for use.

The label or directions must indicate the name of the medicine, specifications, the producer, registration number, batch number of the product, principal components, indications, directions for use dosage, contraindications, adverse reactions and precautions.

Special indications must be printed as required on the labels of narcotics, psychotropic substances, toxic drugs, radioactive drugs and medicines for external use.

Article 38   A pharmaceuticals trading enterprise engaged in the repackaging of medicines must possess the necessary facilities and sanitary conditions suitable for the purpose, and pharmaceutical technicians must be placed in charge of this work. The repackaging records must be complete and accurate.

The repackaged medicine must enclose directions for use, and on the package must be indicated the name of the medicine, specifications, the producter, the batch number of the product, the repackaging unit and the lot number of the repackaged product. If the medicine has a period of validity, it must also be indicated on the new package.

Chapter   VII

Pharmaceuticals Under Special Control

Article 39   The state adopts special measures for the control of narcotics, psychotropic substances, toxic drugs and radioactive drugs. Regulations for the control of these drugs shall be formulated by the State Council.

Article 40   Narcotics, including their mother plants, must be produced only by units jointly designated by the administrative department of health under the State Council and other departments concerned, and must be supplied by units jointly designated by the administrative department of health of provinces, autonomous regions, and municipalities directly under the Central Government and other departments concerned.

Chapter   VIII

Administration of Trademarks
and Advertisements of Pharmaceuticals

Article 41   Registered trademarks must be used for all pharmaceuticals with the exception of traditional Chinese medicinal materials and their preparations in ready-to-use forms. The sale of pharmaceuticals without completing trademark registration shall be prohibited.

The registered trademark must appear on the package and the label of the medicine.

Article 42   Advertisements of pharmaceuticals must be examined and approved by the administrative department of health of the relevant province, autonomous region, or municipality directly under the Central Government. In the absence of such approval, advertisement of any medicine may not be published, broadcast, handed out or posted on walls.

Article 43   Foreign enterprises which apply to advertise pharmaceuticals in China must submit relevant documents of approval by the country (region) in which the pharmaceuticals are produced, directions for use and other relevant materials.

Article 44   Advertisements of pharmaceuticals must be based on the directions for use approved by the administrative department of health under the State Council or the administrative departments of health of provinces, autonomous regions, or municipalities directly under the Central Government.

Chapter   IX

Supervision over Pharmaceuticals

Article 45   The administrative departments of health at or above the county level shall exercise supervisory power over pharmaceuticals.

The administrative departments of health at or above the county level may set up organs for the administration of pharmaceuticals and organs for the inspection of pharmaceuticals.

Article 46   There shall be pharmaceutical inspectors in the administrative departments of health at or above the county level. Pharmaceutical inspectors shall be appointed from among pharmacological technical personnel and issued certificates by the people's governments at the same level.

Article 47   Pharmaceutical inspectors are authorized to exercise, in accordance with the regulations, supervision, inspection and sampling as regards the quality of pharmaceuticals in the producing enterprises, trading enterprises and medical units within their jurisdiction, and when necessary may pick samples at random and ask for relevant data in accordance with regulations. The enterprises and units concerned may not refuse such requests or withhold relevant data. Pharmaceutical inspectors are duty bound to keep confidential the technical information provided by pharmaceutical producing enterprises and scientific research institutions.

Article 48   Pharmaceutical producing enterprises, pharmaceutical trading enterprises and medical institutions shall conduct regular surveys of the quality, curative effects and adverse reactions of the pharmaceuticals they have produced, traded in or used.

When drug poisoning is discovered, the medical institution concerned must promptly report the matter to the local administrative department of health.

Article 49   The organs or personnel in charge of pharmaceutical inspection in pharmaceutical producing enterprises and pharmaceutical trading enterprises shall receive operational guidance from the local pharmaceutical inspection organs.

Chapter X
Legal Responsibility

Article 50   Whoever produces or sells fake medicines shall have his fake medicines and unlawful income confiscated and may concurrently be fined; in addition, he may be ordered to suspend production or business operations pending rectification, or have his Pharmaceutical Producer Licence, Pharmaceutical Trading Enterprise Licence or Dispensing Permit revoked.

An individual who produces or sells fake medicines, or the person directly responsible for a unit which commits this offence, and thereby endangers people's health, shall be investigated for criminal liability under Article 164 of the Criminal Law.

Article 51   Whoever produces or sells medicines of inferior quality shall have his medicines of inferior quality and unlawful income confiscated and may be fined as well. If the circumstances are serious, the unit concerned shall be ordered to suspend production or business operations pending rectification, or have its Pharmaceutical Producer Licence, Pharmaceutical Trading Enterprise Licence or Dispensing Permit revoked.

An individual who produces or sells medicines of inferior quality or the person directly responsible for a unit which commits this offence, and thereby endangers people's health and causes serious consequences, shall be investigated for criminal liability in reference to the provisions of Article 164 of the Criminal Law.

Article 52   Any unit engaged in the production, trading or preparation of medicines without obtaining the Pharmaceutical Producer Licence, Pharmaceutical Trading Enterprise Licence or Dispensing Permit shall be ordered to suspend production, business operations or preparation of such medicines. The medicines and unlawful income shall all be confiscated and a fine may also be imposed.

Article 53   Whoever violates any other provision of this Law on the administration of pharmaceutical production and pharmaceutical trading shall be served a warning or be fined.

Article 54   The decision to mete out administrative sanctions stipulated in this Law shall be made by the administrative departments of health at or above the county level. The decision to mete out administrative sanctions for violations of the provisions of Article 15 or of Chapter VIII on administration of advertisements of this Law shall be made by the administrative departments for industry and commerce.

Punishment by suspension of production or business operations pending rectification for seven days or more, or revocation of the Pharmaceutical Producer Licence or Pharmaceutical Trading Enterprise Licence to be meted out to pharmaceutical producing enterprises or pharmaceutical trading enterprises directly under the jurisdiction of the Central Government or of the people's governments of provinces, autonomous regions, or municipalities directly under the Central Government, shall be submitted by the administrative department of health of the relevant province, autonomous region, or municipality directly under the Central Government to the people's government at the same level for final decision. Punishment by suspension of production or business operations for seven days or more, or revocation of the Pharmaceutical Producer Licence or Pharmaceutical Trading Enterprise Licence, to be meted out to pharmaceutical producing enterprises or pharmaceutical trading enterprises under the jurisdiction of people's governments at or below the city or county level, shall be submitted by the administrative department of health of the people's governments at or below the city or county level to the people's governments at the same level for final decision.

The confiscated pharmaceuticals shall be disposed of under the supervision of the administrative departments of health.

Article 55   If the party concerned does not accept the administrative sanction decided on, it may file suit in the people's court within 15 days after receiving notification of the sanction. However, the said party must immediately carry out the decision on the control of pharmaceuticals made by the administrative department of health. If the party neither complies with the sanction nor files suit within the time limit, the organ which made the decision on the administrative sanction shall apply to the people's court for compulsory execution.

Article 56   If any individual or unit, in violation of this Law, causes drug poisoning, he or it shall be liable for the damage. The victims may request the administrative department of health at or above the county level to handle the matter; if a party does not accept the decision, it may file suit in the people's court. The victims, too, may directly take the case to the people's court.

The claim for compensation must be made within a year from the day on which the victim or his representative was aware or should have been aware of the damage done. No claim for compensation shall be entertained beyond the time limit.

Chapter   XI

Supplementary Provisions

Article 57   For the purpose of this Law, the definitions of the following terms are:

"Pharmaceuticals" means articles intended for use in the prevention, treatment or diagnosis of human diseases, or intended to effect the purposive regulation of human physiological functions, for which indications, usage and dosage are prescribed, including raw traditional Chinese medicinal materials, traditional medicines prepared in ready-to-use forms and other prepared Chinese medicines, medicinal chemicals and their preparations, antibiotics, biochemical medicines, radioactive drugs, serums, vaccines, blood products, diagnostic aids, etc.

"New medicines" means medicines which have not been produced in this country before.

"Supplementary materials" means the excipients and additives used for the production and dispensing of pharmaceuticals.

"Pharmaceutical producing enterprise" means an enterprise exclusively or partly engaged in the production of pharmaceuticals.

"Pharmaceutical trading enterprise" means an enterprise exclusively or partly engaged in the trading of pharmaceuticals.

Article 58   The production of pharmaceuticals referred to in this Law does not include the cultivation, collection and breeding of all categories of medicinal materials used in traditional Chinese medicine.

Article 59   The administrative department of health under the State Council shall, pursuant to this Law, draw up measures for its implementation, which shall enter into force after being submitted to and approved by the State Council.

Measures for the control of pharmaceuticals specially needed by the Chinese People's Army shall be formulated by the competent military department of the state.

Article 60   This Law shall enter into force as of July 1, 1985.

Resolution of the Standing Committee of the National People's Congress Approving the Fire Protection Regulations of the People's Republic of China

(*Adopted on May 11, 1984*)

The Fifth Meeting of the Standing Committee of the Sixth National People's Congress has decided to approve the Fire Protection Regulations of the People's Republic of China, which shall enter into force upon promulgation by the State Council.

Appendix:

Fire Protection Regulations of the People's Republic of China

(Adopted at the Fifth Meeting of the Standing Committee of the Sixth National People's Congress on May 11, 1984, and promulgated by the State Council on May 13, 1984)

Contents

139

Chapter I

General Provisions

Article 1   These Regulations are formulated to strengthen fire protection, safeguard socialist modernization and protect public property and the lives and property of citizens.

Article 2   The policy of "put prevention first and combine prevention with elimination" shall be implemented for fire protection.

Article 3   Fire protection shall be effected and supervised by public security organs.

Fire protection of the various units of the People's Liberation Army, state-owned forests and the underground areas of mines shall be effected and supervised by the departments in charge of them with the assistance of public security organs.

Chapter II

Fire Prevention

Article 4   When building, extending or rebuilding a city, the city planning and construction departments must concurrently plan and build public fire protection facilities, including fire stations, a water supply for fire fighting, fire service communications, and passageways for fire apparatus. In urban areas where existing public fire protection facilities are insufficient or unfit for actual needs, such facilities shall undergo technical renovation, rebuilding or expansion.

Article 5   The design and construction of new, expanded or reconstructed buildings shall conform to the stipulations of the Fire Prevention Code for Architectural Designs issued by the relevant authorities of the State Council.

Article 6   The design and construction of houses in the countryside shall conform to the stipulations of the Fire Prevention Code for Rural Architectural Designs issued by the relevant authorities of the State Council.

Article 7   Outdoor fires in forest areas or on grasslands shall be prohibited during the fire prevention periods in those areas. If it is necessary to build a fire under special circumstances, approval shall be obtained from the people's governments at the county level or their authorized organs, and strict surveillance measures shall be taken in accordance with relevant regulations.

Article 8   New factories, warehouses and special purpose stations and wharves designed for producing, storing, loading and unloading combustible or explosive chemicals shall be built in safe places and shall be examined and approved by the local city or county people's government. If existing establishments gravely interfere with fire safety, the departments in charge shall take effective measures to solve the problem.

Article 9   Units that produce, use, store or transport combustible or explosive chemicals must comply with the regulations issued by the relevant authorities of the State Council concerning the safe control of combustible and explosive chemicals. Persons ignorant of the properties of combustible and explosive chemicals and their safe handling methods shall not be allowed to take part in the handling and safekeeping of such chemicals.

Article 10   The departments in charge of communications and transport, fishery, investigation of marine resources, and prospecting shall regulate fire safety measures according to the particularities of aircraft, vessels and vehicles and shall instruct employees and passengers to strictly abide by those measures.

Article 11   In public places where people congregate, fire escapes and exits must be kept unobstructed. Rules governing the use of fire and electricity and the control of combustibles and explosives shall be established and strictly adhered to. Inspections and patrols shall be reinforced to ensure safety.

Article 12   Units that produce combustible or explosive chemicals shall include with their products information on the ignition points, flash points and explosion limits of the products and precautions against fire and explosion.

Article 13   Enterprises and institutions using new materials, new equipment or new technology must investigate their specific fire hazard characteristics and take proper fire safety measures.

Article 14   A responsibility system for fire prevention shall be enforced in government organs, enterprises and institutions.

Residents' committees in cities and villagers' committees in rural areas shall be responsible for mobilizing and organizing the inhabitants to effectively prevent fires.

Article 15   Government organs, enterprises and institutions shall install appropriate types and quantities of fire-fighting apparatus, equipment and facilities as needed for fire suppression.

Chapter III

Fire Protection Organizations

Article 16   Enterprises and institutions shall organize volunteer fire brigades or select volunteer firemen from among their staff to be responsible for fire prevention and suppression. The necessary expenses shall be borne by the enterprise or institution concerned.

Article 17   Large and medium-sized enterprises and relatively large institutions which have high fire risks and are situated rather far from a local public security fire brigade (station) shall, in light of their needs, set up full-time fire brigades responsible for fire protection in their establishments. The necessary expenses shall be borne by the enterprise or institution concerned.

Article 18   Public security fire brigades (stations) shall be set up in newly constructed cities and extended and reconstructed urban areas on the principle that within five minutes of receiving an alarm a fire engine should be able to reach the fringes of the area for which its fire brigade (station) is responsible. In cities where the existing fire brigades (stations) do not conform to the above provision, more fire brigades (stations) shall be added in stages. In towns and industrial and mining areas, public security fire brigades (stations) shall be set up according to needs. Existing fire brigades (stations) which do not have enough fire-fighting apparatus, equipment and facilities shall make up the insufficiency gradually.

Chapter IV

Fire Fighting

Article 19   When any unit or individual detects a fire, he or it should immediately and accurately report it to the fire brigade and take an active part in fighting the fire.

When a fire breaks out, the unit concerned shall promptly mobilize people to fight it. Neighbouring units should give it active support.

Upon receiving an alarm, a fire brigade shall promptly rush to the scene of the fire to fight it.

Article 20   Fire fighting at the scene of a fire shall be organized and directed by the fire supervision body. The commanding officer at the scene of the fire shall have the authority, according to circumstances, to deploy the fire brigades of enterprises and institutions in a coordinated effort to extinguish the fire.

Article 21   The commanding officer at the scene of a fire shall have the authority to decide on the dismantling of buildings and structures adjacent to the scene of the fire if such dismantling is needed to avoid major losses due to spread of the fire. In an emergency, he shall have the authority to mobilize forces from the departments of communications and transport, water supply, electric power supply, telecommunications, medical and first aid services and environmental sanitation.

Article 22   When fire engines or fire boats are rushing to the scene of a fire, other vehicles, vessels and persons shall make way for them. If necessary, fire engines and fire boats may use roads, open grounds and waterways normally closed to traffic. Traffic controllers shall ensure the quick passage of fire engines and fire boats.

Article 23   Fire engines, fire boats and other fire-fighting apparatus, equipment and facilities may not be used for any purpose unrelated to fire protection, except in emergencies and for providing disaster relief.

Article 24   A unit that has experienced a fire shall, in accordance with the stipulations laid down by the relevant authorities of the State Council, provide medical care and/or pensions for the people wounded or disabled in the course of fighting the fire who were not employees of the state; the unit shall also provide pensions for the families of those killed in the process who were not employees of the state. If the unit that experienced the fire was not responsible for having caused the fire or is truly unable to bear such expenses, or if the fire was caused by a resident, the medical care and pensions shall be provided by the local people's government.

Chapter   V
Fire Supervision

Article 25   The public security organs at the county level and above shall set up fire supervision bodies to be responsible for fire supervision.

Article 26   The fire supervision bodies at various levels shall exercise the following functions and powers:

(1) supervise and inspect fire protection activity in the various departments, units and civilian houses in accordance with these Regulations and relevant government regulations;

(2) spread knowledge of fire protection among the public and oversee the elimination of fire hazards by relevant establishments;

(3) examine the fire safety measures and technical standards adopted by various departments, enterprises and institutions;

(4) supervise and inspect construction projects in the design and construction stages for implementation of the Fire Prevention Code for Architectural Designs and take part in the examination and acceptance of the completed projects;

(5) supervise and inspect the planning and construction of public fire protection facilities in urban construction and see to the maintenance and improvement of urban public fire protection facilities by urban construction and management departments;

(6) keep informed on fire situations and compile statistics on fires;

(7) direct fire-fighting forces and train their officers and firemen;

(8) organize and direct fire fighting in a unified way;

(9) organize investigations into the causes of fires;

(10) direct research in the science and technology of fire protection and evaluate and popularize the results of such research; and

(11) oversee quality control in the production of fire-fighting apparatus and equipment.

Article 27   Upon discovering a fire hazard, the fire supervision body at any level should promptly notify the units or individuals concerned to take measures to eliminate the hazard within a prescribed period.

Article 28   The fire supervision bodies at various levels shall be staffed with fire supervisors who possess professional fire protection knowledge. The fire supervisors shall supervise and inspect fire protection activity in the units and civilian houses in their assigned areas.

Chapter   VI

Awards and Punishments

Article 29   Units and individuals that have made contributions to or performed outstanding services in fire protection shall be commended and given awards by public security organs, higher authorities or their own units.

Article 30   In cases of serious violation of these Regulations and refusal to carry out corrective measures as notified by the fire supervision bodies, the persons responsible shall be punished by the public security organs in accordance with the Regulations on Administrative Penalties for Public Security or shall be subjected to administrative sanctions by relevant authorities.

In the case of a fire due to a violation of these Regulations, the persons responsible shall be investigated for their criminal responsibility in accordance with the law. In cases of minor violations, the persons responsible shall be punished by public security organs in accordance with the Regulations on Administrative Penalties for Public Security or shall be subjected to administrative sanctions by relevant authorities.

Chapter VII

Supplementary Provisions

Article 31 The Ministry of Public Security shall, in accordance with these Regulations, formulate rules for their implementation and shall submit them to the State Council for approval before they are put into effect.

Article 32 These Regulations shall come into force as of October 1, 1984. On the same day, the Fire Supervision Regulations adopted by the Standing Committee of the National People's Congress on November 29, 1957, shall be invalidated.

Decision of the Second Session of the Sixth National People's Congress on the Establishment of the Hainan Administrative Region

(Adopted at the Second Session of the Sixth National People's Congress on May 31, 1984)

Having examined the proposal of the State Council on establishing the People's Government of the Hainan Administrative Region, the Second Session of the Sixth National People's Congress has decided to establish the Hainan Administrative Region, which shall put under its unified jurisdiction Haikou Municipality, the counties of Qiongshan, Qionghai, Wenchang, Wanning, Ding'an, Tunchang, Chengmai, Lingao and Danxian, the Hainan Li and Miao Autonomous Prefecture and Sanya Municipality and the counties of Dongfang, Ledong, Qiongzhong, Baoting, Lingshui, Baisha and Changjiang, which are under the jurisdiction of the prefecture, as well as the islets, reefs and sea areas of Xisha, Nansha and Zhongsha islands. The Hainan Administrative Region shall have its people's congress and people's government as local organs of state power. The regional people's government shall have a chairman and vice-chairmen, to be elected by the people's congress of the administrative region. The People's Government of the Hainan Administrative Region shall be under the leadership of the Guangdong Provincial People's Government. The structure and functions and powers of the state organs of the Hainan Administrative Region shall be stipulated separately.

Supplementary Provisions of the Standing Committee of the National People's Congress Concerning the Time Limits for Handling Criminal Cases

(Adopted at the Sixth Meeting of the Standing Committee of the Sixth National People's Congress, promulgated for implementation by Order No. 15 of the President of the People's Republic of China on July 7, 1984, and effective as of July 7, 1984)

The time limits for handling criminal cases prescribed by the Criminal Procedure Law in the spirit of shortening the time limits as much as possible and guaranteeing the citizens' right of the person are both appropriate and correct. The public security organs and judicial organs shall continue to improve their work, raise the quality of case-handling and work efficiency, conscientiously implement the time limits for case-handling prescribed by the Criminal Procedure Law and, in a practical manner, strive to shorten the time limits as much as possible. Meanwhile, the following supplementary provisions are made in order to solve certain special, concrete problems which have arisen in the process of implementation.

1. In the event that major cases involving crimes committed by a group or major and complex cases involving persons going from place to place committing crimes cannot be concluded within the time limit for holding a defendant in custody during investigation as stipulated in Paragraph 1 of Article 92 of the Criminal Procedure Law, or within the time limit for trial in a case of first instance as stipulated in Article 125, or within the time limit for trial in a case of second instance as stipulated in Article 142, the time limit for holding the defendant in custody during investigation may be extended by two months upon approval or decision by the people's procuratorates of provinces, autonomous regions, or municipalities directly under the Central Government, and the time limit for trial in cases of first and second instances may be extended by one month upon approval or decision by the higher people's courts of provinces, autonomous regions, or municipalities directly under the Central Government.

2. In the event that major and complex criminal cases in remote areas with extremely poor communications cannot be concluded within the time limit stipulated in the Criminal Procedure Law for holding the defendant in custody during investigation or within the time limit for trial in a case

of first or second instance, the time limit for case-handling may be appropriately extended. The extension of the time limit for case-handling and the measures for its examination and approval shall be dealt with in pursuance of item (1) above.

When the time limit for case-handling may be extended in remote areas with extremely poor communications, such areas shall be designated by the standing committees of the people's congresses of the relevant provinces or autonomous regions.

3. If in the course of investigation the defendant is found to have committed other serious crimes, supplementary investigation may be conducted upon approval of or decision by the people's procuratorate, and the time limit for holding the defendant in custody during investigation may be calculated anew.

4. A defendant held in custody who is subject to investigation, prosecution or trial in a case of first or second instance which cannot be concluded within the time limit stipulated in the Criminal Procedure Law and who, if permitted to obtain a guarantor pending trial or to live at home under surveillance, will pose no threat to society may obtain a guarantor pending trial or live at home under surveillance. The period during which he obtains a guarantor pending trial or lives at home under surveillance shall not be counted in the time limit for case-handling as stipulated in the Criminal Procedure Law, but the hearing of the case shall not be suspended.

5. In the event of a case of public prosecution reviewed and brought by the people's procuratorates and heard by a people's court where the defendant is not held in custody, the handling of the case is not subject to the restriction of the time limits stipulated in Articles 97, 125 and 142 of the Criminal Procedure Law, but the hearing of the case shall not be suspended.

6. In the event a case of public prosecution over which a people's procuratorate or people's court has jurisdiction is transferred, the time limit for case-handling shall be reckoned from the date when the new case-handling organ receives the case.

7. In the event a people's court has returned a case to a people's procuratorate for supplementary investigation, the latter shall complete the supplementary investigation within one month. After supplementary investigation has been completed and the case has been returned to the people's court, the court shall calculate anew the time limit for case-hearing.

8. Where a people's court of second instance returns a case for retrial to the people's court which originally handled the case, the latter people's court shall calculate anew the time limit for case-hearing from the date it receives the returned case.

9. The time period during which a defendant undergoes examination for determination of mental illness shall not be counted in the time limit

for case-handling.

10. These Provisions shall go into effect on the day of their promulgation.

Appendix:

The Relevant Articles in the Criminal Procedure Law

Article 92 The time limit for holding a defendant in custody during investigation shall not exceed two months. If the circumstances of a case are complex and the case cannot be concluded before the expiration of that period, an extension of one month may be allowed with the approval of the people's procuratorate at the next higher level.

In the event a particularly grave and complicated case still cannot be concluded within the extension period provided in the preceding paragraph, the Supreme People's Procuratorate shall request the Standing Committee of the National People's Congress to approve a postponement of the hearing of the case.

Article 97 A people's procuratorate shall make a decision within one month on a case that a public security organ has transferred to it with a recommendation to initiate a public prosecution or exempt it from prosecution; an extension of half a month may be allowed for major and complicated cases.

Article 125 A people's court shall pronounce judgment on a case of public prosecution within one month, or one and a half months at the latest, after accepting it for trial.

Article 142 A people's court of second instance shall conclude the trial of a case of appeal or protest within one month, or one and a half months at the latest, after accepting it for trial.

Decision of the Standing Committee of the National People's Congress on Authorizing the State Council to Reform the System of Industrial and Commercial Taxes and Issue Relevant Draft Tax Regulations for Trial Application

(Adopted on September 18, 1984)

The Seventh Meeting of the Standing Committee of the Sixth National People's Congress, having considered the proposal of the State Council, has decided to authorize it to draft regulations relating to taxation and issue them in the form of drafts for trial application while introducing the practice according to which state enterprises pay taxes instead of turning over their profit to the state and in the course of reforming the system of industrial and commercial taxes. The draft regulations shall be revised in light of the experience gained through trial application and shall be submitted to the Standing Committee of the National People's Congress for examination. These draft regulations on taxation to be issued by the State Council for trial application shall not apply to Chinese-foreign equity joint ventures and enterprises with foreign capital.

Decision of the Standing Committee of the National People's Congress on the Establishment of Maritime Courts in Coastal Port Cities

(Adopted at the Eighth Meeting of the Standing Committee of the Sixth National People's Congress and promulgated for implementation by Order No. 20 of the President of the People's Republic of China on November 14, 1984)

To meet the needs in the development of the country's maritime transport and in its economic relations and trade with foreign countries, effectively exercise the country's judicial jurisdiction and handle maritime affairs and maritime trade cases promptly, so as to safeguard the lawful rights and interests of both Chinese and foreign litigants, the following decisions have been made:

1. Maritime courts shall be established in certain coastal port cities according to need.

The establishment of such courts, their alteration and their abolition shall be decided by the Supreme People's Court.

The establishment of adjudicatory apparatus and administrative offices of the maritime courts shall be decided by the Supreme People's Court.

2. The maritime courts shall be responsible to the standing committees of the people's congresses of the municipalities where they are located.

The judicial work of maritime courts shall be subject to supervision by the higher people's courts in their respective localities.

3. The maritime courts shall have jurisdiction over maritime cases and maritime trade cases of first instance; they shall not handle criminal cases or other civil cases.

The designation of the jurisdiction area for each maritime court shall be decided by the Supreme People's Court.

The higher people's court in the locality where a maritime court is located shall have jurisdiction over appeals against the judgments and orders of the maritime court.

4. The president of a maritime court shall be appointed or removed by the standing committee of the people's congress of the city where the court is located, upon a proposal submitted by the chairman of the standing committee of the people's congress.

The vice-presidents, chief judges and associate chief judges of divisions, judges and members of the judicial committee of a maritime court shall be appointed or removed by the standing committee of the people's congress of the city where the court is located, upon a proposal submitted by the president of the maritime court.

1985

1985

Accounting Law of the People's Republic of China

*(Adopted at the Ninth Meeting of the Standing Committee of
the Sixth National People's Congress, promulgated by Order
No. 21 of the President of the People's Republic
of China on January 21, 1985, and
effective as of May 1, 1985)*

Contents

Chapter   I

General Provisions

Article 1   This Law is formulated in order to improve accounting work, to ensure that accounting personnel exercise their functions and powers according to law and to bring into play the role of accounting in upholding the state systems of public finance administration and financial management, protecting socialist public property, strengthening economic management and raising economic results.

Article 2   State enterprises and institutions, government agencies, public organizations and armed forces shall abide by this Law in handling accounting affairs.

Article 3   Accounting offices and accounting personnel must abide by laws and regulations and handle accounting affairs, conduct accounting computation and control and exercise accounting supervision in accordance with the stipulations of this Law.

Article 4   Administrative heads of all localities, departments and units shall direct their accounting offices, accounting personnel and other personnel in implementing this Law and shall ensure that the functions and powers of accounting personnel are not infringed upon. No one is allowed to attack or retaliate against accounting personnel.

Moral encouragement and material awards shall be given to the accounting personnel who have made outstanding achievements in conscientiously implementing this Law and who are devoted to their duty.

Article 5   The department of finance under the State Council shall administer the accounting work throughout the country.

The departments of finance under the local people's governments at various levels shall administer the accounting work of their respective areas.

Article 6   A uniform accounting system of the state shall be formulated by the department of finance under the State Council in accordance with this Law.

The departments of finance under the people's governments of the provinces, autonomous regions, and municipalities directly under the Central Government, the competent departments of the State Council and the General Logistics Department of the Chinese People's Liberation Army may, on condition that this Law and the uniform accounting system of the state are not contravened, formulate accounting systems or supplemental stipulations for their respective areas and departments and submit them to the department of finance under the State Council for examination and approval or for the record.

Chapter II

Accounting Practice

Article 7   Accounting procedures shall be undertaken and accounting conducted with respect to the following transactions:

(1) receipts and disbursements of cash holdings and valuable securities;

(2) receipts, issuances, additions, reductions and use of money and articles of property;

(3) creation and settlement of debts and claims;

(4) increases and decreases of funds, receipts and outlays of appropriations;

(5) computation of revenue, expenses and costs;

(6) computation and treatment of financial results; and

(7) other transactions that are subject to accounting procedures and to accounting.

Article 8 The fiscal year shall start on January 1 and end on December 31 of the Gregorian calendar.

Article 9 Account books shall be kept, using Renminbi yuan as the unit.

Transactions in foreign currency shall be converted into Renminbi in bookkeeping, and the conversion rate used, as well as the amounts in foreign currency, shall be recorded concurrently.

Article 10 Accounting documents, account books, accounting statements and other accounting information shall be authentic, accurate and complete and shall conform to the provisions of the accounting system.

Article 11 In handling the transactions specified in Article 7 of this Law, original documents must be drawn up or obtained, and then promptly filed with the accounting office.

Accounting offices must examine the original documents and prepare accounting vouchers based on the original documents examined.

Article 12 Each unit shall set up its accounting items and account books in accordance with the provisions of the accounting system.

Accounting offices shall keep their books on the basis of the examined original documents and accounting vouchers in accordance with the bookkeeping rules stipulated by the accounting system.

Article 13 Each unit shall set up a property inventory system and ensure that the accounting records conform to the physical assets and cash holdings.

Article 14 Each unit shall prepare its accounting statements on the basis of the accounting records and in accordance with the provisions of the uniform accounting system of the state. The accounting statements shall be reported to the superior competent authorities for compilation and submission to the department of finance and other relevant departments.

Accounting statements shall be signed or sealed by the unit's administrative head, the person in charge of the accounting office and the accountant in charge. If the unit has an accountant-general, he shall also sign or seal the accounting statements.

Article 15 Archives shall be established for accounting documents, account books, accounting statements and other accounting information in accordance with the relevant state provisions, and shall be properly retained. The period of retention of the archives and the procedures for their destruction shall be stipulated jointly by the department of finance under the State Council and the relevant departments.

Chapter   III

Accounting Supervision

Article 16   The accounting office and accounting personnel of a unit shall exercise accounting supervision over the unit.

Article 17   Accounting offices and accounting personnel shall not accept any original documents that are inauthentic or illegitimate. Original documents which are inaccurately and incompletely recorded shall be returned for correction or supplementation.

Article 18   When an accounting office and accounting personnel find that the accounting records do not conform to the physical assets and cash holdings, they shall deal with the issue in accordance with relevant stipulations. If they have no authority to handle the case by themselves, they shall report immediately to the administrative head of their unit, requesting an investigation and a settlement of the issue.

Article 19   An accounting office and accounting personnel shall not handle any receipts or disbursements that violate the stipulations of the state uniform system of public finance administration and system of financial management.

In cases where an accounting office and accounting personnel believe that certain receipts and disbursements are in violation of the state uniform system of public finance administration and financial management, and where the unit's administrative head insists on their being handled, the said accounting office and personnel may carry out the decision made by the administrative head, at the same time making a written report to the head of the superior administrative unit requesting action, and also to the auditing agency. The head of the superior administrative unit must make a decision on the matter within one month from the date of receiving the written report from an accounting office or accounting personnel. Accounting personnel shall also be held liable if they do not submit a report to the head of the superior administrative unit.

Article 20   All units must accept supervision exercised in accordance with laws and relevant state regulations by auditing agencies, departments of finance and tax agencies and must provide them with accounting documents, account books, accounting statements, other accounting information and relevant data. They may not conceal, falsify or refuse to provide such material and information.

Public accountants' offices composed of certified public accountants approved by the department of finance under the State Council or the departments of finance under the people's governments of the provinces, autonomous regions, and municipalities directly under the Central Government may undertake to audit accounts pursuant to the relevant state provisions.

Chapter IV

Accounting Offices and Accounting Personnel

Article 21 According to the needs of its accounting work, each unit shall set up an accounting office or staff a relevant office with accounting personnel and designate an accountant in charge. Large and medium-sized enterprises, institutions and competent departments may have accountants-general. The position of an accountant-general shall be assumed by a person with the technical title of accountant or above.

Accounting offices shall establish an internal auditing system.

A cashier shall not be concurrently in charge of auditing, taking custody of accounting archives or keeping the revenue, expense or claims and liability accounts.

Article 22 The main functions of accounting offices and accounting personnel shall be:

(1) to conduct accounting practice pursuant to the provisions of Chapter II of this Law;

(2) to exercise accounting supervision pursuant to the provisions of Chapter III of this Law;

(3) to formulate specific procedures for handling accounting affairs in their respective units;

(4) to participate in the formulation of economic and business plans, and examine and analyse the results of the execution of budget and financial plans; and

(5) to handle other accounting affairs.

Article 23 Accounting personnel shall be appointed or removed in accordance with the provisions for the limits of authority over personnel administration. The appointment and removal of the persons in charge of accounting offices and the accountants in charge in enterprises or institutions shall be approved by their superior administrative units. If an accountant who is loyal to his duty and adheres to principles is wrongly treated, the superior administrative unit shall instruct the unit in which he works to correct the mistake. If an accountant proves himself unsuitable for accounting work because of dereliction of duty and abandonment of principle, the superior administrative unit shall instruct the unit in which he works to replace him.

Article 24 Accounting personnel who are being transferred to other work or leaving their posts must finalize the handing-over procedure with the persons who are taking over.

The person in charge of the accounting office and the accountant in charge shall supervise handing-over procedures for ordinary accountants. The administrative head of a unit shall supervise handing-over procedures between the person in charge of the accounting office and the accountant in charge; when necessary, the superior administrative unit may send people to participate in the supervision of the hand-over.

Chapter V

Legal Liability

Article 25   Administrative sanctions shall be taken against administrative heads of those units and accounting personnel who have seriously violated the provisions for accounting practice specified in Chapter II of this Law.

Article 26   Administrative sanctions shall be taken against administrative heads of units, accounting personnel and other personnel who have counterfeited, concocted or deliberately destroyed accounting vouchers or account books. When the circumstances are serious, criminal liability shall be investigated in accordance with the Law.

Article 27   Administrative sanctions shall be taken against accounting personnel who have accepted original vouchers that they clearly knew to be inauthentic or illegitimate or who have handled receipts or disbursements that they clearly knew to be in violation of the stipulations of the state uniform systems of public finance administration and financial management, and against administrative heads of relevant units and administrative heads of superior units who have decided to handle, or insisted on handling, receipts or disbursements that they clearly knew to be in violation of the stipulations of the state uniform systems of public finance administration and financial management. Criminal liability shall be investigated in accordance with the law in cases where the state has suffered grave economic losses.

Article 28   Administrative sanctions shall be taken against heads of superior administrative units who have received written reports from accounting personnel pursuant to the provisions of the second paragraph of Article 19 of this Law but fail to make a decision on the matter without any justifiable reason within the stipulated period of time, thus causing grave financial consequences.

Article 29   Administrative sanctions shall be taken against administrative heads of units and other personnel who attack or retaliate against accounting personnel who perform their duties pursuant to this Law. Criminal liability shall be investigated if the circumstances are serious.

Chapter VI

Supplementary Provisions

Article 30   Procedures for the administration of accounting work of urban and rural economic collectives shall be jointly formulated by the department of finance under the State Council and the relevant competent authorities according to the principles of this Law.

Article 31   This Law shall come into force on May 1, 1985.

Law of the People's Republic of China on Economic Contracts Involving Foreign Interest

(Adopted at the Tenth Session of the Standing Committee of the Sixth National People's Congress, promulgated by Order No. 22 of the President of the People's Republic of China on March 21, 1985, and effective as of July 1, 1985)

Contents

Chapter   I

General Provisions

Article 1   This Law is formulated with a view to protecting the lawful rights and interests of the parties to Chinese-foreign economic contracts and promoting the development of China's foreign economic relations.

Article 2   This Law shall apply to economic contracts concluded between enterprises or other economic organizations of the People's Republic of China and foreign enterprises, other economic organizations or individuals. (hereinafter referred to as "contracts"). However, this provision shall not apply to international transport contracts.

Article 3   Contracts shall be concluded according to the principle of equality and mutual benefit and the principle of achieving agreement through consultation.

Article 4   In concluding a contract, the parties must abide by the law of the People's Republic of China and shall not harm the public interest of the People's Republic of China.

Article 5   The parties to a contract may choose the proper law applicable to the settlement of contract disputes. In the absence of such a choice by the parties, the law of the country which has the closest connection with the contract shall apply.

The law of the People's Republic of China shall apply to contracts that are to be performed within the territory of the People's Republic of China, namely contracts for Chinese-foreign equity joint ventures, Chinese-foreign contractual joint ventures and Chinese-foreign cooperative exploration and development of natural resources.

For matters that are not covered in the law of the People's Republic of China, international practice shall be followed.

Article 6   Where an international treaty which is relevant to a contract, and to which the People's Republic of China is a contracting party or a signatory, has provided differently from the law of the People's Republic of China, the provisions of the international treaty shall prevail, with the exception of those clauses on which the People's Republic of China has declared reservation.

Chapter   II

The Conclusion of Contracts

Article 7   A contract shall be formed as soon as the parties to it have reached a written agreement on the terms and have signed the contract. If an agreement is reached by means of letters, telegrams or telex and one party requests a signed letter of confirmation, the contract shall be formed only after the letter of confirmation is signed.

Contracts which are subject to the approval of the state, as provided for by the laws or administrative regulations of the People's Republic of China, shall be formed only after such approval is granted.

Article 8   Appendices specified in a contract shall be integral parts of the contract.

Article 9   Contracts that violate the law or the public interest of the People's Republic of China shall be void.

In case any terms in a contract violate the law or the public interest of the People's Republic of China, the validity of the contract shall not be affected if such terms are cancelled or modified by the parties through consultations.

Article 10   Contracts that are concluded by means of fraud or duress shall be void.

Article 11   A party which is responsible for the invalidity of a contract shall be liable for the losses suffered by the other party as a result of the contracts becoming invalid.

Article 12   A contract shall, in general, contain the following terms:

(1) the corporate or personal names of the contracting parties and their nationalities and principal places of business or domicile;

(2) the date and place of the signing of the contract;

(3) the type of contract and the kind and scope of the object of the contract;

(4) The technical conditions, quality, standard, specifications and quantity of the object of the contract;

(5) the time limit, place and method of performance;

(6) the price, amount and method of payment, and various incidental charges;

(7) whether the contract is assignable and, if it is, the conditions for its assignment;

(8) liability to pay compensation and other liabilities for breach of contract;

(9) the ways for settling contract disputes; and

(10) the language(s) in which the contract is to be written and its validity.

Article 13   So far as it may require, a contract shall provide for the limits of the risks to be borne by the parties in performing the object; if necessary, it shall provide for the coverage of insurance for the object.

Article 14   Where a contract needs to be performed continuously over a long period, the parties shall set a period of validity for the contract and may also stipulate conditions for its extension and its termination before its expiry.

Article 15   In the contract the parties may agree to provide a guaranty. The guarantor shall be held liable within the agreed scope of guaranty.

Chapter   III

The Performance of Contracts
and Liability for Breach of Contract

Article 16   A contract shall be legally binding as soon as it is established in accordance with the law. The parties shall perform their obligations stipulated in the contract. No party shall unilaterally modify or rescind the contract.

Article 17   A party may temporarily suspend its performance of the contract if it has conclusive evidence that the other party is unable to perform the contract. However, it shall immediately inform the other party of such suspension. It shall perform the contract if and when the other party provides a sure guarantee for performance of the contract. If a party suspends performance of the contract without conclusive evidence of the other party's inability to perform the contract, it shall be liable for breach of contract.

Article 18   If a party fails to perform the contract or its performance of the contractual obligations does not conform to the agreed terms, which constitutes a breach of contract, the other party is entitled to claim damages or demand other reasonable remedial measures. If the losses suffered by the other party cannot be completely made up after the adoption of such remedial measures, the other party shall still have the right to claim damages.

Article 19   The liability of a party to pay compensation for the breach of a contract shall be equal to the loss suffered by the other party as a consequence of the breach. However, such compensation may not exceed the loss which the party responsible for the breach ought to have foreseen at the time of the conclusion of the contract as a possible consequence of a breach of contract.

Article 20   The parties may agree in a contract that, if one party breaches the contract, it shall pay a certain amount of breach of contract damages to the other party; they may also agree upon a method for calculating the damages resulting from such a breach.

The breach of contract damages as stipulated in the contract shall be regarded as compensation for the losses resulting from breach of contract. However, if the contractually agreed breach of contract damages are far more or far less than is necessary to compensate for the losses resulting from the breach, the party concerned may request an arbitration body or a court to reduce or increase them appropriately.

Article 21   If both parties breach the contract, each shall be commensurately liable for the breach of contract that is its responsibility.

Article 22   A party which suffers losses resulting from a breach of contract by the other party shall promptly take appropriate measures to prevent the losses from becoming severer. If the losses are aggravated as a result of its failure to adopt appropriate measures, it shall not be entitled to claim compensation for the aggravated part of the losses.

Article 23   If a party fails to pay on time any amount stipulated as payable in the contract or any other amount related to the contract that is payable, the other party is entitled to interest on the amount in arrears. The method for calculating the interest may be specified in the contract.

Article 24   If a party is prevented from performing all or part of its obligations owing to force majeure, it shall be relieved of all or part of its obligations.

If a party cannot perform its obligations within the contractually agreed time limit owing to force majeure, it shall be relieved of the liability for delayed performance during the aftereffect of the event.

Force majeure means an event that the parties could not have foreseen at the time of conclusion of the contract, both parties being unable to either avoid or overcome its occurrence and consequences.

The scope of force majeure may be specified in the contract.

Article 25 The party which fails to perform wholly or in part its contractual obligations owing to force majeure shall promptly inform the other party so as to mitigate possible losses inflicted on the other party, and shall also provide a certificate issued by the relevant agency within a reasonable period of time.

Chapter IV

The Assignment of Contracts

Article 26 When a party assigns, wholly or in part, its contractual rights and obligations to a third party, it must obtain the consent of the other party.

Article 27 In the case of a contract which, according to the laws or administrative regulations of the People's Republic of China, is to be formed with the approval of the state, the assignment of the contractual rights and obligations shall be subject to the approval of the authority which approved the contract, unless otherwise stipulated in the approved contract.

Chapter V

The Modification, Rescission and Termination of Contracts

Article 28 A contract may be modified if both parties agree through consultation.

Article 29 A party shall have the right to notify the other party that a contract is rescinded in any of the following situations:

(1) if the other party has breached the contract, thus adversely affecting the economic benefits they expected to receive at the time of the conclusion of the contract;

(2) if the other party fails to perform the contract within the time limit agreed upon in the contract, and again fails to perform it within the reasonable period of time allowed for delayed performance;

(3) if all the obligations under the contract cannot be performed owing

to force majeure; or

(4) if the contractually agreed conditions for the rescission of the contract are present.

Article 30   For a contract consisting of several independent parts, some may be rescinded according to the provisions of the preceding article while the other parts remain valid.

Article 31   A contract shall be terminated in any one of the following situations:

(1) if the contract has already been performed in accordance with the agreed terms;

(2) if an arbitration body or a court has decided that the contract shall be terminated; or

(3) if the parties agree through consultation to terminate the contract.

Article 32   Notices or agreements on the modification or rescission of contracts shall be made in writing.

Article 33   In the case of a contract which, according to the laws or administrative regulations of the People's Republic of China, is to be established with the approval of the state, any significant modification of the contract shall be subject to the approval of the authority which approved the contract, and the rescission of the contract shall be filed with the same authority for the record.

Article 34   The modification, rescission or termination of a contract shall not affect the rights of the parties to claim damages.

Article 35   The contractually agreed terms for the settlement of disputes shall not become invalid because of the rescission or termination of a contract.

Article 36   The contractually agreed terms for the settlement of accounts and liquidation of a contract shall not become invalid because of the rescission or termination of the contract.

Chapter VI

The Settlement of Disputes

Article 37   If disputes over a contract develop, the parties shall, as far as possible, settle them through consultation, or through mediation by a third party.

If the parties are unwilling to settle their dispute through consultation or mediation, or if consultation or mediation proves unsuccessful, they may, in accordance with the arbitration clause provided in the contract or a written arbitration agreement reached by the parties afterwards, submit the dispute to a Chinese arbitration body or any other arbitration body for arbitration.

Article 38   If no arbitration clause is provided in the contract, and a written arbitration agreement is not reached afterwards, the parties may bring suit in a people's court.

Chapter VII

Supplementary Provisions

Article 39   The time limit for filing suit or applying for arbitration in a dispute over a contract for the purchase and sale of goods shall be four years, counting from the day when the party was aware or ought to have been aware of its rights' being infringed upon. The time limit for filing suit or applying for arbitration in a dispute over any other contract shall be stipulated separately by law.

Article 40   If new legal provisions are formulated while contracts for Chinese-foreign equity joint ventures, Chinese-foreign contractual joint ventures, or Chinese-foreign cooperative exploration and development of natural resources, which have been concluded with the approval of the state, are being performed within the territory of the People's Republic of China, the performance may still be based on the terms of the contracts.

Article 41   This Law may apply to contracts concluded before it goes into effect if this is agreed to by the parties through consultation.

Article 42   The State Council shall, in accordance with this Law, formulate rules for its implementation.

Article 43   This Law shall go into effect on July 1, 1985.

Law of Succession of the People's Republic of China

(Adopted at the Third Session of the Sixth National People's Congress,
promulgated by Order No. 24 of the President of the
People's Republic of China on April 10, 1985,
and effective as of October 1, 1985)

Contents

Chapter   I

General Provisions

Article 1   This Law is enacted pursuant to the provisions of the Constitution of the People's Republic of China with a view to protecting the right of citizens to inherit private property.

Article 2   Succession begins at the death of a citizen.

Article 3   Estate denotes the lawful property owned by a citizen personally at the time of his death, which consists of:

(1) his income;

(2) his houses, savings and articles of everyday use;

(3) his forest trees, livestock and poultry;

(4) his cultural objects, books and reference materials;

(5) means of production lawfully owned by him;

(6) his property rights pertaining to copyright and patent rights; and

(7) his other lawful property.

Article 4   Personal benefits accruing from a contract entered into by an individual are heritable in accordance with the provisions of this Law. Contracting by an individual, if permitted by law to be continued by the successor, shall be treated in accordance with the terms of the contract.

Article 5   Succession shall, after its opening, be handled in accordance with the provisions of statutory succession; where a will exists, it shall be handled in accordance with testamentary succession or as legacy; where there is an agreement for legacy in return for support, the former shall be handled in accordance with the terms of the agreement.

Article 6   The right to inheritance or legacy of a competent person shall be exercised on his behalf by his statutory agent.

The right to inheritance or legacy of a person with limited capacity shall be exercised on his behalf by his statutory agent or by such person himself after obtaining the consent of his statutory agent.

Article 7   A successor shall be disinherited upon his commission of any one of the following acts:

(1) intentional killing of the decedent;

(2) killing any other successor in fighting over the estate;

(3) a serious act of abandoning or maltreating the decedent; or

(4) a serious act of forging, tampering with or destroying the will.

Article 8   The time limit for institution of legal proceedings pertaining to disputes over the right to inheritance is two years, counting from the day the successor became or should have become aware of the violation of his right to inheritance. No legal proceedings, however, may be instituted after the expiration of a period of 20 years from the day succession began.

Chapter   II

Statutory Succession

Article 9   Males and females are equal in their right to inheritance.

Article 10   The estate of the decedent shall be inherited in the following order:

First in order: spouse, children, parents.

Second in order: brothers and sisters, paternal grand parents, maternal grandparents.

When succession opens, the successor(s) first in order shall inherit to the exclusion of the successor(s) second in order. The successor(s) second in order shall inherit in default of any successor first in order.

The "children" referred to in this Law include legitimate children, illegitimate children and adopted children, as well as step-children who supported or were supported by the decedent.

The "parents" referred to in this Law include natural parents and adoptive parents, as well as step-parents who supported or were supported by the decedent.

The "brothers and sisters" referred to in this Law include blood brothers and sisters, brothers and sisters of half blood, adopted brothers and sisters, as well as step-brothers and step-sisters who supported or were supported by the decedent.

Article 11   Where a decedent survived his child, the direct lineal descendants of the predeceased child shall inherit in subrogation. Descendants who inherit in subrogation generally shall take only the share of the estate their father or mother was entitled to.

Article 12   Widowed daughters-in-law or sons-in-law who have made the predominant contributions in maintaining their parents-in-law shall, in relationship to their parents-in-law, be regarded as successors first in order.

Article 13   Successors same in order shall, in general, inherit in equal shares.

At the time of distributing the estate, due consideration shall be given to successors who are unable to work and have special financial difficulties.

At the time of distributing the estate, successors who have made the predominant contributions in maintaining the decedent or have lived with the decedent may be given a larger share.

At the time of distributing the estate, successors who had the ability and were in a position to maintain the decedent but failed to fulfil their duties shall be given no share or a smaller share of the estate.

Successors may take unequal shares if an agreement to that effect is reached among them.

Article 14   An appropriate share of the estate may be given to a person, other than a successor, who depended on the support of the decedent and who neither can work nor has a source of income, or to a person, other than a successor, who was largely responsible for supporting the decedent.

Article 15   Questions pertaining to succession should be dealt with through consultation by and among the successors in the spirit of mutual understanding and mutual accommodation, as well as of amity and unity. The time and mode for partitioning the estate and the shares shall be decided by the successors through consultation. If no agreement is reached through consultation, they may apply to a People's Mediation Committee for mediation or institute legal proceedings in a people's court.

Chapter   III

Testamentary Succession and Legacy

Article 16   A citizen may, by means of a will made in accordance with the provisions of this Law, dispose of the property he owns and may appoint a testamentary executor for the purpose.

A citizen may, by making a will, designate one or more of the statutory successors to inherit his personal property.

A citizen may, by making a will, donate his personal property to the state or a collective, or bequeath it to persons other than the statutory successors.

Article 17   A notarial will is one made by a testator through a notary agency.

A testator-written will is one made in the testator's own handwriting and signed by him, specifying the date of its making.

A will written on behalf of the testator shall be witnessed by two or more witnesses, of whom one writes the will, dates it and signs it along with the other witness or witnesses and with the testator.

A will made in the form of a sound-recording shall be witnessed by two or more witnesses.

A testator may, in an emergency situation, make a nuncupative will, which shall be witnessed by two or more witnesses. When the emergency situation is over and if the testator is able to make a will in writing or in the form of a sound-recording, the nuncupative will he has made shall be invalidated.

Article 18   None of the following persons shall act as a witness of a will:

(1) persons with no capacity or with limited capacity;

(2) successors and legatees; or

(3) persons whose interests are related to those of the successors and legatees.

Article 19   Reservation of a necessary portion of an estate shall be made in a will for a successor who neither can work nor has a source of income.

Article 20   A testator may revoke or alter a will he previously made.

Where several wills that have been made conflict with one another in content, the last one shall prevail.

A notarial will may not be revoked or altered by a testator-written will, a will written on behalf of the testator, a will in the form of a sound-recording or a nuncupative will.

Article 21   Where there are obligations attached to testamentary succession or legacy, the successor or legatee shall perform them. Anyone who fails to perform the obligations without proper reasons may, upon request by a relevant organization or individual, entail nullification of his right to inheritance by a people's court.

Article 22   Wills made by persons with no capacity or with limited capacity shall be void.

Wills shall manifest the genuine intention of the testators; those made under duress or as a result of fraud shall be void.

Forged wills shall be void.

Where a will has been tampered with, the affected parts of it shall be void.

Chapter IV

Disposition of the Estate

Article 23   After the opening of succession, a successor who has knowledge of the death should promptly notify the other successors and the testamentary executor. If none of the successors knows about the death or if there is no way to make the notification, the organization to which the decedent belonged before his death or the residents' committee or villagers' committee at his place of residence shall make the notification.

Article 24   Anyone who has in his possession the property of the decedent shall take good care of such property and no one is allowed to misappropriate it or contend for it.

Article 25   A successor who, after the opening of succession, disclaims inheritance should make known his decision before the disposition of the estate. In the absence of such an indication, he is deemed to have accepted the inheritance.

A legatee should, within two months from the time he learns of the legacy, make known whether he accepts it or disclaims it. In the absence of such an indication within the specified period, he is deemed to have disclaimed the legacy.

Article 26   If a decedent's estate is partitioned, half of the joint property acquired by the spouses in the course of their matrimonial life shall, unless otherwise agreed upon, be first allotted to the surviving spouse as his or her own property; the remainder shall constitute the decedent's estate.

If the decedent's estate is a component part of the common property of his family, that portion of the property belonging to the other members of the family shall first be separated at the time of the partitioning of the decedent's estate.

Article 27   Under any of the following circumstances, the part of the estate affected shall be dealt with in accordance with statutory succession:

(1) where inheritance is disclaimed by a testamentary successor or the legacy is disclaimed by a legatee;

(2) where a testamentary successor is disinherited;

(3) where a testamentary successor or legatee predeceases the testator;

(4) where an invalidated portion of the will involves part of the estate; or

(5) where no disposition is made under the will for part of the estate.

Article 28   At the time of the partitioning of the estate, reservation shall be made for the share of an unborn child. The share reserved shall, if the baby is stillborn, be dealt with in accordance with statutory succession.

Article 29   The partitioning of a decedent's estate shall be conducted in a way beneficial to the requirements of production and livelihood; it shall not diminish the usefulness of the estate.

If the estate is unsuitable for partitioning, it may be disposed of by such means as price evaluation, appropriate compensation or co-ownership.

Article 30   A surviving spouse who re-marries is entitled to dispose of the property he or she has inherited, subject to no interference by any other person.

Article 31   A citizen may enter into a legacy-support agreement with a person who, in accordance with the agreement, assumes the duty to support the former in his or her lifetime and attends to his or her interment after death, in return for the right to legacy.

A citizen may enter into a legacy-support agreement with an organization under collective ownership which, in accordance with the agreement, assumes the duty to support the former in his or her lifetime and attends to his or her interment after death, in return for the right to legacy.

Article 32   An estate which is left with neither a successor nor a legatee shall belong to the state or, where the decedent was a member of an organization under collective ownership before his or her death, to such an organization.

Article 33   The successor to an estate shall pay all taxes and debts payable by the decedent according to law, up to the actual value of such estate, unless the successor pays voluntarily in excess of the limit.

The successor who disclaims inheritance assumes no responsibility for the payment of taxes and debts payable by the decedent according to law.

Article 34   The carrying out of a legacy shall not affect the payment of taxes and debts payable by the legator according to law.

Chapter V

Supplementary Provisions

Article 25   The people's congress of a national autonomous area may, in accordance with the principles of this Law and the actual practices of the local nationality or nationalities with regard to property inheritance, enact adaptive or supplementary provisions. Provisions made by autonomous regions shall be reported to the Standing Committee of the National People's Congress for the record. Provisions made by autonomous prefectures or autonomous counties shall become effective after being reported to and approved by the standing committee of the people's congress of the relevant province or autonomous region and shall be reported to the Standing Committee of the National People's Congress for the record.

Article 36   For inheritance by a Chinese citizen of an estate outside the People's Republic of China or of an estate of a foreigner within the People's Republic of China, the law of the place of domicile of the decedent shall apply in the case of movable property; in the case of immovable property, the law of the place where the property is located shall apply.

For inheritance by a foreigner of an estate within the People's Republic of China or of an estate of a Chinese citizen outside the People's Republic of China, the law of the place of domicile of the decedent shall apply in the case of movable property; in the case of immovable property, the law of the place where the property is located shall apply.

Where treaties or agreements exist between the People's Republic of China and foreign countries, matters of inheritance shall be handled in accordance with such treaties or agreements.

Article 37   This Law shall go into effect as of October 1, 1985.

Grassland Law of the People's Republic of China

(Adopted at the 11th Meeting of the Standing Committee of the Sixth National People's Congress, promulgated by Order No. 26 of the President of the People's Republic of China on June 18, 1985, and effective as of October 1, 1985)

Article 1　This Law is formulated in accordance with the provisions of the Constitution of the People's Republic of China with a view to improving the protection, management and development of grasslands and ensuring their rational use; protecting and improving the ecological environment; modernizing animal husbandry; enhancing the prosperity of the local economies of the national autonomous areas; and meeting the needs of socialist construction and the people's life.

Article 2　This Law shall be applicable to all grasslands within the territory of China, including hills and lands covered with grass.

Article 3　The department of farming and animal husbandry under the State Council shall be in charge of administration concerning the grasslands in the whole country. The departments of farming and animal husbandry of the local people's governments at the county level and above shall be in charge of administration concerning the grasslands in their respective administrative areas.

Article 4　The grasslands are owned by the state, that is, by the whole people, with the exception of the grasslands that are owned by collectives in accordance with the law.

Grasslands under ownership by the whole people may be assigned to collectives for long-term use. Grasslands under ownership by the whole people, those under collective ownership, and those under ownership by the whole people that are assigned to collectives for long-term use may be contracted by collectives or individuals for pursuits in animal husbandry.

With respect to grasslands used by units under ownership by the whole people, the local people's governments at the county level or above shall register such grasslands, issue certificates to the said units after verification and thus establish their right to use such grasslands. With respect to grasslands under collective ownership and those under ownership by the whole people that are assigned to collectives for long-term use, the local people's governments at the county level shall register such grasslands, issue certificates to the collectives after verification and thus establish their right of ownership of the grasslands or their right to use them.

The right to own or use grasslands shall be protected by law and may not be infringed upon by any unit or individual.

Article 5 If there is a need for temporary adjustments in the use of grasslands under special circumstances, such as in the event of natural disasters, the matter shall be settled by the parties concerned through negotiation on the principles of voluntariness and mutual benefit. Where there is a need for temporary adjustments in the use of grasslands that cross the borders of different counties, the county people's governments concerned shall sponsor negotiations for the settlement of the matter.

Article 6 Disputes over the right of ownership of grasslands or the right to use them shall be settled by the parties concerned through negotiation on the principle of mutual understanding and mutual accommodation in the interest of unity. If no agreement can be reached through such negotiation, the disputes shall be handled by the people's governments.

Disputes over the right of ownership of grasslands or the right to use them that arise between units under ownership by the whole people, between units under collective ownership or between units under ownership by the whole people and those under collective ownership shall be handled by the people's governments at the county level or above.

Disputes over the right to use grasslands that arise between individuals, between individuals and units under ownership by the whole people or between individuals and units under collective ownership shall be handled by the people's governments at the township or county level.

If the parties concerned disagree with the decision made by the people's government, they may file suit in a people's court within one month after they have been informed of the decision.

Pending the settlement of a dispute, none of the parties concerned may destroy the resources of the grasslands in question or the facilities therein.

Article 7 When grasslands owned by collectives are to be requisitioned for state construction the matter shall be handled in accordance with the provisions of the Regulations Concerning Land Requisition for State Construction.

If grasslands under ownership by the whole people that are assigned to collectives for long-term use are to be used for state construction, due compensation shall be paid to the collectives concerned and proper arrangements made for the productive pursuits and livelihood of herdsmen with reference to the provisions of the Regulations Concerning Land Requisition for State Construction.

If grasslands in national autonomous areas are to be requisitioned or used for state construction, due consideration shall be given to the interests of the national autonomous areas and arrangements made in favour of the economic development of those areas.

The temporary use of grasslands for state construction shall be effected in accordance with the provisions of the Regulations Concerning Land Requisition for State Construction. When the period of use expires, the unit that has used the grasslands shall restore the grassland vegetation.

Article 8   The local people's governments at various levels shall be responsible for conducting general surveys of grassland resources within their respective administrative areas and formulating plans for the development of animal husbandry, which shall be incorporated into the plans for national economic development, in order to improve the protection of the grasslands, promote their development and ensure their rational use, and increase the capacity for raising livestock on the grasslands.

Article 9   The state shall encourage scientific research in animal husbandry on the grasslands in order to raise the scientific and technological level in this field of endeavour.

The state shall encourage the growing of grass in farming, forestry and pastoral areas and in cities and towns so as to promote the development of animal husbandry and improve the ecology.

The state shall protect the ecology of the grasslands, to prevent and control pollution.

Article 10   Rigorous measures shall be adopted to protect the vegetation of the grasslands; land reclamation and destruction of grasslands shall be prohibited. Reclamation of limited stretches of grassland by users of such land must be approved by the local people's governments at the county level or above. Where land reclamation has already caused aridity or serious soil erosion, the local people's governments at the county level or above shall close the area for a limited time and order the reclaimers to restore the vegetation and defer farming for a return to animal husbandry.

Article 11   Persons who wish to cut shrubs, dig medicinal herbs or wild plants on the grasslands, scrape alkaline earth off the grasslands or move away fertile soil must secure the agreement of the users of the grasslands and the approval of the people's governments at the township or county level; they must operate within the designated areas, fill the holes in the ground immediately after digging and keep part of the mother plants intact.

Cutting or digging shrubs, medicinal herbs or other sand-fixation plants on desert or semi-desert grass ands or in arid areas shall be prohibited. No one may collect rare and precious wild plants from the grasslands without the approval of a people's government at the county level.

Article 12   Grasslands shall be used rationally and overgrazing prevented. Where aridity, degeneration or soil erosion occurs as a result of overgrazing, users of the grasslands shall be required to reduce grazing and resow forage grass so as to restore vegetation. Where man-made grasslands have already been established, extra control shall be administered; they shall be rationally managed and used in a scientific way, so as to prevent degeneration.

Article 13   The local people's governments at various levels shall take measures to combat grassland pests and mice and protect beneficial animals and birds that feed on pests and mice.

Article 14   The local people's governments at various levels shall take measures to prevent and treat endemic diseases among livestock and diseases contracted commonly by both human beings and livestock in grassland areas.

Hunters of wild animals on the grasslands shall be required to observe strictly the regulations of the local people's governments concerning the prevention of epidemic diseases.

Article 15   Motor vehicle drivers shall take care to protect the grasslands when driving across them. Where there are regular highways, vehicles may not deviate from them.

Purchasers of domestic animals shall drive and graze them along designated routes and may not contend with herdsmen over grazing grounds or water resources.

Article 16   Efforts shall be strengthened to prevent fires on the grasslands, implementing the principle of "put prevention first and combine prevention with elimination." A responsibility system for fire prevention shall be instituted. Fire prevention rules and pledges shall be formulated and specific periods shall be designated for fire prevention on the grasslands. During those periods, safety measures shall be adopted and rigorously administered. When a grassland fire breaks out, masses of people should be organized promptly to put it out, the cause of the fire and the losses sustained should be determined through investigation and the case should be handled without delay.

Article 17   Units or individuals that have achieved outstanding success in protecting, managing and developing the grasslands or in developing animal husbandry on the grasslands shall be given commendation or material awards by the local people's governments at various levels.

Article 18   When a person's right of ownership of grasslands or his right to use them has been infringed upon, he may apply for settlement to the farming and animal husbandry department of the local people's government at the county level or above. The farming and animal husbandry department concerned shall have the power to order the infringing party to stop such infringement and compensate for the losses sustained by the victim. The victim may also directly file suit in a people's court.

Article 19   The farming and animal husbandry departments of the local people's governments at the county level or above shall have the power to order anyone who reclaims grassland in violation of the provisions of this

Law to stop reclaiming it and restore vegetation; a fine may be imposed in serious cases.

Article 20   If anyone damages the vegetation of the grasslands by cutting or digging sand-fixation plants or other wild plants or by moving away soil in violation of the provisions of this Law, the people's governments at the township level and the farming and animal husbandry departments of the people's governments at the county level shall have the power to stop him and order him to restore the vegetation and compensate for the losses. A fine may be imposed in serious cases.

Article 21   If a party concerned disagrees with the decision on a fine or compensation as made by the relevant farming and animal husbandry department of a local people's government or by a people's government at the township level, it may file suit in a people's court within one month of being informed of the decision. If upon the expiration of the period a party concerned has neither filed suit nor obeyed the decision by paying the fine, the relevant farming and animal husbandry department of the local people's government or the people's government at the township level may request the people's court for compulsory execution.

Article 22   The farming and animal husbandry department under the State Council shall, in accordance with this Law, formulate rules for its implementation and shall submit them to the State Council for approval before they are put into effect.

The standing committees of the people's congresses of autonomous regions and provinces may formulate rules for the implementation of this Law in accordance with the provisions of the Constitution and the principles laid down in this Law and in the light of the characteristics of their respective localities, and they shall submit the rules to the Standing Committee of the National People's Congress for the record.

Article 23   This Law shall come into force as of October 1, 1985.

Metrology Law of the
People's Republic of China

*(Adopted at the 12th Meeting of the Standing Committee of the Sixth
National People's Congress, promulgated by Order No. 28 of
the President of the People's Republic of China on September 6,
1985, and effective as of July 1, 1986)*

Contents

Chapter   I

General Provisions

Article 1 This Law is formulated to strengthen the metrological supervision and administration, to ensure the uniformity of the national system of units of measurement and the accuracy and reliability of the values of quantities, so as to contribute to the development of production, trade and science and technology, to meet the needs of socialist modernization and to safeguard the interests of the state and the people.

Article 2 Within the territory of the People's Republic of China, this Law must be abided by in establishing national primary standards of measurement and standards of measurement, in conducting metrological verification, and in the manufacture, repair, sale or use of measuring instruments.

Article 3 The state shall adopt the International System of Units (SI).

The International System of Units and other units of measurement adopted by the state shall be the national legal units of measurement. The names and symbols of the national legal units of measurement shall be promulgated by the State Council.

Non-national legal units of measurement shall be abrogated. Measures for the abrogation shall be stipulated by the State Council.

Article 4   The metrological administrative department of the State Council shall exercise unified supervision over and administration of metrological work throughout the country.

The metrological administrative departments of the local people's governments at and above the county level shall exercise supervision over and administration of metrological work within their respective administrative areas.

Chapter   II

Primary Standards of Measurement, Standards of Measurement and Metrological Verification

Article 5   The metrological administrative department of the State Council shall be responsible for establishing all kinds of primary standards of measurement, which shall serve as the ultimate basis for unifying the values of quantities of the country.

Article 6   The metrological administrative departments of the local people's governments at or above the county level may, according to the needs of their respective areas, establish public standards of measurement, which shall be put into use after being checked and found to be qualified by the metrological administrative department of the people's government at the next higher level.

Article 7   The competent department concerned of the State Council and the competent department concerned of the people's governments of the provinces, autonomous regions, and municipalities directly under the Central Government may, in light of their own specific needs, establish standards of measurement for their own use. The ultimate standard of measurement of each kind shall be put into use after being checked and found to be qualified by the metrological administrative authorities of the people's government at the corresponding level.

Article 8   Enterprises or institutions may, according to their needs, establish standards of measurement for their own use. The ultimate standard of measurement of each kind shall be put into use after being checked and found to be qualified by the metrological administrative department of the people's government concerned.

Article 9   The metrological administrative departments of the people's governments at or above the county level shall make compulsory verification of the public standards of measurement, the ultimate standards of measurement used in the departments, enterprises and institutions as well as the working measuring instruments used in settling trade accounts, safety protection, medical and health work, or environmental monitoring that are listed in the compulsory verification catalogue. Those measuring instruments which have not been submitted for verification as required and those which have been checked and found to be unqualified shall not be used. The catalogue of the working measuring instruments subject to compulsory verification and the measures for the administration of such instruments shall be stipulated by the State Council.

Standards of measurement and working measuring instruments other than those referred to in the preceding paragraph shall be verified at regular intervals by the users themselves or by the metrological verification institutions. The metrological administrative departments of the people's governments at or above the county level shall supervise and inspect such verification.

Article 10   Metrological verification shall be conducted according to the National Metrological Verification System. The National Metrological Verification System shall be worked out by the metrological administrative department of the State Council.

Metrological verification must be carried out in accordance with the regulations governing metrological verification. The national metrological verification regulations shall be formulated by the metrological administrative department of the State Council. In the case of certain instruments that are not covered in the national metrological verification regulations, the competent departments of the State Council and the metrological administrative departments of the people's governments of provinces, autonomous regions, and municipalities directly under the Central Government shall respectively formulate departmental and local verification regulations. Such verification regulations shall be submitted to the metrological administrative department of the State Council for the record.

Article 11   Metrological verification shall, according to the principle of economy and rationality, be carried out on the spot or in the vicinity.

Chapter III

Administrative Control of Measuring Instruments

Article 12   An enterprise or institution which is to engage in manufacturing or repairing measuring instruments must have facilities, personnel and verification appliances appropriate to the measuring instruments it is to manufacture or repair and, after being checked and considered as qualified by the metrological administrative department of the people's government at or above the county level, obtain a Licence for Manufacturing Measuring Instruments or a Licence for Repairing Measuring Instruments.

The administrative departments for industry and commerce shall not issue a business licence to an enterprise engaged in manufacturing or repairing measuring instruments which has not obtained a Licence for Manufacturing Measuring Instruments or a Licence for Repairing Measuring Instruments.

Article 13   When an enterprise or institution manufacturing measuring instruments undertakes to manufacture new types of measuring instruments which it has not previously manufactured, such measuring instruments may be put into production only after the metrological performance of the sample products has been checked and found to be qualified by the metrological administrative department of a people's government at or above the provincial level.

Article 14   Without the approval of the metrological administrative department of the State Council, measuring instruments with non-legal units of measurement which have been abrogated by the State Council, and other measuring instruments which are banned by the State Council, shall not be manufactured, sold or imported.

Article 15   An enterprise or institution engaged in manufacturing or repairing measuring instruments must verify the measuring instruments it has manufactured or repaired, guarantee the metrological performance of the products and issue certificates of inspection for the qualified products.

The metrological administrative department of the people's governments at or above the county level shall supervise and inspect the quality of the measuring instruments manufactured or repaired.

Article 16   Measuring instruments imported from abroad may be sold only after having been verified and found to be up to standard by the metrological administrative department of the people's government at or above the provincial level.

Article 17   When using measuring instruments, no person shall be allowed to impair their accuracy, thereby prejudicing the interests of the state and consumers.

Article 18   Self-employed workers or merchants may manufacture or repair simple measuring instruments.

Any self-employed worker or merchant who is to engage in manufacturing or repairing measuring instruments may apply for a business licence from the administrative department for industry and commerce provided he has been tested and found to be qualified by the metrological administrative department of a people's government at the county level, and issued a Licence for Manufacturing Measuring Instruments or a Licence for

Repairing Measuring Instruments.

The types of measuring instruments which can be manufactured or repaired by self-employed workers or merchants shall be determined by the metrological administrative department of the State Council, which shall also adopt measures for their control.

Chapter IV

Metrological Supervision

Article 19 The metrological administrative department of the people's governments at or above the county level may, according to their needs, appoint metrological supervisors. The measures for the administration of the metrological supervisors shall be formulated by the metrological administrative department of the State Council.

Article 20 The metrological administrative department of the people's governments at or above the county level may, according to their needs, set up metrological verification organs or authorize the metrological verification institutions of other establishments to carry out compulsory verification and other verification and testing tasks.

The personnel carrying out the tasks of verification and testing mentioned in the preceding paragraph must be tested for their qualifications.

Article 21 Any dispute over the accuracy of measuring instruments shall be handled in accordance with the data provided after verification with the national primary standards of measurement or public standards of measurement.

Article 22 A product quality inspection agency which is to provide notarial data on the quality of products for society must be checked for its capability and reliability of metrological verification and testing by the metrological administrative department of a people's government at or above the provincial level.

Chapter V

Legal Liability

Article 23 Whoever without a Licence for Manufacturing Measuring Instruments or a Licence for Repairing Measuring Instruments manufactures or repairs measuring instruments shall be ordered to stop his production or business operations. His unlawful income shall be confiscated and a fine may concurrently be imposed.

Article 24   Whoever manufactures or sells a new type of measuring instrument which has not been checked and found to be qualified shall be ordered to stop the manufacture or sale of that new product. His unlawful income shall be confiscated and he may concurrently be punished by a fine.

Article 25   Whoever manufactures, repairs or sells unqualified measuring instruments shall have his unlawful income confiscated and a fine may concurrently be imposed.

Article 26   Whoever uses measuring instruments subject to compulsory verification without having filed an application for verification as required or continues to use measuring instruments which have been checked but found to be unqualified shall be ordered to stop the use and may concurrently be punished by a fine.

Article 27   Whoever uses unqualified measuring instruments or impairs the accuracy of measuring instruments, thus causing losses to the state and consumers, shall be ordered to make compensation for the losses and shall have his measuring instruments and unlawful income confiscated and may concurrently be punished by a fine.

Article 28   Whoever manufactures, sells or uses measuring instruments for the purpose of deceiving consumers shall have his measuring instruments and unlawful income confiscated and may concurrently be punished by a fine. If the circumstances are serious, the individual or the person in the unit who is directly responsible shall be investigated for his criminal responsibility according to the crimes of swindling or speculation.

Article 29   When any individual or unit,in violation of the provisions of this Law, manufactures, repairs or sells unqualified measuring instruments leading to people's injury or death or causing major property losses, the individual or the person in the unit who is directly responsible shall be investigated for his criminal responsibility by reference to the provisions of Article 187 of the Criminal Law.

Article 30   A metrological supervisor who transgresses the law and neglects his duty, where the circumstances are serious, shall be investigated for criminal responsibility pursuant to the relevant provisions of the Criminal Law. If the circumstances are minor, he shall be given an administrative sanction.

Article 31   The administrative sanction provided for in this Law shall be determined by the metrological administrative department of a people's government at or above the county level. The administrative sanction provided for in Article 27 of this Law may also be determined by the administrative departments for industry and commerce.

Article 32   A party who refuses to accept the decision of the administrative sanction may, within 15 days after receipt of the notification of the decision, file suit in a people's court. If within that time limit the party does not file suit or comply with the penalty of paying a fine and having his unlawful income confiscated, the administrative authorities which have made the decision of the administrative sanction may request the people's court for compulsory execution.

Chapter VI

Supplementary Provisions

Article 33 Measures for the administration of and supervision over metrological work in the Chinese People's Liberation Army and in units under the jurisdiction of the Commission on Science, Technology and Industry for National Defence shall be formulated separately by the State Council and the Central Military Commission in accordance with this Law.

Article 34 The metrological administrative department of the State Council shall, in accordance with this Law, formulate rules for its implementation, which shall go into effect after being submitted to and approved by the State Council.

Article 35 This Law shall go into effect on July 1, 1986.

Regulations of the People's Republic of China Concerning Resident Identity Cards

(Adopted at the 12th Meeting of the Standing Committee of the Sixth National People's Congress, promulgated for implementation by Order No. 29 of the President of the People's Republic of China on September 6, 1985, and effective as of September 6, 1985)

Article 1   These Regulations are formulated in order to prove the identity of residents, facilitate citizens' social activities, maintain public order and guarantee citizens' lawful rights and interests.

Article 2   Chinese citizens who have reached the age of 16 and who reside in the People's Republic of China shall obtain by application a resident identity card of the People's Republic of China in accordance with the provisions of these Regulations.

Soldiers of the People's Liberation Army and members of the People's Armed Police Force who are in active service shall dispense with resident identity cards; instead they shall have servicemen's identity cards or armed policemen's identity cards issued to them respectively by the Central Military Commission of the People's Republic of China and the General Headquarters of the Chinese People's Armed Police Force.

Article 3   The items to be registered in a resident identity card shall include name, sex, nationality, birth date and address.

These items shall be registered in the standard language used throughout the country.

In a national autonomous area, the organ exercising autonomy may decide to use at the same time the language of the minority nationality concerned or to choose one of the languages commonly used in the area, depending on the specific local condition.

Article 4   There are three different terms of validity of resident identity cards: 10 years, 20 years and an indefinite number of years. Those in the 16 to 25 age bracket shall be issued resident identity cards valid for 10 years; those in the 26 to 45 age bracket shall be issued resident identity cards valid for 20 years; and those who are over 46 shall be issued resident identity cards valid indefinitely.

Article 5   Public security organs shall be responsible for the printing, issuance and control of resident identity cards.

Article 6   Citizens shall apply for resident identity cards from the

188

residence registration organs at the places where their permanent residence is registered, and shall go through the prescribed procedures for applying for and obtaining such cards.

Article 7   An overseas Chinese who returns to China for permanent residence shall, when going through the formalities of residence registration, apply for a resident identity card.

Article 8   When the term of validity of a resident identity card has expired, or the items registered in it need to be modified or corrected, or the card has been so seriously damaged that what is registered becomes illegible, the bearer shall report the matter and apply for a new card according to the relevant provisions; those who have lost their identity cards shall report the loss and apply for new ones.

Article 9   Citizens who are enlisted in active service shall hand in their resident identity cards when going through the formalities to cancel their resident registration; when they retire from active service, they shall have their resident identity cards back or apply for new ones.

Article 10   If persons who are sentenced to criminal detention, fixed-term imprisonment or more severe punishment or who are undergoing rehabilitation through labour, as well as those who are held in custody, have not yet applied for resident identity cards, they shall not be issued such cards during the period when they are serving their sentences, undergoing rehabilitation through labour, or are held in custody; those who have already obtained their resident identity cards shall, according to stipulations, be divested of their cards by the executing organs. All these persons shall, upon their release or termination of rehabilitation through labour, apply for resident identity cards or get their original ones back.

Article 11   Citizens leaving the country who are required to cancel their residence registration shall hand in their resident identity cards when going through formalities for such cancellation.

Article 12   When a citizen dies, the public security organ shall revoke his or her resident identity card.

Article 13   When performing its duties, the public security organ shall have the power to examine a citizen's resident identity card, and the citizen shall not refuse to be examined.

When on-duty public security personnel examine citizens' resident identity cards, they shall produce their own service cards. The public security organ shall not withhold a citizen's resident identity card except for a person who is subject to coercive measures under the Criminal Procedure Law of the People's Republic of China.

Article 14   When handling matters involving their political and economic rights and interests as well as their rights and interests in social life, citizens may produce their resident identity cards to prove their identities. The relevant units may not withhold their resident identity cards or demand to take them as security.

Article 15   Those who come under one of the following categories shall be penalized in accordance with relevant provisions of the Regulations of the People's Republic of China Concerning Security Control and Punishment:

(1) those who refuse examination of their resident identity cards by a public security organ;

(2) those who transfer or loan their resident identity cards to others;

(3) those who use resident identity cards other than their own; and

(4) those who wilfully damage others' resident identity cards.

Article 16   Whoever forges, falsifies or steals a resident identity card, if the circumstances are serious, shall be penalized according to Article 167 of the Criminal Law of the People's Republic of China.

Article 17   Personnel of the public security organs who engage in malpractices for the benefit of their friends or infringe on citizens' lawful rights and interests while enforcing these Regulations shall be subject to administrative sanctions. If the circumstances of their cases are serious enough to constitute criminal offenses, criminal responsibility shall be investigated in accordance with the law.

Article 18   These Regulations shall not apply to aliens and stateless persons who reside in the People's Republic of China.

Article 19   Rules for the implementation of these Regulations shall be formulated by the Ministry of Public Security and put into effect after being submitted to and approved by the State Council.

Article 20   These Regulations shall go into effect on the day of their promulgation.

Law of the People's Republic of China on Control of the Entry and Exit of Aliens

(Adopted at the 13th Meeting of the Standing Committee of the Sixth National People's Congress, promulgated by Order No. 31 of the President of the People's Republic of China on November 22, 1985, and effective as of February 1, 1986)

Contents

Chapter   I

General Provisions

Article 1   This Law is formulated with a view to safeguarding the sovereignty of the People's Republic of China, maintaining its security and public order and facilitating international exchange.

This Law is applicable to aliens entering, leaving and transiting the territory of the People's Republic of China and to those residing and travelling in China.

Article 2   Aliens must obtain the permission of the competent authorities of the Chinese Government in order to enter, transit or reside in China.

Article 3   For entry, exit and transit, aliens must pass through ports open to aliens or other designated ports and must be subject to inspection by the frontier inspection offices.

For entry, exit and transit, foreign-owned means of transport must pass through ports open to aliens or other designated ports and must be subject to inspection and supervision by the frontier inspection offices.

Article 4   The Chinese Government shall protect the lawful rights and interests of aliens on Chinese territory.

Freedom of the person of aliens is inviolable. No alien may be arrested except with the approval or by decision of a people's procuratorate or by decision of a people's court, and arrest must be made by a public security organ or state security organ.

Article 5   Aliens in China must abide by Chinese laws and may not endanger the state security of China, harm public interests or disrupt public order.

Chapter   II

Entry into the Country

Article 6   For entry into China, aliens shall apply for visas from Chinese diplomatic missions, consular offices or other resident agencies abroad authorized by the Ministry of Foreign Affairs. In specific situations aliens may, in compliance with the provisions of the State Council, apply for visas to visa-granting offices at ports designated by the competent authorities of the Chinese Government.

The entry of nationals from countries having visa agreements with the Chinese Government shall be handled in accordance with those agreements.

In cases where another country has special provisions for Chinese citizens entering and transiting that country, the competent authorities of the Chinese Government may adopt reciprocal measures contingent on the circumstances.

Visas are not required for aliens in immediate transit on connected international flights who hold passenger tickets and stay for no more than 24 hours in China entirely within airport boundaries. Anyone desiring to leave the airport temporarily must obtain permission from the frontier inspection office.

Article 7   When applying for various kinds of visas, aliens shall present valid passports and, if necessary, provide pertinent evidence.

Article 8   Aliens who have been invited or hired to work in China shall, when applying for visas, produce evidence of the invitation or employment.

Article 9   Aliens desiring to reside permanently in China shall, when applying for visas, present status-of-residence identification forms. Applicants may obtain such forms from public security organs at the place where they intend to reside.

Article 10   The competent authorities of the Chinese Government shall issue appropriate visas to aliens according to the purposes stated in their entry applications.

Article 11   When an aircraft or a vessel navigating international routes arrives at a Chinese port, the captain or his agent must submit a passenger name list to the frontier inspection office; a foreign aircraft or vessel must also provide a name list of its crew members.

Article 12   Aliens who are considered a possible threat to China's state security and public order shall not be permitted to enter China.

Chapter   III

Residence

Article 13   For residence in China, aliens must possess identification papers or residence certificates issued by the competent authorities of the Chinese Government.

The term of validity of identification papers or residence certificates shall be determined according to the purposes of entry.

Aliens residing in China shall submit their certificates to the local public security organs for examination within the prescribed period of time.

Article 14   Aliens who, in compliance with Chinese laws, find it necessary to establish prolonged residence in China for the purpose of investing in China or engaging in cooperative projects with Chinese enterprises or institutions in the economic, scientific, technological and cultural fields, or for other purposes, are eligible for prolonged or permanent residence in China upon approval by the competent authorities of the Chinese Government.

Article 15   Aliens who seek asylum for political reasons shall be permitted to reside in China upon approval by the competent authorities of the Chinese Government.

Article 16   Aliens who fail to abide by Chinese laws may have their period of stay in China curtailed or their status of residence in China annulled by the competent authorities of the Chinese Government.

Article 17   For a temporary overnight stay in China, aliens shall complete registration procedures pursuant to the relevant provisions.

Article 18   Aliens holding residence certificates who wish to change their place of residence in China must complete removal formalities pursuant to the relevant provisions.

Article 19   Aliens who have not acquired residence certificates or who are on a study programme in China may not seek employment in China without permission of the competent authorities of the Chinese Government.

Chapter   IV

Travel

Article 20   Aliens who hold valid visas or residence certificates may travel to places open to aliens as designated by the Chinese Government.

Article 21   Aliens desiring to travel to places closed to aliens must apply to local public security organs for travel permits.

Chapter   V

Exit from the Country

Article 22   For exit from China, aliens shall present their valid passports or other valid certificates.

Article 23   Aliens belonging to any of the following categories shall not be allowed to leave China:

(1) defendants in criminal cases or criminal suspects confirmed by a public security organ, a people's procuratorate or a people's court;

(2) persons who, as notified by a people's court, shall be denied exit owing to involvement in unresolved civil cases; and

(3) persons who have committed other acts in violation of Chinese law who have not been dealt with and against whom the competent authorities consider it necessary to institute prosecution.

Article 24   Frontier inspection offices shall have the power to stop aliens belonging to any of the following categories from leaving the country and to deal with them according to law:

(1) holders of invalid exit certificates;

(2) holders of exit certificates other than their own; and

(3) holders of forged or altered exit certificates.

Chapter   VI

Administrative Organs

Article 25   China's diplomatic missions, consular offices and other resident agencies abroad authorized by the Ministry of Foreign Affairs shall be the Chinese Government's agencies abroad to handle aliens' applications for entry and transit.

The Ministry of Public Security, its authorized local public security organs, the Ministry of Foreign Affairs and its authorized local foreign affairs departments shall be the Chinese Government's agencies in China to handle aliens' applications for entry, transit, residence and travel.

Article 26   The authorities handling aliens' applications for entry, transit, residence and travel shall have the power to refuse to issue visas and certificates or to cancel visas and certificates already issued or declare them invalid.

The Ministry of Public Security and the Ministry of Foreign Affairs may, when necessary, alter decisions made by their respectively authorized agencies.

Article 27   An alien who enters or resides in China illegally may be detained for examination or be subjected to residential surveillance or deportation by a public security organ at or above the county level.

Article 28   While performing their duties, foreign affairs police of the public security organs at or above the county level shall have the power to examine the passports and other certificates of aliens. When conducting such examinations, the foreign affairs police shall produce their own service certificates, and relevant organizations or individuals shall have the duty to offer them assistance.

Chapter VII

Penalties

Article 29   If a person, in violation of the provisions of this Law, enters or leaves China illegally, establishes illegal residence or makes an illegal stopover in China, travels to places closed to aliens without a valid travel document, forges or alters an entry or exit certificate, uses another person's certificate as his own or transfers his certificate, he may be penalized by a public security organ at or above the county level with a warning, a fine or detention for not more than ten days. If the circumstances of the case are serious enough to constitute a crime, criminal responsibility shall be investigated in accordance with the law.

If an alien subject to a fine or detention by a public security organ refuses to accept the penalty, he may, within 15 days of receiving notification, appeal to the public security organ at the next higher level, which shall make the final decision; he may also directly file suit in the local people's court.

Article 30   In cases where a person commits any of the acts stated in Article 29 of this Law, if the circumstances are serious, the Ministry of Public Security may impose a penalty by ordering him to leave the country within a certain time or may expel him from the country.

Chapter   VIII

Supplementary Provisions

Article 31   For the purposes of this Law the term "alien" means any person not holding Chinese nationality according to the Nationality Law of the People's Republic of China.

Article 32   Transitory entry into and exit from China by aliens who are nationals of a country adjacent to China and who reside in areas bordering on China shall be handled according to any relevant agreements between the two countries or, in the absence of such agreements, according to the relevant provisions of the Chinese Government.

Article 33   The Ministry of Public Security and the Ministry of Foreign Affairs shall, pursuant to this Law, formulate rules for its implementation, which shall go into effect after being submitted to and approved by the State Council.

Article 34   Affairs concerning members of foreign diplomatic missions and consular offices in the People's Republic of China and other aliens who enjoy diplomatic privileges and immunities, after their entry into China, shall be administered in accordance with the relevant provisions of the State Council and its competent departments.

Article 35   This Law shall go into effect on February 1, 1986.

Law of the People's Republic of China on the Control of the Exit and Entry of Citizens

(Adopted at the 13th Meeting of the Standing Committee of the Sixth National People's Congress, promulgated by Order No. 32 of the President of the People's Republic of China on November 22, 1985, and effective as of February 1, 1986)

Contents

Chapter I

General Provisions

Article 1 This Law is formulated with a view to safeguarding the legitimate rights and interests of Chinese citizens with respect to their exit from and entry into China's territory and to promoting international exchange.

Article 2 Chinese citizens may leave or enter the country with valid passports or other valid certificates issued by the competent departments of the State Council or other departments authorized by them. They shall not be required to apply for visas.

Article 3 For exit and entry, Chinese citizens shall pass through open ports or other designated ports and shall be subject to inspection by the frontier inspection offices.

Article 4 After leaving the country, Chinese citizens may not commit any act harmful to the security, honour or interests of their country.

Chapter   II

Exit from the Country

Article 5   Chinese citizens who desire to leave the country for private purposes shall apply to the public security organs of the city or county in which their residence is registered. Approval shall be granted except in cases prescribed in Article 8 of this Law.

The public security organs shall decide, within a specified time, whether to approve or disapprove the citizens' applications for leaving the country for private purposes, and shall notify the applicants accordingly.

Article 6   In the case of Chinese citizens leaving the country on official business, the units sending them abroad shall apply to the Ministry of Foreign Affairs or the local foreign affairs department authorized by the ministry for the citizens' exit certificates and acquire the certificates for them.

Article 7   In the case of seamen leaving the country to perform their duties, the Bureau of Harbour Superintendence or a harbour superintendent authorized by the bureau shall acquire the exit certificates for them.

Article 8   Approval to exit the country shall not be granted to persons belonging to any of the following categories:

(1) defendants in criminal cases or criminal suspects confirmed by a public security organ, a people's procuratorate or a people's court;

(2) persons who, as notified by a people's court, shall be denied exit owing to involvement in unresolved civil cases;

(3) convicted persons serving their sentences;

(4) persons undergoing rehabilitation through labour; and

(5) persons whose exit from the country will, in the opinion of the competent department of the State Council, be harmful to state security or cause a major loss to national interests.

Article 9   The frontier inspection offices shall have the power to stop persons belonging to any of the following categories from leaving the country and to deal with them according to law:

(1) holders of invalid exit certificates;

(2) holders of exit certificates other than their own; and

(3) holders of forged or altered exit certificates.

Chapter   III

Entry into the Country

Article 10   Chinese citizens residing abroad who desire to return to

China for permanent residence shall complete the relevant procedures at the Chinese diplomatic missions, consular offices or other agencies located abroad that are authorized by the Ministry of Foreign Affairs, or at the public security organs of the relevant provinces, autonomous regions, or municipalities directly under the Central Government.

Article 11   After their entry into China, Chinese citizens who have come for permanent residence or employment shall register for prolonged residence in accordance with the provisions for the administration of residence. Those who have entered for a temporary stay shall register for temporary residence in accordance with the same provisions.

Chapter IV

Administrative Organs

Article 12   Passports for Chinese citizens going abroad on official business shall be issued by the Ministry of Foreign Affairs or by the local foreign affairs departments authorized by the ministry. Seamen's papers shall be issued by the Bureau of Harbour Superintendence or a harbour superintendent authorized by the bureau. Passports for Chinese citizens going abroad for private purposes shall be issued by the Ministry of Public Security or by local public security organs authorized by the ministry.

Passports and certificates which Chinese citizens apply for abroad shall be issued by the Chinese diplomatic missions, consular offices or other agencies located abroad authorized by the Ministry of Foreign Affairs.

Article 13   The Ministry of Public Security, the Ministry of Foreign Affairs, the Bureau of Harbour Superintendence and other agencies that issue passports and certificates shall have the power to cancel passports and certificates issued by them or by their authorized agencies, or to declare such passports and certificates invalid.

Chapter V

Penalties

Article 14   Any person who, in violation of the provisions of this Law, leaves or enters the country illegally, forges or alters an exit or entry certificate, uses another person's certificate as his own or transfers his certificate may be given a warning or placed in detention for not more than ten days by a public security organ. If the circumstances of the case are serious enough to constitute a crime, criminal responsibility shall be investigated in accordance with the Law.

Article 15 If a citizen subject to the penalty of detention by a public security organ refuses to accept the penalty, he may, within 15 days of receiving notification, appeal to the public security organ at the next higher level, which shall make the final decision; he may also directly file suit in the local people's court.

Article 16 Where a state functionary charged with implementing this Law takes advantage of his position and power to extort and accept bribes, he shall be punished according to the Criminal Law of the People's Republic of China and the Decision of the Standing Committee of the National People's Congress Regarding the Severe Punishment of Criminals Who Seriously Undermine the Economy. If he has committed any other act involving violation of the Law and dereliction of duty which is serious enough to constitute a crime, his criminal responsibility shall be investigated according to the relevant provisions of the Criminal Law of the People's Republic of China.

Chapter VI

Supplementary Provisions

Article 17 Control measures governing Chinese citizens' travels to and from the Hong Kong or the Macao region shall be separately formulated by the relevant departments of the State Council.

Article 18 Transitory exit from and entry into China by Chinese citizens residing in areas bordering on a neighbouring country shall be handled according to any relevant agreements between the two countries or, in the absence of such agreements, according to the relevant provisions of the Chinese Government.

The exit and entry of crews of transnational trains, crews of civil aviation planes operating international flights and the railway functionaries working in China's border areas shall be handled according to relevant agreements and provisions.

Article 19 The Ministry of Public Security, the Ministry of Foreign Affairs and the Ministry of Communications shall, pursuant to this Law, formulate rules for its implementation, which shall go into effect after being submitted to and approved by the State Council.

Article 20 This Law shall go into effect as of February 1, 1986.

Decision of the Third Session of the Sixth National People's Congress on Authorizing the State Council to Formulate Interim Provisions or Regulations Concerning the Reform of the Economic Structure and the Open Policy

(Adopted at the Third Session of the Sixth National People's Congress on April 10, 1985)

With a view to ensuring the smooth progress of the reform of the economic structure and the implementation of the open policy, the Third Session of the Sixth National People's Congress has decided to authorize the State Council to formulate, promulgate and implement, whenever necessary, interim provisions or regulations concerning the reform of the economic structure and the open policy in accordance with the Constitution without contravening the relevant laws and the basic principles of the relevant decisions of the National People's Congress and its Standing Committee, and to report them to the Standing Committee of the National People's Congress for the record. These provisions and regulations shall be made into law by the National People's Congress or its Standing Committee after they are tested in practice and when conditions are ripe.

Decision of the Third Session of the Sixth National People's Congress on Establishing the Drafting Committee of the Basic Law for Hong Kong Special Administrative Region of the People's Republic of China

(Adopted at the Third Session of the Sixth National People's Congress on April 10, 1985)

The Third Session of the Sixth National People's Congress of the People's Republic of China has decided to establish the Drafting Committee for the Basic Law of the Hong Kong Special Administrative Region of the People's Republic of China, which shall be in charge of drafting the Basic Law of the Hong Kong Special Administrative Region.

The Drafting Committee for the Basic Law of the Hong Kong Special Administrative Region shall be responsible to the National People's Congress and, when the Congress is not in session, to its Standing Committee.

The Drafting Committee for the Basic Law of the Hong Kong Special Administrative Region shall be composed of people from various quarters and of experts, including those from among the compatriots in Hong Kong. The name list shall be decided upon and announced by the Standing Committee of the National People's Congress.

Resolution of the Standing Committee of the National People's Congress on Acquainting Citizens with Basic Knowledge of Law

(Adopted at the 13th Meeting of the Standing Committee of the Sixth National People's Congress on November 22, 1985)

In the interest of developing socialist democracy and improving the socialist legal system, it is necessary to place the law in the hands of the masses of people so that they will know what the law is, abide by the law, acquire a sense of legality and learn to use the law as a weapon against all acts committed in violation of the Constitution and the law. This will contribute towards safeguarding the lawful rights and interests of citizens and ensuring the enforcement of the Constitution and the law. A major effort to publicize the legal system and popularize basic knowledge of law among citizens is of great significance to the consolidation of the socialist legal system, the ensurance of long-term stability in the country, the promotion of material and cultural progress in our socialist society, and the realization of our country's objectives and general task in the new period. The 13th Meeting of the Standing Committee of the Sixth National People's Congress takes the view that the draft resolution submitted by the State Council concerning the popularization of basic knowledge of law among citizens is very important and timely, and resolves as follows:

1. Beginning in 1986, a programme of education aimed at popularizing basic knowledge of law among all citizens capable of understanding it shall be carried out in well-planned steps over a period of about five years. Such education shall gradually be institutionalized and regularized.

2. The popularization of basic knowledge of law is intended, first and foremost, for cadres at all levels and for young people. In particular, leading cadres at all levels shall set examples for studying the laws, understanding them and acting by them.

3. The popularization of basic knowledge of law shall focus on the Constitution and cover the essentials of the basic laws, such as those of civil and criminal law and the law concerning the structure of the state, as well as basic knowledge of laws which have much to do with the vast numbers of cadres and people. Different departments shall devote more attention to basic knowledge of the laws pertinent to their respective pursuits, and in

various regions pertinent laws may be chosen for study according to the needs.

4. Schools are important places for popularizing basic knowledge of law. Universities, secondary schools, primary schools and schools belonging to various other categories shall all offer courses for legal education or incorporate such education in related courses, include both in the curriculum, and combine legal education with moral and ideological-political education.

5. It is necessary to write or compile concise and popular readers on basic knowledge of law and to conduct publicity and education for the popularization of such knowledge by closely linking it with reality and employing a variety of forms. Such education shall be conducted in an accurate, popular, vivid and wholesome way. Solid work must be stressed in order to achieve good results and avoid a formalistic way of doing things.

6. The popularization of basic knowledge of law shall be conducted under the leadership of the Communist Party of China and by setting in motion and relying upon the forces of society as a whole. All state organs, armed forces, political parties and public organizations, enterprises and institutions shall earnestly educate the citizens in their respective organizations and establishments for the popularization of basic knowledge of law. Newspapers and periodicals, news agencies, radio and television stations, publishing houses and institutions in the field of literature and art shall all take up the publicity and education on legality and popularization of basic knowledge of law as an important regular task. The standing committees of the local people's congresses and the local people's governments at all levels shall provide competent leadership for the implementation of this resolution by working out a realistic and feasible plan and taking effective measures to carry it out earnestly.

1986

Fisheries Law of the People's Republic of China

(Adopted at the 14th Meeting of the Standing Committee of the National People's Congress, promulgated by Order No. 34 of the President of the People's Republic of China on January 20, 1986, and effective as of July 1, 1986)

Contents

Chapter I

General Provisions

Article 1 This Law is formulated for the purpose of enhancing the protection, increase, development and reasonable utilization of fishery resources, developing artificial cultivation, protecting fishery workers' lawful rights and interests and boosting fishery production, so as to meet the requirements of socialist construction and the needs of the people.

Article 2 All productive activities of fisheries, such as aquaculture and catching or harvesting of aquatic animals and plants in the inland waters, tidal flats and territorial waters of the People's Republic of China, or in other sea areas under the jurisdiction of the People's Republic of China, must be conducted in accordance with this Law.

Article 3 In fishery production, the state shall adopt a policy that calls for simultaneous development of aquaculture, fishing and processing, with special emphasis on aquaculture and with priority given to different pursuits in accordance with local conditions.

People's governments at various levels shall include fishery production in their economic development plans and take measures to enhance the overall planning and comprehensive utilization of water areas.

Article 4   The state shall encourage research in fishery science and technology and popularization of advanced technology in order to raise the level of the country's fishery science and technology.

Article 5   People's governments at various levels shall give moral encouragement or material awards to units and individuals who make outstanding contributions to the increase and protection of fishery resources, to development of fishery production, or to research in fishery science and technology.

Article 6   The department of fishery administration under the State Council shall be in charge of the administration of fisheries throughout the country. Departments of fishery administration under people's governments at or above the county level shall be in charge of fisheries in their respective areas. These departments shall be authorized to set up fishery superintendency agencies in important fishing areas and fishing ports.

Departments of fishery administration under people's governments at or above the county level and their fishery superintendency agencies may appoint fishery inspectors who will carry out assignments that those departments and agencies entrust to them.

Article 7   State superintendence of fisheries shall operate under the principle of unified leadership and decentralized administration.

Marine fishery shall be under the superintendence of departments of fishery administration under the people's governments of provinces, autonomous regions and centrally administered municipalities contiguous to the sea, with the exception of those sea areas and fishing grounds with specially designated fishery resources that the State Council has put under direct administration of its fishery department and subordinate fishery superintendency agencies.

Fishery in rivers and lakes shall be subject to the superintendence of the departments of fishery administration under the relevant people's governments at or above the county level in accordance with administrative divisions. Fishery administration for water areas that straddle several administrative divisions shall be decided by the relevant people's governments at or above the county level through consultation or placed under departments of fishery administration of people's governments at the next higher level and their subordinate fishery superintendency agencies.

Article 8   Foreigners and foreign fishing vessels must obtain permission from the relevant department under the State Council before entering the territorial waters of the People's Republic of China to carry on fishery production or investigations of fishery resources, and must abide by this Law and other related laws and regulations of the People's Republic of

China. If those persons and vessels belong to countries that have signed relevant accords or agreements with the People's Republic of China, their activities shall be conducted in accordance with those accords or agreements.

State fishery administration and fishing port superintendency agencies shall exercise administrative and supervisory authority over external relations pertaining to fisheries and fishing ports.

Chapter II

Aquaculture

Article 9   The state shall encourage units owned by the whole people, units under collective ownership and individuals to make the best use of suitable water surfaces and tidal flats to develop aquaculture.

Article 10   In conformity with the overall arrangement made by the state for utilization of water areas, people's governments at or above the county level may assign state-owned water surfaces and tidal flats that have been designated for aquaculture to units owned by the whole people and units under collective ownership to develop aquaculture, and after examining their qualifications grant those units aquaculture licences to confirm their rights to the use of such water surfaces and tidal flats.

Water surfaces and tidal flats used by units owned by the whole people, water surfaces and tidal flats owned by collectives, and those owned by the whole people but used by units under collective ownership may all be contracted to collectives or individuals to develop aquaculture.

Ownership and rights to the use of water surfaces and tidal flats shall be protected by law and shall not be subject to encroachment by any units or individuals.

Article 11   If any units or individuals that use water surfaces and tidal flats owned by the whole people for aquaculture neglect them for 12 months without a proper reason, the agencies granting aquaculture licences shall order those units or individuals to develop and utilize them within a certain period of time and if the order is not carried out within the time limit, their aquaculture licences may be revoked.

Article 12   Disputes over the ownership and rights to the use of water surfaces or tidal flats that arise between units owned by the whole people, between units under collective ownership or between units owned by the whole people and units under collective ownership shall be solved through consultation between the parties concerned. If no agreement is reached through consultation, the disputes shall be handled by a people's government at or above the county level. If a party refuses to accept the decision of the people's government, it may file suit in a people's court within 30 days after receiving notification of the decision.

Before disputes over ownership and rights to the use of certain water surfaces or tidal flats are solved, no party may disrupt fishery production in the disputed areas.

Article 13   Requisitioning of collectively owned water surfaces and tidal flats for state construction shall be conducted in accordance with the Regulations on Requisition of Land for State Construction.

When state-owned water surfaces and tidal flats that have been allotted to units owned by the whole people and units under collective ownership for aquaculture are requisitioned for state construction, the construction units shall give those units appropriate compensation.

Chapter   III

Fishing

Article 14   The state shall encourage and support the development of offshore and deep-sea fisheries and make rational arrangement of fishing capacity for inland and inshore fisheries.

Article 15   Any unit or individual that wants to engage in offshore or deep-sea fishing must obtain permission from the department of fishery administration under the State Council; the state shall give support or preferential treatment in the form of funds, materials and technology, and in matters of taxation.

Article 16   Any unit or individual that intends to engage in inland water or inshore fishing must first apply to departments of fishery administration for fishing licences. Licences for using large trawls and purse seines in marine fishing shall be granted upon approval by the department of fishery administration under the State Council. Other fishing licences shall be granted upon approval by local people's governments at or above the county level, but the fishing licences for marine operations that have been issued must not allow uses of trawls and other fishing gear which exceed quotas set by the state. Concrete measures shall be worked out by the people's governments of provinces, autonomous regions, and municipalities directly under the Central Government.

Fishing licences may not be sold, leased or transferred by other illegal means, and they may not be altered.

Article 17   Units and individuals engaging in inland water and inshore fisheries must conduct their operations in accordance with their licences concerning the types of operation, location, time limits and quantity of fishing gear, and they must also abide by the relevant regulations on protection of fishery resources.

Article 18 All fishing vessels that are built, rebuilt, purchased or imported must be examined and inspected by fishing vessel inspection agencies before they are launched for operation. Concrete administrative measures shall be formulated by the department of fishery administration under the State Council.

Chapter IV

Increase and Protection of Fishery Resources

Article 19 Departments of fishery administration under the people's governments at or above the county level shall work out overall plans and take measures to increase fishery resources in the fishery waters under their jurisdiction. These departments may collect fees from the units and individuals profiting from the use of such waters and devote the money thus collected to the increase and protection of fishery resources. The procedures for collecting such fees shall be formulated by the department of fishery administration and the department of finance under the State Council, and must be approved by the State Council before going into effect.

Article 20 Use of explosives and poisons in fishing shall be prohibited. It shall not be permitted to fish in prohibited fishing areas and during closed seasons, to fish with gear and methods banned by the fishery authority or to use fishing nets with meshes smaller than the minimum prescribed sizes.

Departments of fishery administration under the people's governments at or above the county level shall designate species under special protection, prohibited fishing areas and closed seasons, fishing gear and methods that are to be banned or restricted and the minimum sizes for the mesh of nets, as well as other measures for the protection of fishery resources.

Article 21 Catching fry of aquatic animals of important economic value shall be prohibited. Catching fry of aquatic animals of important economic value or spawning aquatic animals under protection for artificial breeding or for other special purposes must be approved by the department of fishery administration under the State Council or by departments of fishery administration under the people's governments of provinces, autonomous regions, and municipalities directly under the Central Government, and it must be conducted in the designated areas and times and strictly in accordance with the quotas assigned.

Measures shall be adopted to protect fry of aquatic animals when channeling or using water from water areas that specialize in producing such fry.

Article 22   When building sluices and dams on the migration routes of fish, shrimp and crabs which will have serious effects on fishery resources, the construction units must build fish passages or adopt other remedial measures.

Article 23   For water bodies that are used for fisheries and also serve the purposes of water storage and regulation and irrigation, the departments concerned shall fix the lowest water level required for fishery.

Article 24   It shall be forbidden to reclaim land from lakes. Without approval from a people's government at or above the county level, it shall not be allowed to enclose tidal flats for cultivation and no one shall be allowed to reclaim land from water areas that are used as major seedling producing centres and aquatic breeding grounds.

Article 25   To conduct underwater explosions, exploration and construction that may have serious effects on fishery resources, the construction units shall consult in advance with the department of fishery administration under the relevant people's government at or above the county level and take measures to prevent or minimize the damage to fishery resources. In case any damage to fishery resources occurs therefrom, the relevant people's government at or above the county level shall order the responsible party to pay compensation.

Article 26   In accordance with the Marine Environmental Protection Law and the Water Pollution Prevention Law, people's governments at all levels shall take measures to protect and improve the ecosystem of fishery waters, prevent pollution and investigate the responsibility of any unit or individual that pollutes the fishery waters.

Article 27   Protection shall be provided to rare aquatic animals whose capture is banned by the state. In case there is a special need to catch them, the matter shall be handled in accordance with the relevant laws and regulations.

Chapter   V

Legal Liability

Article 28   Anyone who uses explosives or poisons in fishing, fishes in violation of the regulations on prohibited fishing areas and closed seasons, uses prohibited fishing gear and methods or catches rare aquatic animals under state protection without permission shall have his catch and unlawful income confiscated and be fined; in addition, his fishing gear may be confiscated and his fishing licence revoked. In serious cases, criminal responsibility of the individual or the persons of a unit who are directly responsible shall be investigated in accordance with Article 129 of the

Criminal Law.

Article 29   Anyone who poaches on or seizes others' aquatic products, or damages others' aquaculture water bodies and facilities shall be ordered by the department of fishery administration or its subordinate fishery superintendency agencies to compensate for the damages and shall concurrently be fined. In serious cases or if the damage is great, criminal responsibility of the individual or the persons of a unit who are directly responsible shall be investigated in accordance with Articles 151 and 156 of the Criminal Law.

Article 30   Anyone who fishes without a fishing licence obtained in accordance with this Law shall have his catches and unlawful income confiscated and may concurrently be fined. In serious cases his fishing gear may also be confiscated.

Article 31   Anyone who fishes in violation of the type of operation, location, time limit and amount of fishing gear stipulated in his licence, shall have his catches and unlawful income confiscated and a fine may concurrently be imposed. In serious cases his fishing gear may also be confiscated and his fishing licence revoked.

Article 32   Anyone who trades in, leases or transfers fishing licences by other illegal means shall have his unlawful income confiscated and his fishing licence revoked and may concurrently be fined.

Article 33   The administrative sanctions stipulated in this Law shall be decided by departments of fishery administration or their subordinate fishery superintendency agencies. Any party who refuses to accept the decision on an administrative sanction may file suit in a people's court within 30 days after receiving notification of the decision. If the party neither files suit nor complies with the decision within the time limit, the agency that made the decision shall request the people's court to compel execution of the decision. However, a party which is engaged in maritime operations must comply with the sanction before filing suit.

Chapter   VI

Supplementary Provisions

Article 34   The department of fishery administration under the State Council shall, in accordance with this Law, formulate rules for its implementation, which shall go into effect after being submitted to and approved by the State Council.

The standing committees of people's congresses of provinces, autonomous regions, and municipalities directly under the Central Government may formulate measures of implementation in accordance with this Law and the rules for its implementation.

Article 35   This Law shall come into force as of July 1, 1986.

Mineral Resources Law of the People's Republic of China

(Adopted at the 15th Meeting of the Standing Committee of the Sixth National People's Congress, promulgated by Order No. 36 of the President of the People's Republic of China on March 19, 1986, and effective as of October 1, 1986)

Contents

Chapter I

General Provisions

Article 1 This Law is formulated in accordance with the Constitution of the People's Republic of China, with a view to developing the mining industry, to promoting the exploration, development, utilization and protection of mineral resources and to ensuring the present and long-term requirements of socialist modernization.

Article 2 This Law must be observed in exploring and exploiting mineral resources within the territory of the People's Republic of China and in the sea areas under its jurisdiction.

Article 3 Mineral resources shall be owned by the state. The state ownership of mineral resources, either near the earth's surface or underground, shall not change with the ownership or right to the use of the land which the mineral resources are attached to.

The state shall safeguard the rational development and utilization of mineral resources. Seizing or damaging mineral resources by any means and by any organization or individual shall be forbidden. People's governments at all levels must make serious efforts to protect mineral resources.

Anyone who wishes to explore mineral resources shall register according to law. Anyone who wishes to exploit mineral resources shall apply for the right of mining. The state shall protect lawful rights of exploration and mining from violation and protect order in production and other work in the mining and exploration areas from interference and disruption.

Mining rights may not be sold, leased or put in pledge.

Article 4   The state-operated mining enterprises shall be the principal force in exploiting mineral resources. The state shall guarantee the consolidation and expansion of state-operated mining enterprises.

The state shall encourage, direct and help the collective mining enterprises of township and towns to develop.

By administrative measures, the state shall direct, help and supervise individuals to conduct mining according to law.

Article 5   The state shall adopt the policy that mineral resources are to be mined with compensation. Anyone who exploits mineral resources must pay resources tax and compensation in accordance with relevant state provisions.

Article 6   With regard to the exploration and development of mineral resources, the state shall practise the policy of unified planning, rational distribution, comprehensive exploration, rational exploitation and comprehensive utilization.

Article 7   The state shall encourage scientific-technical research on the exploration and development of mineral resources, popularize advanced technology and raise the scientific-technical level of mineral exploration and development.

Article 8   Any organization or individual that has achieved remarkable success in the exploration, development and protection of mineral resources and in scientific-technical research shall be rewarded by the people's governments at various levels.

Article 9   The department in charge of geology and mineral resources under the State Council shall be responsible for supervision and administration of the exploration and development of mineral resources throughout the country. Other departments concerned under the State Council shall assist the department in charge of geology and mineral resources under the State Council in supervising and administering the exploration and exploitation of mineral resources.

The departments in charge of geology and mineral resources under the people's governments of provinces, autonomous regions, and municipalities directly under the Central Government shall be in charge of supervising and administering the exploration and exploitation of mineral resources within their respective administrative areas. Other departments concerned under the people's governments of provinces, autonomous regions, and municipalities directly under the Central Government shall assist the departments in charge of geology and mineral resources at the same level in supervising and administering the exploration and exploitation of mineral resources.

Chapter II

Registration for Mineral Exploration and Examination and Approval of Mineral Exploitation

Article 10 The state shall adopt a unified registration system for mineral exploration. The department in charge of geology and mineral resources under the State Council shall be responsible for registering the exploration of mineral resources. The State Council may authorize relevant departments to handle registration of the exploitation of special kinds of mineral ores. The scope and procedures for registration of mineral exploration shall be formulated by the State Council.

Article 11 The mineral reserves approval agency of the State Council or mineral reserves approval agencies of provinces, autonomous regions, and municipalities directly under the Central Government shall be responsible for the examination and approval of the prospecting reports to be used for mine construction designing and shall, within the prescribed time limit, give official replies to the units that submitted the reports. Unless a prospecting report is approved, it may not be used as the basis for mine construction designing.

Article 12 Archives of mineral exploration results and statistics of reserves of various kinds of minerals shall be subject to unified management, and shall be collected or compiled for submission to the competent authorities in accordance with the stipulations of the State Council.

Article 13 The establishment of state-operated mining enterprises shall be approved respectively by the State Council, the relevant department in charge under the State Council and the people's governments of provinces, autonomous regions, or municipalities directly under the Central Government.

In the case of a state-operated mining enterprise which shall be established with the approval of the State Council or its relevant department in charge, the department in charge of geology and mineral resources under the State Council shall, before approval is granted, verify the proposed limits of mining operations and comprehensive utilization plan and write down its comments; after the approval is given, it shall issue a mining licence according to the approval document. Mining licences for specific kinds of minerals may be issued by a relevant department authorized by the State Council. In the case of a state-operated mining enterprise which shall be established with the approval of the people's government of a province, autonomous region, or municipality directly under the Central Government, the department in charge of geology and mineral resources under that people's government shall, before approval is granted, verify the proposed limits of mining operations and comprehensive utilization plan and write down its comments after the approval is given; it shall issue a mining licence according to the approval document.

Article 14   Procedures for the examination and approval of the establishment of collective mining enterprises of villages and towns, for the issuance of mining licences and for the administration of mining by individuals shall be formulated by the standing committees of the people's congresses of provinces, autonomous regions, or municipalities directly under the Central Government.

Article 15   Mining areas which are to be exploited under the state plan, those which are of great value to the national economy and special kinds of minerals for which protective mining is prescribed by the state, shall be exploited by the state in a planned way. No unit or individual may be permitted to exploit them without the approval of the department in charge under the State Council.

Article 16   After defining, according to law, the limits of the mining areas that are to be exploited under the state plan, mining areas that are of great value to the national economy and mining areas of mining enterprises, the competent departments responsible for defining such areas shall inform the relevant people's government at the county level to make a public announcement.

Any change in the mining area of a mining enterprise must be reported to and approved by the original approval department, and a new mining licence must be obtained from the department that issued the original mining licence.

No unit or individual may enter and mine in the mining area of a mining enterprise that have acquired the mining rights.

Article 17   Unless approved by the competent department authorized by the State Council, no one may exploit mineral deposits in the following places:

(1) within demarcated areas of harbours, airports and national defence projects or installations;

(2) within a certain distance from important industrial districts, large-scale water conservancy works or municipal engineering installations of cities and towns;

(3) within certain limits on both sides of railways and important

highways;

(4) within certain limits on both sides of important rivers and embankments;

(5) nature reserves and important scenic spots designated by the state, major sites of immovable historical relics and places of historical interest and scenic beauty that are under state protection; and

(6) other areas where mineral exploitation is forbidden by the state.

Article 18   If a mine is to be closed down, a report must be prepared with information about the mining operations, hidden dangers, land reclamation and utilization, and environmental protection, and an application for approval must be filed in accordance with the relevant state provisions.

Article 19   If, in the course of mineral exploration or exploitation, rare geologic phenomena or ancient cultural remains of major scientific and cultural value are discovered, they shall be protected and reported immediately to the relevant departments.

Chapter III

Mineral Exploration

Article 20   Regional geologic surveys shall be carried out in accordance with the unified state plan. Reports on regional geologic surveys and the appended maps and other data shall be examined and accepted according to state regulations and then provided to relevant departments for use.

Article 21   In conducting a general survey of mineral resources, while surveying for the chief kind of mineral deposits, a preliminary comprehensive assessment shall be made of the minerogenetic conditions involving all paragenetic or associated mineral ores and of the economic perspective of those mineral ores in the area being surveyed.

Article 22   In prospecting for mineral deposits, a comprehensive assessment of the paragenetic and associated mineral ores of commercial value within the mining area must be made and their reserves calculated. Any prospecting report without such comprehensive assessment shall not be approved. However, an exception shall be made of the mineral deposit prospecting items for which the planning department of the State Council has made other stipulations.

Article 23   In conducting general surveys and prospecting of special kinds of fragile non-metallic minerals, fluid minerals, combustible, explosive and soluble minerals and minerals containing radioactive elements, methods prescribed by the competent departments of people's governments at or above the provincial level must be used, and necessary technical installations and safety measures must be provided.

Article 24   The original geological record, maps, and other data of mineral exploration, rock cores, test samples, specimens of other material objects, and various exploration marks shall be protected and preserved in accordance with the relevant provisions.

Article 25   Prospecting reports on mineral deposits and other valuable exploration data shall be provided for use with compensation in accordance with the provisions made by the State Council.

Chapter   IV

Mineral Exploitation

Article 26   Before a mining enterprise is established, the approval authority shall examine its application as to the limits of its mining area, design or mining plan, production technique and safety and environmental protection measures in accordance with the law and relevant state provisions. Approval shall be granted if it finds the enterprise meets these requirements.

Article 27   In exploiting mineral resources, a mining enterprise must adopt rational sequence and methods of mining and the proper ore-dressing technology. The recovery rate and impoverishment rate in mining and recovery rate in ore-dressing of a mining enterprise shall meet the design requirements.

Article 28   While exploiting the chief mineral deposit, its paragenetic and associated mineral ores having commercial value shall be comprehensively exploited and utilized in accordance with a unified plan, so as to avoid waste. Effective protective measures shall be adopted to avoid loss and damage to ores that cannot be exploited in a comprehensive way or that must be exploited simultaneously but cannot be comprehensively utilized for the time being, and to tailings containing useful components.

Article 29   In exploiting mineral resources, it is essential to abide by the state provisions for labour safety and hygiene and have the necessary conditions to ensure safety in production.

Article 30   In exploiting mineral resources, it is essential to observe the legal provisions on environmental protection to prevent pollution of the environment.

In mining mineral resources, attention shall be paid to using land economically. In case cultivated land, grassland or forest land is damaged owing to mining, the relevant mining enterprise shall take measures to utilize the lands affected, such as by reclamation, tree planting and grass planting, as appropriate to the local conditions.

Anyone who, in mining mineral deposits, causes losses to the production and livelihood of other persons shall be liable to compensation and adopt the necessary remedial measures.

Article 31   Before the construction of railways, factories, reservoirs, oil pipelines, transmission lines and various large structures or architectural complexes, the units responsible for the construction must obtain information from departments in charge of geology and mineral resources under the people's governments of provinces, autonomous regions, or centrally administered municipalities where the units are located, about the distribution and mining of mineral resources in the areas where the construction projects are to be built. Those projects shall not be built over important mineral deposits unless approved by departments authorized by the State Council.

Article 32   As prescribed by the State Council, mineral products to be purchased exclusively by designated units may not be purchased by any other units or individuals; excavators of such minerals shall not sell their products to non-designated units.

Article 33   In exploiting mineral resources in national autonomous areas, the state shall give due consideration to the interests of those areas and make arrangements favourable to the areas' economic construction and to the production and livelihood of the people of local minority nationalities.

The organs of self-government of national autonomous areas shall, in accordance with legal provisions and the unified state plan, have priority for rationally developing and utilizing the mineral resources that may be developed by local authorities.

Chapter   V

Collective Mining Enterprises of Villages and Towns and Mining by Individuals

Article 34   The state shall adopt a policy of vigorous support, rational planning, correct guidance and powerful administration with regard to collective mining enterprises of villages and towns and mining by individuals. It shall encourage collective mining enterprises of townships and towns to exploit mineral resources within the areas designated by the state, and permit individuals to exploit scattered and dispersed mineral deposits, as well as sand, stone and clay usable only for common building materials, and small amounts of minerals for their own use in daily life.

The state shall direct and help collective mining enterprises of villages and towns and individual miners to raise unceasingly their technical level, and to increase the mineral resource utilization rate and economic effects.

Departments in charge of geology and mineral resources, geological units and state-operated mining enterprises shall, on the principles of vigorous support and mutual benefit, provide geological data and technical service with compensation to collective mining enterprises of villages and towns and individual miners.

Article 35   Existing collective mining enterprises of villages and towns, located within the mining area of a mining enterprise which is to be established with the approval of the State Council or the relevant department in charge under the State Council, shall be closed down or carry on mining in other designated places. The unit that undertakes to open the mine shall give rational compensation to the closed-down enterprise and make appropriate arrangements for the masses' livelihood. According to its overall arrangement, the state-operated mining enterprise may also enter into joint operation with the collective mining enterprises.

Article 36   Under the general arrangement of the state-operated mining enterprises and with the approval of higher authorities, collective mining enterprises of villages and towns may exploit marginal and scattered ores within the limits of the state-operated mining enterprises, provided that they apply for mining licences as required.

Article 37   Collective mining enterprises of villages and towns and individuals engaged in mining shall raise their technical level and increase the mineral recovery rate. Abusive or wasteful exploitation which is destructive to mineral resources shall be forbidden.

Collective mining enterprises of villages and towns must survey and draw maps showing the correlation between surface and underground workings.

Article 38   People's governments at and above the county level shall direct and help collective mining enterprises of villages and towns and individuals engaged in mining in carrying out technological transformation, improving business management and ensuring safety in production.

Chapter   VI

Legal Liability

Article 39   Anyone who, in violation of the provisions of this Law, mines without a mining licence, enters without authorization and mines in mining areas that the state has planned to develop, in mining areas with ores of significant value to the national economy, or in others' mining areas, or exploits special kinds of minerals that the state has prescribed for protective exploitation shall be ordered to stop excavation, compensate for the losses caused, have his extracted mineral products and unlawful proceeds confiscated, and may be fined concurrently. If the party refuses to stop mining and thus causes damage to mineral resources, the persons directly responsible shall be investigated for criminal responsibility in accordance with the provisions of Article 156 of the Criminal Law.

Article 40   Anyone who mines beyond the approved limits of his mining area shall be ordered to return to his own area and compensate for the losses caused, shall have the mineral products extracted outside his area and his unlawful proceeds confiscated, and may be fined concurrently. If the offender refuses to return to his own mining area and causes damage to mineral resources, his mining licence shall be revoked and the persons directly responsible shall be investigated for criminal responsibility in accordance with the provisions of Article 156 of the Criminal Law.

Article 41   Anyone who steals or seizes mineral products or other property of mining enterprises or exploration units, damages mining or exploration facilities, or disrupts order in production and other work in mining areas or in areas of exploration operation shall be investigated for criminal responsibility in accordance with relevant provisions of the Criminal Law; if the circumstances are obviously minor, the offender shall be punished in accordance with relevant provisions of the Penalty Regulations Regarding Public Security Administration.

Article 42   Anyone who sells, leases or transfers mineral resources by other means shall have his unlawful proceeds confiscated and be fined.

Anyone who sells a mining right or puts it in pledge shall have his unlawful proceeds confiscated, be fined and have his mining licence revoked.

Article 43   Anyone who, in violation of the provisions of this Law, purchases or sells mineral products which are to be purchased exclusively by the state shall have such products and his unlawful proceeds confiscated and may be fined concurrently. If the circumstances are serious, criminal responsibility shall be investigated in accordance with the provisions of Articles 117 and 118 of the Criminal Law.

Article 44   Anyone who, in violation of the provisions of this Law, exploits mineral resources in a destructive way and causes heavy damage to mineral resources shall be ordered to compensate for the losses caused and be fined. If the circumstances are serious, the offender's mining licence may be revoked.

Article 45   The administrative penalties prescribed in Articles 39, 40 and 42 of this Law shall be decided by municipal or county people's governments. The administrative penalties prescribed in Article 43 shall be decided by the administrative departments for industry and commerce. The administrative penalties prescribed in Article 44 shall be decided by departments in charge of geology and mineral resources under the people's governments of provinces, autonomous regions, or municipalities directly under the Central Government. The penalty of revoking the mining licence of a mining enterprise, the opening of which was approved by the State Council or its relevant department, shall be reported to the people's government of a province, autonomous region, or municipality directly under the Central Government for approval.

Article 46   A party who refuses to accept the decision on administrative penalties may, within 15 days after receiving notification of the decision, bring suit in a people's court. If the party neither brings suit nor complies with the decision on a fine and confiscation of the unlawful proceeds within the time limit, the agency that made the decison shall request the people's court to compel execution of the decision.

Article 47   Disputes over the limits of mining areas between mining enterprises shall be settled by the parties through consultation; if no agreement is reached through consultation, the relevant local government at or above the county level shall handle the case on the basis of the limits that have been verified and fixed according to law. Disputes over the limits of mining areas that straddle provinces, autonomous regions, or municipalities directly under the Central Government shall be settled by the people's governments of the relevant provinces, autonomous regions' or municipalities through consultation. If no agreement is reached through consultation, the disputes shall be settled by the State Council.

Chapter   VII

Supplementary Provisions

Article 48   Rules for the implementation of this Law shall be formulated by the State Council.

Article 49   This Law shall go into effect on October 1, 1986.

Article 50   Before this Law goes into effect, anyone who exploited mineral resources without going through approval procedures, having the mining area delimited and obtaining a mining licence shall complete the formalities in accordance with relevant provisions of this Law.

General Principles of the Civil Law of the People's Republic of China

(Adopted at the Fourth Session of the Sixth National People's Congress, promulgated by Order No. 37 of the President of the People's Republic of China on April 12, 1986, and effective as of January 1, 1987)

Contents

Chapter   I

Basic Principles

Article 1   This Law is formulated in accordance with the Constitution and the actual situation in our country, drawing upon our practical experience in civil activities, for the purpose of protecting the lawful civil rights and interests of citizens and legal persons and correctly adjusting civil relations, so as to meet the needs of the developing socialist modernization.

Article 2   The Civil Law of the People's Republic of China shall adjust property relationships and personal relationships between civil subjects with equal status, that is, between citizens, between legal persons and between citizens and legal persons.

Article 3   Parties to a civil activity shall have equal status.

Article 4   In civil activities, the principles of voluntariness, fairness, making compensation for equal value, honesty and credibility shall be observed.

Article 5   The lawful civil rights and interests of citizens and legal persons shall be protected by law; no organization or individual may infringe upon them.

Article 6   Civil activities must be in compliance with the law; where there are no relevant provisions in the law, they shall be in compliance with state policies.

Article 7   Civil activities shall have respect for social ethics and shall not harm the public interest, undermine state economic plans or disrupt social economic order.

Article 8   The law of the People's Republic of China shall apply to civil activities within the People's Republic of China, except as otherwise stipulated by law.

The stipulations of this Law as regards citizens shall apply to foreigners and stateless persons within the People's Republic of China, except as otherwise stipulated by law.

Chapter II

Citizen (Natural Person)

Section 1

Capacity for Civil Rights and Capacity for Civil Conduct

Article 9   A citizen shall have the capacity for civil rights from birth to death and shall enjoy civil rights and assume civil obligations in accordance with the law.

Article 10   All citizens are equal as regards their capacity for civil rights.

Article 11   A citizen aged 18 or over shall be an adult. He shall have full capacity for civil conduct, may independently engage in civil activities and shall be called a person with full capacity for civil conduct.

A citizen who has reached the age of 16 but not the age of 18 and whose main source of income is his own labour shall be regarded as a person with full capacity for civil conduct.

Article 12   A minor aged 10 or over shall be a person with limited capacity for civil conduct and may engage in civil activities appropriate to his age and intellect; in other civil activities, he shall be represented by his agent *ad litem* or participate with the consent of his agent *ad litem*.

A minor under the age of 10 shall be a person having no capacity for civil conduct and shall be represented in civil activities by his agent *ad litem*.

Article 13   A mentally ill person who is unable to account for his own conduct shall be a person having no capacity for civil conduct and shall be represented in civil activities by his agent *ad litem*.

A mentally ill person who is unable to fully account for his own conduct shall be a person with limited capacity for civil conduct and may engage in civil activities appropriate to his mental health; in other civil activities, he shall be represented by his agent *ad litem* or participate with the consent of his agent *ad litem*.

Article 14   The guardian of a person without or with limited capacity for civil conduct shall be his agent *ad litem*.

Article 15   The domicile of a citizen shall be the place where his residence is registered; if his habitual residence is not the same as his domicile, his habitual residence shall be regarded as his domicile.

Section 2

Guardianship

Article 16   The parents of a minor shall be his guardians.

If the parents of a minor are dead or lack the competence to be his guardian, a person from the following categories who has the competence to be a guardian shall act as his guardian:

(1) paternal or maternal grandparent;

(2) elder brother or sister; or

(3) any other closely connected relative or friend willing to bear the responsibility of guardianship and having approval from the units of the minor's parents or from the neighbourhood or village committee in the place of the minor's residence.

In case of a dispute over guardianship, the units of the minor's parents or the neighbourhood or village committee in the place of his residence shall appoint a guardian from among the minor's near relatives. If disagreement over the appointment leads to a lawsuit, the people's court shall make a ruling.

If none of the persons listed in the first two paragraphs of this article is available to be the guardian, the units of the minor's parents, the neighbourhood or village committee in the place of the minor's residence or the civil affairs department shall act as his guardian.

Article 17   A person from the following categories shall act as guardian for a mentally ill person without or with limited capacity for civil conduct:

(1) spouse;

(2) parent;

(3) adult child;

(4) any oher near relative;

(5) any other closely connected relative or friend willing to bear the responsibility of guardianship and having approval from the unit to which the mentally ill person belongs or from the neighbourhood or village committee in the place of his residence.

In case of a dispute over guardianship, the unit to which the mentally ill person belongs or the neighbourhood or village committee in the place of his residence shall appoint a guardian from among his near relatives. If disagreement over the appointment leads to a lawsuit, the people's court shall make a ruling.

If none of the persons listed in the first paragraph of this article is available to be the guardian, the unit to which the mentally ill person belongs, the neighbourhood or village committee in the place of his residence or the civil affairs department shall act as his guardian.

Article 18   A guardian shall fulfil his duty of guardianship and protect the person, property and other lawful rights and interests of his ward. A guardian shall not handle the property of his ward unless it is in the ward's interests.

A guardian's rights to fulfil his guardianship in accordance with the law shall be protected by law.

If a guardian does not fulfil his duties as guardian or infringes upon the lawful rights and interests of his ward, he shall be held responsible; if a guardian causes any property loss for his ward, he shall compensate for such loss. The people's court may disqualify a guardian based on the application of a concerned party or unit.

Article 19   A person who shares interests with a mental patient may apply to a people's court for a declaration that the mental patient is a person without or with limited capacity for civil conduct.

With the recovery of the health of a person who has been declared by a people's court to be without or with limited capacity for civil conduct, and upon his own application or that of an interested person, the people's court may declare him to be a person with limited or full capacity for civil conduct.

Section 3

Declarations of Missing Persons and Death

Article 20   If a citizen's whereabouts have been unknown for two years, an interested person may apply to a people's court for a declaration of the citizen as missing.

If a person's whereabouts become unknown during a war, the calculation of the time period in which his whereabouts are unknown shall begin on the final day of the war.

Article 21   A missing person's property shall be placed in the custody of his spouse, parents, adult children or other closely connected relatives or friends. In case of a dispute over custody, if the persons stipulated above are unavailable or are incapable of taking such custody, the property shall be placed in the custody of a person appointed by the people's court.

Any taxes, debts and other unpaid expenses owed by a missing person shall defrayed by the custodian out of the missing person's property.

Article 22   In the event that a person who has been declared missing reappears or his whereabouts are ascertained, the people's court shall, upon his own application or that of an interested person, revoke the declaration of his missing-person status.

Article 23   Under either of the following circumstances, an interested person may apply to the people's court for a declaration of a citizen's death:

(1) if the citizen's whereabouts have been unknown for four years or

(2) if the citizen's whereabouts have been unknown for two years after the date of an accident in which he was involved.

If a person's whereabouts become unknown during a war, the calculation of the time period in which his whereabouts are unknown shall begin on the final day of the war.

Article 24   In the event that a person who has been declared dead reappears or it is ascertained that he is alive, the people's court shall, upon his own application or that of an interested person, revoke the declaration of his death.

Any civil juristic acts performed by a person with capacity for civil conduct during the period in which he has been declared dead shall be valid.

Article 25   A person shall have the right to request the return of his property, if the declaration of his death has been revoked. Any citizen or organization that has obtained such property in accordance with the Inheritance Law shall return the original items or make appropriate compensation if the original items no longer exist.

Section 4

Individual Businesses and Leaseholding Farm Households

Article 26   "Individual businesses" refers to businesses run by individual citizens who have been lawfully registered and approved to engage in industrial or commercial operation within the sphere permitted by law. An individual business may adopt a shop name.

Article 27   "Leaseholding farm households" refers to members of a rural collective economic organization who engage in commodity production under a contract and within the spheres permitted by law.

Article 28   The legitimate rights and interests of individual businesses and leaseholding farm households shall be protected by law.

Article 29   The debts of an individual business or a leaseholding farm household shall be secured with the individual's property if the business is operated by an individual and with the family's property if the business is operated by a family.

Section 5

Individual Partnership

Article 30   "Individual partnership" refers to two or more citizens associated in a business and working together, with each providing funds, material objects, techniques and so on according to an agreement.

Article 31   Partners shall make a written agreement covering the funds each is to provide, the distribution of profits, the responsibility for debts, the entering into and withdrawal from partnership, the ending of partnership and other such matters.

Article 32   The property provided by the partners shall be under their unified management and use.

The property accumulated in a partnership operation shall belong to all the partners.

Article 33   An individual partnership may adopt a shop name; it shall be approved and registered in accordance with the law and conduct business operations within the range as approved and registered.

Article 34   The operational activities of an individual partnership shall be decided jointly by the partners, who each shall have the right to carry out and supervise those activities.

The partners may elect a responsible person. All partners shall bear civil liability for the operational activities of the responsible person and other personnel.

Article 35   A partnership's debts shall be secured with the partners' property in proportion to their respective contributions to the investment or according to the agreement made.

Partners shall undertake joint liability for their partnership's debts, except as otherwise stipulated by law. Any partner who overpays his share of the partnership's debts shall have the right to claim compensation from the other partners.

Chapter   III

Legal Persons

Section   1

General Stipulations

Article 36   A legal person shall be an organization that has capacity for civil rights and capacity for civil conduct and independently enjoys civil rights and assumes civil obligations in accordance with the law.

A legal person's capacity for civil rights and capacity for civil conduct shall begin when the legal person is established and shall end when the legal person terminates.

Article 37   A legal person shall have the following qualifications:

(1) establishment in accordance with the law;

(2) possession of the necessary property or funds;

(3) possession of its own name, organization and premises; and

(4) ability to independently bear civil liability.

Article 38   In accordance with the law or the articles of association of the legal person, the responsible person who acts on behalf of the legal person in exercising its functions and powers shall be its legal representative.

Article 39   A legal person's domicile shall be the place where its main administrative office is located.

Article 40   When a legal person terminates, it shall go into liquidation in accordance with the law and discontinue all other activities.

Section 2
Enterprise as Legal Person

Article 41   An enterprise owned by the whole people or under collective ownership shall be qualified as a legal person when it has sufficient funds as stipulated by the state; has articles of association, an organization and premises; has the ability to independently bear civil liability; and has been approved and registered by the competent authority.

A Chinese-foreign equity joint venture, Chinese-foreign contractual joint venture or foreign-capital enterprise established within the People's Republic of China shall be qualified as a legal person in China if it has the qualifications of a legal person and has been approved and registered by the administrative agency for industry and commerce in accordance with the law.

Article 42   An enterprise as legal person shall conduct operations within the range approved and registered.

Article 43   An enterprise as legal person shall bear civil liability for the operational activities of its legal representatives and other personnel.

Article 44   If an enterprise as legal person is divided or merged or undergoes any other important change, it shall register the change with the registration authority and publicly announce it.

When an enterprise as legal person is divided or merged, its rights and obligations shall be enjoyed and assumed by the new legal person that results from the change.

Article 45   An enterprise as legal person shall terminate for any of the following reasons:

(1) if it is dissolved by law;

(2) if it is disbanded;

(3) if it is declared bankrupt in accordance with the law; or

(4) for other reasons.

Article 46   When an enterprise as legal person terminates, it shall cancel its registration with the registration authority and publicly announce the termination.

Article 47   When an enterprise as legal person is disbanded, it shall establish a liquidation organization and go into liquidation. When an enterprise as legal person is dissolved or is declared bankrupt, the competent authority or a people's court shall organize the organs and personnel concerned to establish a liquidation organization to liquidate the enterprise.

Article 48   An enterprise owned by the whole people, as legal person, shall bear civil liability with the property that the state authorizes it to manage. An enterprise under collective ownership, as legal person, shall bear civil liability with the property it owns. A Chinese-foreign equity joint venture, Chinese-foreign contractual joint venture or foreign-capital enterprise as legal person shall bear civil liability with the property it owns, except as stipulated otherwise by law.

Article 49   Under any of the following circumstances, an enterprise as legal person shall bear liability, its legal representative may additionally be given administrative sanctions and fined and, if the offence constitutes a crime, criminal responsibility shall be investigated in accordance with the law:

(1) conducting illegal operations beyond the range approved and registered by the registration authority;

(2) concealing facts from the registration and tax authorities and practising fraud;

(3) secretly withdrawing funds or hiding property to evade repayment of debts;

(4) disposing of property without authorization after the enterprise is dissolved, disbanded or declared bankrupt;

(5) failing to apply for registration and make a public announcement promptly when the enterprise undergoes a change or terminates, thus causing interested persons to suffer heavy losses;

(6) engaging in other activities prohibited by law, damaging the interests of the state or the public interest.

Section 3

Official Organ, Institution and Social Organization as Legal Person

Article 50   An independently funded official organ shall be qualified as a legal person on the day it is established.

If according to law an institution or social organization having the qualifications of a legal person needs not go through the procedures for registering as a legal person, it shall be qualified as a legal person on the day it is established; if according to law it does need to go through the registration procedures, it shall be qualified as a legal person after being approved and registered.

Section 4

Economic Association

Article 51   If a new economic entity is formed by enterprises or an enterprise and an institution that engage in economic association and it independently bears civil liability and has the qualifications of a legal person, the new entity shall be qualified as a legal person after being approved and registered by the competent authority.

Article 52   If the enterprises or an enterprise and an institution that engage in economic association conduct joint operation but do not have the qualifications of a legal person, each party to the association shall, in proportion to its respective contribution to the investment or according to the agreement made, bear civil liability with the property each party owns or manages. If joint liability is specified by law or by agreement, the parties shall assume joint liability.

Article 53   If the contract for economic association of enterprises or of an enterprise and an institution specifies that each party shall conduct operations independently, it shall stipulate the rights and obligations of each party, and each party shall bear civil liability separately.

Chapter   IV

Civil Juristic Acts and Agency

Section   1
Civil Juristic Acts

Article 54   A civil juristic act shall be the lawful act of a citizen or legal person to establish, change or terminate civil rights and obligations.

Article 55   A civil juristic act shall meet the following requirements:

(1) the actor has relevant capacity for civil conduct;

(2) the intention expressed is genuine; and

(3) the act does not violate the law or the public interest.

Article 56   A civil juristic act may be in written, oral or other form. If the law stipulates that a particular form be adopted, such stipulation shall be observed.

Article 57   A civil juristic act shall be legally binding once it is instituted. The actor shall not alter or rescind his act except in accordance with the law or with the other party's consent.

Article 58   Civil acts in the following categories shall be null and void:

(1) those performed by a person without capacity for civil conduct;

(2) those that according to law may not be independently performed by a person with limited capacity for civil conduct;

(3) those performed by a person against his true intentions as a result of cheating, coercion or exploitation of his unfavourable position by the other party;

(4) those that performed through malicious collusion are detrimental

to the interest of the state, a collective or a third party;

(5) those that violate the law or the public interest;

(6) economic contracts that violate the state's mandatory plans; and

(7) those that performed under the guise of legitimate acts conceal illegitimate purposes.

Civil acts that are null and void shall not be legally binding from the very beginning.

Article 59   A party shall have the right to request a people's court or an arbitration agency to alter or rescind the following civil acts:

(1) those performed by an actor who seriously misunderstood the contents of the acts;

(2) those that are obviously unfair.

Rescinded civil acts shall be null and void from the very beginning.

Article 60   If part of a civil act is null and void, it shall not affect the validity of other parts.

Article 61   After a civil act has been determined to be null and void or has been rescinded, the party who acquired property as a result of the act shall return it to the party who suffered a loss. The erring party shall compensate the other party for the losses it suffered as a result of the act; if both sides are in error, they shall each bear their proper share of the responsibility.

If the two sides have conspired maliciously and performed a civil act that is detrimental to the interests of the state, a collective or a third party, the property that they thus obtained shall be recovered and turned over to the state or the collective, or returned to the third party.

Article 62   A civil juristic act may have conditions attached to it. Conditional civil juristic acts shall take effect when the relevant conditions are met.

Section 2

Agency

Article 63   Citizens and legal persons may perform civil juristic acts through agents

An agent shall perform civil juristic acts in the principal's name within the scope of the power of agency. The principal shall bear civil liability for the agent's acts of agency.

Civil juristic acts that should be performed by the principal himself, pursuant to legal provisions or the agreement between the two parties, shall not be entrusted to an agent.

Article 64   Agency shall include entrusted agency, statutory agency and appointed agency.

An entrusted agent shall exercise the power of agency as entrusted by the principal; a statutory agent shall exercise the power of agency as prescribed by law; and an appointed agent shall exercise the power of agency as designated by a people's court or the appointing unit.

Article 65 A civil juristic act may be entrusted to an agent in writing or orally. If legal provisions require the entrustment to be written, it shall be effected in writing.

Where the entrustment of agency is in writing, the power of attorney shall clearly state the agent's name, the entrusted tasks and the scope and duration of the power of agency, and it shall be signed or sealed by the principal.

If the power of attorney is not clear as to the authority conferred, the principal shall bear civil liability towards the third party, and the agent shall be held jointly liable.

Article 66 The principal shall bear civil liability for an act performed by an actor with no power of agency, beyond the scope of his power of agency or after his power of agency has expired, only if he recognizes the act retroactively. If the act is not so recognized, the performer shall bear civil liability for it. If a principal is aware that a civil act is being executed in his name but fails to repudiate it, his consent shall be deemed to have been given.

An agent shall bear civil liability if he fails to perform his duties and thus causes damage to the principal.

If an agent and a third party in collusion harm the principal's interests, the agent and the third party shall be held jointly liable.

If a third party is aware that an actor has no power of agency, is overstepping his power of agency, or his power of agency has expired and yet joins him in a civil act and thus brings damage to other people, the third party and the actor shall be held jointly liable.

Article 67 If an agent is aware that the matters entrusted are illegal but still carries them out, or if a principal is aware that his agent's acts are illegal but fails to object to them, the principal and the agent shall be held jointly liable.

Article 68 If in the principal's interests an entrusted agent needs to transfer the agency to another person, he shall first obtain the principal's consent. If the principal's consent is not obtained in advance, the matter shall be reported to him promptly after the transfer, and if the principal objects, the agent shall bear civil liability for the acts of the transferee; however, an entrusted agency transferred in emergency circumstances in order to safeguard the principal's interests shall be excepted.

Article 69 An entrusted agency shall end under any of the following circumstances:

(1) when the period of agency expires or when the tasks entrusted are completed;

(2) when the principal rescinds the entrustment or the agent declines

the entrustment;

(3) when the agent dies;

(4) when the principal loses his capacity for civil conduct; or

(5) when the principal or the agent ceases to be a legal person.

Article 70 A statutory or appointed agency shall end under any of the following circumstances:

(1) when the principal gains or recovers capacity for civil conduct;

(2) when the principal or the agent dies;

(3) when the agent loses capacity for civil conduct;

(4) when the people's court or the unit that appointed the agent rescinds the appointment; or

(5) when the guardian relationship between the principal and the agent ends for other reasons.

Chapter V

Civil Rights

Section 1

Property Ownership and Related Property Rights

Article 71 "Property ownership" means the owner's rights to lawfully possess, utilize, profit from and dispose of his property.

Article 72 Property ownership shall not be obtained in violation of the law.

Unless the law stipulates otherwise or the parties concerned have agreed on other arrangements, the ownership of property obtained by contract or by other lawful means shall be transferred simultaneously with the property itself.

Article 73 State property shall be owned by the whole people.

State property is sacred and inviolable, and no organization or individual shall be allowed to seize, encroach upon, privately divide, retain or destroy it.

Article 74 Property of collective organizations of the working masses shall be owned collectively by the working masses. This shall include:

(1) land, forests, mountains, grasslands, unreclaimed land, beaches and other areas that are stipulated by law to be under collective ownership;

(2) property of collective economic organizations;

(3) collectively owned buildings, reservoirs, farm irrigation facilities and educational, scientific, cultural, health, sports and other facilities; and

(4) other property that is collectively owned.

Collectively owned land shall be owned collectively by the village peasants in accordance with the law and shall be worked and managed by village agricultural production cooperatives, other collective agricultural economic organizations or villagers' committees. Land already under the ownership of the township (town) peasants' collective economic organizations may be collectively owned by the peasants of the township (town).

Collectively owned property shall be protected by law, and no organization or individual may seize, encroach upon, privately divide, destroy or illegally seal up, distrain, freeze or confiscate it.

Article 75   A citizen's personal property shall include his lawfully earned income, housing, savings, articles for daily use, objets d'art, books, reference materials, trees, livestock, as well as means of production the law permits a citizen to possess and other lawful property.

A citizen's lawful property shall be protected by law, and no organization or individual may appropriate, encroach upon, destroy or illegally seal up, distrain, freeze or confiscate it.

Article 76   Citizens shall have the right of inheritance under the law.

Article 77   The lawful property of social organizations, including religious organizations, shall be protected by law.

Article 78   Property may be owned jointly by two or more citizens or legal persons.

There shall be two kinds of joint ownership, namely co-ownership by shares and common ownership. Each of the co-owners by shares shall enjoy the rights and assume the obligations respecting the joint property in proportion to his share. Each of the common owners shall enjoy the rights and assume the obligations respecting the joint property.

Each co-owner by shares shall have the right to withdraw his own share of the joint property or transfer its ownership. However, when he offers to sell his share, the other co-owners shall have a right of pre-emption if all other conditions are equal.

Article 79   If the owner of a buried or concealed object is unknown, the object shall belong to the state. The unit that receives the object shall commend or give a material reward to the unit or individual that turns in the object.

Lost-and-found objects, flotsam and stray animals shall be returned to their rightful owners, and any costs thus incurred shall be reimbursed by the owners.

Article 80   State-owned land may be used according to law by units under ownership by the whole people; it may also be lawfully assigned for use by units under collective ownership. The state shall protect the usufruct of the land, and the usufructuary shall be obligated to manage, protect and properly use the land.

The right of citizens and collectives to contract for management of land under collective ownership or of state-owned land under collective use shall be protected by law. The rights and obligations of the two contracting parties shall be stipulated in the contract signed in accordance with the law.

Land may not be sold, leased, mortgaged or illegally transferred by any other means.

Article 81 State-owned forests, mountains, grasslands, unreclaimed land, beaches, water surfaces and other natural resources may be used according to law by units under ownership by the whole people; or they may also be lawfully assigned for use by units under collective ownership. The state shall protect the usufruct of those resources, and the usufructuary shall be obliged to manage, protect and properly use them.

State-owned mineral resources may be mined according to law by units under ownership by the whole people and units under collective ownership; citizens may also lawfully mine such resources. The state shall protect lawful mining rights.

The right of citizens and collectives to lawfully contract for the management of forests, mountains, grasslands, unreclaimed land, beaches and water surfaces that are owned by collectives or owned by the state but used by collectives shall be protected by law. The rights and obligations of the two contracting parties shall be stipulated in the contract in accordance with the law.

State-owned mineral resources and waters as well as forest land, mountains, grasslands, unreclaimed land and beaches owned by the state and those that are lawfully owned by collectives may not be sold, leased, mortgaged or illegally transferred by any other means.

Article 82 Enterprises under ownership by the whole people shall lawfully enjoy the rights of management over property that the state has authorized them to manage and operate, and the rights shall be protected by law.

Article 83 In the spirit of helping production, making things convenient for people's lives, enhancing unity and mutual assistance, and being fair and reasonable, neighbouring users of real estate shall maintain proper neighbourly relations over such matters as water supply, drainage, passageway, ventilation and lighting. Anyone who causes obstruction or damage to his neighbour, shall stop the infringement, eliminate the obstruction and compensate for the damage.

Section 2

Creditors' Rights

Article 84 A debt represents a special relationship of rights and obligations established between the parties concerned, either according to the agreed terms of a contract or legal provisions. The party entitled to the rights shall be the creditor, and the party assuming the obligations shall be the debtor.

The creditor shall have the right to demand that the debtor fulfil his obligations as specified by the contract or according to legal provisions.

Article 85   A contract shall be an agreement whereby the parties establish, change or terminate their civil relationship. Lawfully established contracts shall be protected by law.

Article 86   When there are two or more creditors to a deal, each creditor shall be entitled to rights in proportion to his proper share of the credit. When there are two or more debtors to a deal, each debtor shall assume obligations in proportion to his proper share of the debt.

Article 87   When there are two or more creditors or debtors to a deal, each of the joint creditors shall be entitled to demand that the debtor fulfil his obligations, in accordance with legal provisions or the agreement between the parties; each of the joint debtors shall be obliged to perform the entire debt, and the debtor who performs the entire debt shall be entitled to ask the other joint debtors to reimburse him for their shares of the debt.

Article 88   The parties to a contract shall fully fulfil their obligations pursuant to the terms of the contract.

If a contract contains ambiguous terms regarding quality, time limit for performance, place of performance, or price, and the intended meaning cannot be determined from the context of relevant terms in the contract, and if the parties cannot reach an agreement through consultation, the provisions below shall apply:

(1) If quality requirements are unclear, state quality standards shall apply; if there are no state quality standards, generally held standards shall apply.

(2) If the time limit for performance is unclear, the debtor may at his convenience fulfil his obligations towards the creditor; the creditor may also demand at any time that the debtor perform his obligations, but sufficient notice shall be given to the debtor.

(3) If the place of performance is unclear, and the payment is money, the performance shall be effected at the seat or place of residence of the party receiving the payment; if the payment is other than money, the performance shall be effected at the seat or place of residence of the party fulfilling the obligations.

(4) If the price agreed by the parties is unclear, the state-fixed price shall apply. If there is no state-fixed price, the price shall be based on market price or the price of a similar article or remuneration for a similar service.

If the contract does not contain an agreed term regarding rights to patent application, any party who has completed an invention-creation shall have the right to apply for a patent.

If the contract does not contain an agreed term regarding rights to the use of scientific and technological research achievements, the parties shall all have the right to use such achievements.

Article 89   In accordance with legal provisions the agreement between the parties on the performance of a debt may be guaranteed using the methods below:

(1) A guarantor may guarantee to the creditor that the debtor shall perform his debt. If the debtor defaults, the guarantor shall perform the debt or bear joint liability according to agreement. After performing the debt, the guarantor shall have the right to claim repayment from the debtor.

(2) The debtor or a third party may offer a specific property as a pledge. If the debtor defaults, the creditor shall be entitled to keep the pledge to offset the debt or have priority in satisfying his claim out of the proceeds from the sale of the pledge pursuant to relevant legal provisions.

(3) Within the limits of relevant legal provisions, a party may leave a deposit with the other party. After the debtor has discharged his debt, the deposit shall either be retained as partial payment of the debt or be returned. If the party who leaves the deposit defaults, he shall not be entitled to demand the return of the deposit; if the party who accepts the deposit defaults, he shall repay the deposit in double.

(4) If a party has possession of the other party's property according to contract and the other party violates the contract by failing to pay a required sum of money within the specified time limit, the possessor shall have a lien on the property and may keep the retained property to offset the debt or have priority in satisfying his claim out of the proceeds from the sale of the property pursuant to relevant legal provisions.

Article 90   Legitimate loan relationships shall be protected by law.

Article 91   If a party to a contract transfers all or part of his contractual rights or obligations to a third party, he shall obtain the other party's consent and may not seek profits therefrom. Contracts which according to legal provisions are subject to state approval, such as transfers, must be approved by the authority that originally approved the contract, unless the law or the original contract stipulates otherwise.

Article 92   If profits are acquired improperly and without a lawful basis, resulting in another person's loss, the illegal profits shall be returned to the person who suffered the loss.

Article 93   If a person acts as manager or provides services in order to protect another person's interests when he is not legally or contractually obligated to do so, he shall be entitled to claim from the beneficiary the expenses necessary for such assistance.

Section 3

Intellectual Property Rights

Article 94   Citizens and legal persons shall enjoy rights of authorship (copyrights) and shall be entitled to sign their names as authors, issue and publish their works and obtain remuneration in accordance with the law.

Article 95   The patent rights lawfully obtained by citizens and legal persons shall be protected by law.

Article 96   The rights to exclusive use of trademarks obtained by legal persons, individual businesses and individual partnerships shall be protected by law.

Article 97   Citizens who make discoveries shall be entitled to the rights of discovery. A discoverer shall have the right to apply for and receive certificates of discovery, bonuses or other awards.

Citizens who make inventions or other achievements in scientific and technological research shall have the right to apply for and receive certificates of honour, bonuses or other awards.

Section 4
Personal Rights

Article 98   Citizens shall enjoy the rights of life and health.

Article 99   Citizens shall enjoy the right of personal name and shall be entitled to determine, use or change their personal names in accordance with relevant provisions. Interference with, usurpation of and false representation of personal names shall be prohibited.

Legal persons, individual businesses and individual partnerships shall enjoy the right of name. Enterprises as legal persons, individual businesses and individual partnerships shall have the right to use and lawfully assign their own names.

Article 100   Citizens shall enjoy the right of portrait.

The use of a citizen's portrait for profit without his consent shall be prohibited.

Article 101   Citizens and legal persons shall enjoy the right of reputation. The personality of citizens shall be protected by law, and the use of insults, libel or other means to damage the reputation of citizens or legal persons shall be prohibited.

Article 102   Citizens and legal persons shall enjoy the right of honour. It shall prohibited to unlawfully divest citizens and legal persons of their honorary titles.

Article 103   Citizens shall enjoy the right of marriage by choice. Mercenary marriages, marriages upon arbitrary decision by any third party and any other acts of interference in the freedom of marriage shall be prohibited.

Article 104   Marriage, the family, old people, mothers and children shall be protected by law.

The lawful rights and interests of the handicapped shall be protected by law.

Article 105   Women shall enjoy equal civil rights with men.

Chapter VI

Civil Liability

Section 1
General Stipulations

Article 106 Citizens and legal persons who breach a contract or fail to fulfil other obligations shall bear civil liability.

Citizens and legal persons who through their fault encroach upon state or collective property or the property or person of other people shall bear civil liability.

Civil liability shall still be borne even in the absence of fault, if the law so stipulates.

Article 107 Civil liability shall not be borne for failure to perform a contract or damage to a third party if it is caused by force majeure, except as otherwise provided by law.

Article 108 Debts shall be cleared. If a debtor is unable to repay his debt immediately, he may repay by instalments with the consent of the creditor or a ruling by a people's court. If a debtor is capable of repaying his debt but refuses to do so, repayment shall be compelled by the decision of a people's court.

Article 109 If a person suffers damages from preventing or stopping encroachment on state or collective property, or the property or person of a third party, the infringer shall bear responsibility for compensation, and the beneficiary may also give appropriate compensation.

Article 110 Citizens or legal persons who bear civil liability shall also be held for administrative responsibility if necessary. If the acts committed by citizens and legal persons constitute crimes, criminal responsibility of their legal representatives shall be investigated in accordance with the law.

Section 2
Civil Liability for Breach of Contract

Article 111 If a party fails to fulfil its contractual obligations or violates the terms of a contract while fulfilling the obligations, the other party shall have the right to demand fulfilment or the taking of remedial measures and claim compensation for its losses.

Article 112 The party that breaches a contract shall be liable for compensation equal to the losses consequently suffered by the other party.

The parties may specify in a contract that if one party breaches the contract it shall pay the other party a certain amount of breach of contract damages; they may also specify in the contract the method of assessing the compensation for any losses resulting from a breach of contract.

Article 113   If both parties breach the contract, each party shall bear its respective civil liability.

Article 114   If one party is suffering losses owing to the other party's breach of contract, it shall take prompt measures to prevent the losses from increasing; if it does not promptly do so, it shall not have the right to claim compensation for the additional losses.

Article 115   A party's right to claim compensation for losses shall not be affected by the alteration or termination of a contract.

Article 116   If a party fails to fulfil its contractual obligations on account of a higher authority, it shall first compensate for the losses of the other party or take other remedial measures as contractually agreed and then the higher authority shall be responsible for settling the losses it sustained.

Section 3

Civil Liability for
Infringement of Rights

Article 117   Anyone who encroaches on the property of the state, a collective or another person shall return the property; failing that, he shall reimburse its estimated price.

Anyone who damages the property of the state, a collective or another person shall restore the property to its original condition or reimburse its estimated price. If the victim suffers other great losses therefrom, the infringer shall compensate for those losses as well

Article 118   If the rights of authorship (copyrights), patent rights, rights to exclusive use of trademarks, rights of discovery, rights of invention or rights for scientific and technological research achievements of citizens or legal persons are infringed upon by such means as plagiarism, alteration or imitation, they shall have the right to demand that the infringement be stopped, its ill effects be eliminated and the damages be compensated for.

Article 119   Anyone who infringes upon a citizen's person and causes him physical injury shall pay his medical expenses and his loss in income due to missed working time and shall pay him living subsidies if he is disabled; if the victim dies, the infringer shall also pay the funeral expenses, the necessary living expenses of the deceased's dependents and other such expenses.

Article 120   If a citizen's right of personal name, portrait, reputation or honour is infringed upon, he shall have the right to demand that the infringement be stopped, his reputation be rehabilitated, the ill effects be eliminated and an apology be made; he may also demand compensation for losses.

The above paragraph shall also apply to infringements upon a legal person's right of name, reputation or honour.

Article 121   If a state organ or its personnel, while executing its duties, encroaches upon the lawful rights and interests of a citizen or legal person and causes damage, it shall bear civil liability.

Article 122   If a substandard product causes property damage or physical injury to others, the manufacturer or seller shall bear civil liability according to law. If the transporter or storekeeper is responsible for the matter, the manufacturer or seller shall have the right to demand compensation for its losses.

Article 123   If any person causes damage to other people by engaging in operations that are greatly hazardous to the surroundings, such as operations conducted high aboveground, or those involving high pressure, high voltage, combustibles, explosives, highly toxic or radioactive substances or high-speed means of transport, he shall bear civil liability; however, if it can be proven that the damage was deliberately caused by the victim, he shall not bear civil liability.

Article 124   Any person who pollutes the environment and causes damage to others in violation of state provisions for environmental protection and the prevention of pollution shall bear civil liability in accordance with the law.

Article 125   Any constructor who engages in excavation, repairs or installation of underground facilities in a public place, on a roadside or in a passageway without setting up clear signs and adopting safety measures and thereby causes damage to others shall bear civil liability.

Article 126   If a building or any other installation or an object placed or hung on a structure collapses, detaches or drops down and causes damage to others, its owner or manager shall bear civil liability, unless he can prove himself not at fault.

Article 127   If a domesticated animal causes harm to any person, its keeper or manager shall bear civil liability. If the harm occurs through the fault of the victim, the keeper or manager shall not bear civil liability; if the harm occurs through the fault of a third party, the third party shall bear civil liability.

Article 128   A person who causes harm in exercising justifiable defence shall not bear civil liability. If justifiable defence exceeds the limits of necessity and undue harm is caused, an appropriate amount of civil liability shall be borne.

Article 129   If harm occurs through emergency actions taken to avoid danger, the person who gave rise to the danger shall bear civil liability. If the danger arose from natural causes, the person who took the emergency actions may either be exempt from civil liability or bear civil liability to an appropriate extent. If the emergency measures taken are improper or exceed the limits of necessity and undue harm is caused, the person who took the emergency action shall bear civil liability to an appropriate extent.

Article 130   If two or more persons jointly infringe upon another person's rights and cause him damage, they shall bear joint liability.

Article 131   If a victim is also at fault for causing the damage, the civil liability of the infringer may be reduced.

Article 132   If none of the parties is at fault in causing damage, they may share civil liability according to the actual circumstances.

Article 133   If a person without or with limited capacity for civil conduct causes damage to others, his guardian shall bear civil liability. If the guardian has done his duty of guardianship, his civil liability may be appropriately reduced.

If a person who has property but is without or with limited capacity for civil conduct causes damage to others, the expenses of compensation shall be paid from his property. Shortfalls in such expenses shall be appropriately compensated for by the guardian unless the guardian is a unit.

Section   4
Methods of Bearing Civil Liability

Article 134   The main methods of bearing civil liability shall be:
(1) cessation of infringements;
(2) removal of obstacles;
(3) elimination of dangers;
(4) return of property;
(5) restoration of original condition;
(6) repair, reworking or replacement;
(7) compensation for losses;
(8) payment of breach of contract damages;
(9) elimination of ill effects and rehabilitation of reputation; and
(10) extension of apology.

The above methods of bearing civil liability may be applied exclusively or concurrently.

When hearing civil cases, a people's court, in addition to applying the above stipulations, may serve admonitions, order the offender to sign a pledge of repentance, and confiscate the property used in carrying out illegal activities and the illegal income obtained therefrom. It may also impose fines or detentions as stipulated by law.

Chapter   VII

Limitation of Action

Article 135   Except as otherwise stipulated by law, the limitation of action regarding applications to a people's court for protection of civil rights shall be two years.

Article 136   The limitation of action shall be one year in cases concerning the following:

(1) claims for compensation for bodily injuries;

(2) sales of substandard goods without proper notice to that effect;

(3) delays in paying rent or refusal to pay rent; or

(4) loss of or damage to property left in the care of another person.

Article 137   A limitation of action shall begin when the entitled person knows or should know that his rights have been infringed upon. However, the people's court shall not protect his rights if 20 years have passed since the infringement. Under special circumstances, the people's court may extend the limitation of action.

Article 138   If a party chooses to fulfil obligations voluntarily after the limitation of action has expired, he shall not be subject to the limitation.

Article 139   A limitation of action shall be suspended during the last six months of the limitation if the plaintiff cannot exercise his right of claim because of force majeure or other obstacles. The limitation shall resume on the day when the grounds for the suspension are eliminated.

Article 140   A limitation of action shall be discontinued if suit is brought or if one party makes a claim for or agrees to fulfilment of obligations. A new limitation shall be counted from the time of the discontinuance.

Article 141   If the law has other stipulations concerning limitation of action, those stipulations shall apply.

Chapter   VIII

Application of Law in Civil Relations with Foreigners

Article 142   The application of law in civil relations with foreigners shall be determined by the provisions in this chapter.   .

If any international treaty concluded or acceded to by the People's Republic of China contains provisions differing from those in the civil laws of the People's Republic of China, the provisions of the international treaty shall apply, unless the provisions are ones on which the People's Republic of China has announced reservations.

International practice may be applied to matters for which neither the law of the People's Republic of China nor any international treaty concluded or acceded to by the People's Republic of China has any provisions.

Article 143   If a citizen of the People's Republic of China settles in a foreign country, the law of that country may be applicable as regards his capacity for civil conduct.

Article 144   The ownership of immovable property shall be bound by the law of the place where it is situated.

Article 145   The parties to a contract involving foreign interests may choose the law applicable to settlement of their contractual disputes, except as otherwise stipulated by law.

If the parties to a contract involving foreign interests have not made a choice, the law of the country to which the contract is most closely connected shall be applied.

Article 146   The law of the place where an infringing act is committed shall apply in handling compensation claims for any damage caused by the act. If both parties are citizens of the same country or have established domicile in another country, the law of their own country or the country of domicile may be applied.

An act committed outside the People's Republic of China shall not be treated as an infringing act if under the law of the People's Republic of China it is not considered an infringing act.

Article 147   The marriage of a citizen of the People's Republic of China to a foreigner shall be bound by the law of the place where they get married, while a divorce shall be bound by the law of the place where a court accepts the case.

Article 148   Maintenance of a spouse after divorce shall be bound by the law of the country to which the spouse is most closely connected.

Article 149   In the statutory succession of an estate, movable property shall be bound by the law of the decedent's last place of residence, and immovable property shall be bound by the law of the place where the property is situated.

Article 150   The application of foreign laws or international practice in accordance with the provisions of this chapter shall not violate the public interest of the People's Republic of China.

Chapter   IX

Supplementary Provisions

Article 151   The people's congresses of the national autonomous areas may formulate separate adaptive or supplementary regulations or provisions in accordance with the principles of this Law and in light of the characteristics of the local nationalities. Those formulated by the people's congresses of autonomous regions shall be submitted in accordance with the law to the Standing Committee of the National People's Congress for approval or for the record. Those formulated by the people's congresses of autonomous prefectures or autonomous counties shall be submitted to the standing committee of the people's congress in the relevant province or autonomous region for approval.

Article 152   If an enterprise owned by the whole people has been established with the approval of the competent authority of a province, autonomous region or centrally administered municipality or at a higher level and it has already been registered with the administrative agency for industry and commerce, before this Law comes into force, it shall automatically qualify as a legal person without having to re-register as such.

Article 153   For the purpose of this Law, "force majeure" means unforeseeable, unavoidable and insurmountable objective conditions.

Article 154   Time periods referred to in the Civil Law shall be calculated by the Gregorian calendar in years, months, days and hours.

When a time period is prescribed in hours, calculation of the period shall begin on the prescribed hour. When a time period is prescribed in days, months and years, the day on which the period begins shall not be counted as within the period; calculation shall begin on the next day.

If the last day of a time period falls on a Sunday or an official holiday, the day after the holiday shall be taken as the last day.

The last day shall end at 24:00 hours. If business hours are applicable, the last day shall end at closing time.

Article 155   In this Law, the terms "not less than," "not more than," "within" and "expires" shall include the given figure; the terms "under" and "beyond" shall not include the given figure.

Article 156   This Law shall come into force on January 1, 1987.

Compulsory Education Law
of the People's Republic of China

*(Adopted at the Fourth Session of the Sixth National People's
Congress, promulgated by Order No. 38 of the President
of the People's Republic of China on April 12, 1986,
and effective as of July 1, 1986)*

Article 1   This Law is formulated, in accordance with the Constitution and the actual conditions in China, for the purpose of promoting elementary education and the building of a socialist society that is advanced culturally and ideologically as well as materially.

Article 2   The state shall institute a system of nine-year compulsory education. The authorities of provinces, autonomous regions, and municipalities directly under the Central Government shall decide on measures to promote compulsory education, in accordance with the degree of economic and cultural development in their own localities.

Article 3   In compulsory education, the state policy on education must be implemented to improve the quality of instruction and enable children and adolescents to achieve all-round development—morally, intellectually and physically—so as to lay the foundation for improving the quality of the entire nation and for cultivating well-educated and self-disciplined builders of socialism with high ideals and moral integrity.

Article 4   The state, the community, schools and families shall, in accordance with the law, safeguard the right to compulsory education of school-age children and adolescents.

Article 5   All children who have reached the age of six shall enrol in school and receive compulsory education for the prescribed number of years, regardless of sex, nationality or race. In areas where that is not possible, the beginning of schooling may be postponed to the age of seven.

Article 6   Schools shall promote the use of *putonghua* (common speech based on Beijing pronunciation), which is in common use throughout the nation.

Schools in which the majority of students are of minority nationalities may use the spoken and written languages of those nationalities in instruction.

Article 7   Compulsory education shall be divided into two stages: primary school education and junior middle school education. Once primary education has been made universal, junior middle school education shall follow. The department in charge of education under the State Council shall decide on the duration of each stage.

Article 8   Under the leadership of the State Council, local authorities shall assume responsibility for compulsory education, and it shall be administered at different levels.

The department in charge of education under the State Council shall, in accordance with the needs of the socialist modernization and with the physical and mental development of children and adolescents, decide on the teaching methods, the courses to be offered and their content, and the selection of textbooks for compulsory education.

Article 9   Local people's governments at various levels shall establish primary schools and junior middle schools at such locations that children and adolescents can attend schools near their homes.

Local people's governments shall establish special schools (or classes) for children and adolescents who are blind, deaf-mute or retarded.

The state shall encourage enterprises, institutions and other segments of society to establish schools of the types prescribed by this Law, under unified administration by local people's governments and in compliance with the basic requirements of the state.

Appropriate facilities for compulsory education must be included in the plans for construction and development of both urban and rural areas.

Article 10   The state shall not charge tuition for students receiving compulsory education.

The state shall establish a system of grants-in-aid to support the school attendance of poor students.

Article 11   When children have reached school age, their parents or guardians shall send them to school to receive compulsory education for the prescribed number of years.

If, on account of illness or other special circumstances, school-age children or adolescents need to postpone enrollment or be exempted from schooling, their parents or guardians shall submit an application to that effect to the local people's government for approval.

No organization or individual shall employ school-age children or adolescents who should receive compulsory education.

Article 12   The State Council and the local people's governments at various levels shall be responsible for raising funds for the operating expenses and capital construction investment needed for the implementation of compulsory education, and the funds must be fully guaranteed.

State appropriations for compulsory education shall increase at a faster rate than regular state revenues, and the average expenditure on education per student shall also increase steadily.

In accordance with the provisions of the State Council, the local people's governments at various levels shall levy a surtax for education, which shall be used mainly for compulsory education.

The state shall subsidize those areas that are unable to introduce compulsory education because of financial difficulties.

The state shall encourage individuals and all segments of society to make donations to help develop education.

The state shall assist areas inhabited by minority nationalities to implement compulsory education by providing them with teachers and funds.

Article 13   The state shall take measures to strengthen and develop normal schools and colleges in order to accelerate the training of teachers, so as to ensure, in a planned way, that all primary school teachers have received at least secondary normal school education and that all junior middle school teachers have received at least higher normal school education.

The state shall establish a system to test the qualifications of teachers and shall issue qualification certificates to those who pass the test.

All graduates of normal schools and colleges must engage in educational work, as required by the relevant regulations. The state shall encourage teachers to make education their long-term career.

Article 14   Teachers should be respected by the public. The state shall safeguard the teachers' lawful rights and interests, and take measures to raise their social status and improve their material benefits. It shall reward outstanding educational workers.

Teachers should be committed to the cause of socialist educaton, endeavour to raise their own ideological and cultural levels as well as professional competence, show concern for their students and be devoted to their duties.

Article 15   The local people's governments at various levels must create conditions for all school-age children and adolescents to enrol in schools and receive compulsory education. In cases where school-age children or adolescents do not enrol in school and receive compulsory education, with the exception of those who, on account of illness or other special circumstances, are allowed by the local people's governments not to go to school, the local people's governments shall admonish and criticize the parents or guardians of those children or adolescents, and adopt effective measures to order them to send the children or wards to school.

In cases where organizations or individuals employ school-age children or adolescents for work, the local people's governments shall admonish and criticize them and shall order them to stop such employment. In serious cases, the offenders may be fined, ordered to suspend their business operations or have their business licences revoked.

Article 16   No organization or individual may appropriate, withhold or misuse funds earmarked for compulsory education, disrupt order in education, or occupy or damage school buildings, grounds or facilities.

It shall be forbidden to insult or assault teachers. It shall be forbidden to inflict physical punishment on students.

No one may make use of religion to engage in activities which interfere with the implementation of compulsory education.

Persons who violate the provisions of the preceding two paragraphs shall be subject to administrative sanctions or penalties depending on the circumstances. In case damage is caused, the offender shall be ordered to make compensation. If the circumstances are serious and a crime is committed, criminal responsibility shall be investigated in accordance with the law.

Article 17   The department in charge of education under the State Council shall, in accordance with this Law, formulate rules for its implementation, which shall come into force after being submitted to and approved by the State Council,

The standing committees of the people's congresses of provinces, autonomous regions, and municipalities directly under the Central Government may formulate specific measures for implementation in accordance with this Law and their local conditions.

Article 18   This law shall go into effect as of July 1, 1986.

Law of the People's Republic of China on Foreign-Capital Enterprises

*(Adopted at the Fourth Session of the Sixth National People's
Congress, promulgated by Order No. 39 of the
President of the People's Republic of China
and effective as of April 12, 1986)*

Article 1   With a view to expanding economic cooperation and technical exchange with foreign countries and promoting the development of China's national economy, the People's Republic of China permits foreign enterprises, other foreign economic organizations and individuals (hereinafter collectively referred to as "foreign investors") to set up enterprises with foreign capital in China and protects the lawful rights and interests of such enterprises.

Article 2   As mentioned in this Law, "enterprises with foreign capital" refers to those enterprises established in China by foreign investors, exclusively with their own capital, in accordance with relevant Chinese laws. The term does not include branches set up in China by foreign enterprises and other foreign economic organizations.

Article 3   Enterprises with foreign capital shall be established in such a manner as to help the development of China's national economy; they shall use advanced technology and equipment or market all or most of their products outside China.

Provisions shall be made by the State Council regarding the lines of business which the state forbids enterprises with foreign capital to engage in or on which it places certain restrictions.

Article 4   The investments of a foreign investor in China, the profits it earns and its other lawful rights and interests are protected by Chinese law.

Enterprises with foreign capital must abide by Chinese laws and regulations and must not engage in any activities detrimental to China's public interest.

Article 5   The state shall not nationalize or requisition any enterprise with foreign capital. Under special circumstances, when public interest requires, enterprises with foreign capital may be requisitioned by legal procedures and appropriate compensation shall be made.

Article 6   The application to establish an enterprise with foreign capital shall be submitted for examination and approval to the department under the State Council which is in charge of foreign economic relations and trade, or to another agency authorized by the State Council. The authorities in charge of examination and approval shall, within 90 days from the date they receive such application, decide whether or not to grant approval.

Article 7   After an application for the establishment of an enterprise with foreign capital has been approved, the foreign investor shall, within 30 days from the date of receiving a certificate of approval, apply to the industry and commerce administration authorities for registration and obtain a business licence. The date of issue of the business licence shall be the date of the establishment of the enterprise.

Article 8   An enterprise with foreign capital which meets the conditions for being considered a legal person under Chinese law shall acquire the status of a Chinese legal person, in accordance with the law.

Article 9   An enterprise with foreign capital shall make investments in China within the period approved by the authorities in charge of examination and approval. If it fails to do so, the industry and commerce administration authorities may cancel its business licence.

The industry and commerce administration authorities shall inspect and supervise the investment situation of an enterprise with foreign capital.

Article 10   In the event of a separation, merger or other major change, an enterprise with foreign capital shall report to and seek approval from the authorities in charge of examination and approval, and register the change with the industry and commerce administration authorities.

Article 11   The production and operating plans of enterprises with foreign capital shall be reported to the competent authorities for the record.

Enterprises with foreign capital shall conduct their operations and management in accordance with the approved articles of association, and shall be free from any interference.

Article 12   When employing Chinese workers and staff, an enterprise with foreign capital shall conclude contracts with them according to law, in which matters concerning employment, dismissal, remuneration, welfare benefits, labour protection and labour insurance shall be clearly prescribed.

Article 13   Workers and staff of enterprises with foreign capital may organize trade unions in accordance with the law, in order to conduct trade union activities and protect their lawful rights and interests.

The enterprises shall provide the necessary conditions for the activities of the trade unions in their respective enterprises.

Article 14   An enterprise with foreign capital must set up account books in China, conduct independent accounting, submit the fiscal reports and statements as required and accept supervision by the financial and tax authorities.

If an enterprise with foreign capital refuses to maintain account books in China, the financial and tax authorities may impose a fine on it, and the industry and commerce administration authorities may order it to suspend operations or may revoke its business licence.

Article 15   Within the scope of the operations approved, enterprises with foreign capital may purchase, either in China or from the world market, raw and semi-processed materials, fuels and other materials they need. When these materials are available from both sources on similar terms, first priority should be given to purchases in China.

Article 16   Enterprises with foreign capital shall apply to insurance companies in China for such kinds of insurance coverage as are needed.

Article 17   Enterprises with foreign capital shall pay taxes in accordance with relevant state provisions for tax payment, and may enjoy preferential treatment for reduction of or exemption from taxes.

An enterprise that reinvests its profits in China after paying the income tax, may, in accordance with relevant state provisions, apply for refund of a part of the income tax already paid on the reinvested amount.

Article 18   Enterprises with foreign capital shall handle their foreign exchange transactions in accordance with the state provisions for foreign exchange control.

Enterprises with foreign capital shall open an account with the Bank of China or with a bank designated by the state agency exercising foreign exchange control.

Enterprises with foreign capital shall manage to balance their own foreign exchange receipts and payments. If, with the approval of the competent authorities, the enterprises market their products in China and consequently experience an imbalance in foreign exchange, the said authorities shall help them correct the imbalance.

Article 19   The foreign investor may remit abroad profits that are lawfully earned from an enterprise with foreign capital, as well as other lawful earnings and any funds remaining after the enterprise is liquidated.

Wages, salaries and other legitimate income earned by foreign employees in an enterprise with foreign capital may be remitted abroad after the payment of individual income tax in accordance with the law.

Article 20   With respect to the period of operations of an enterprise with foreign capital, the foreign investor shall report to and secure approval from the authorities in charge of examination and approval. For an extension of the period of operations, an application shall be submitted to the said authorities 180 days before the expiration of the period. The authorities in charge of examination and approval shall, within 30 days from the date such application is received, decide whether or not to grant the extension.

Article 21   When terminating its operations, an enterprise with foreign capital shall promptly issue a public notice and proceed with liquidation in accordance with legal procedure.

Pending the completion of liquidation, a foreign investor may not dispose of the assets of the enterprise except for the purpose of liquidation.

Article 22   At the termination of operations, the enterprise with foreign capital shall nullify its registration with the industry and commerce administration authorities and hand in its business licence for cancellation.

Article 23   The department under the State Council which is in charge of foreign economic relations and trade shall, in accordance with this Law, formulate rules for its implementation, which shall go into effect after being submitted to and approved by the State Council.

Article 24   This Law shall go into effect on the day of its promulgation.

Land Administration Law of the People's Republic of China

*(Adopted at the 16th Meeting of the Standing Committee of the Sixth
National People's Congress, promulgated by Order No. 41
of the President of the People's Republic of China
on June 25, 1986, and effective
as of January 1, 1987)*

Contents

Chapter   I

General Provisions

Article 1   This Law is formulated in order to strengthen land administration, maintain the socialist public ownership of land, protect and develop land resources, make proper use of land, effectively protect cultivated land and meet the needs of socialist modernization.

Article 2   The People's Republic of China shall practise socialist public ownership of land, namely ownership by the whole people and collective ownership by the working people.

No unit or individual may seize, buy, sell or lease land or make any other unlawful transfer of land.

The state may, in the public interest, lawfully requisition land owned by collectives.

Article 3   People's governments at all levels must observe and implement the guiding principles of valuing land highly and using land rationally, draw up overall plans, strengthen land administration, protect and develop land resources, and prevent acts of unlawful possession of cultivated land and abuse of land.

Article 4 The people's governments shall reward the units or individuals that gain prominent achievements in protecting and developing land resources, using land rationally and carrying out relevant scientific research.

Article 5 The land administration department under the State Council shall be in charge of the unified administration of the land throughout the country.

The land administration departments of local people's governments at and above the county level shall be in charge of the unified administration of the land in their respective administrative areas. The provinces, autonomous regions, and municipalities directly under the Central Government shall set up relevant agencies according to actual requirements.

People's governments at the township level shall be in charge of land administration in their respective administrative areas.

Chapter II

Ownership of Land and Right
to the Use of Land

Article 6 Land in the urban areas of cities shall be owned by the whole people, namely, owned by the state.

Land in rural and suburban areas shall be owned by collectives, except for those portions which belong to the state in accordance with the law; house sites and private plots of cropland and hilly land shall also be owned by collectives.

Article 7 State-owned land may be lawfully determined to be used by units under ownership by the whole people or units under collective ownership. State-owned land and collective-owned land may be lawfully determined to be used by individuals. Units and individuals that use land shall have the obligation to protect and manage the land and make rational use of such land.

Article 8 Collective-owned land shall belong lawfully to peasant collectives of a village and shall be operated and managed by agricultural collective economic organizations such as village agricultural producers' cooperatives or villagers' committees. Ownership of land already belonging to peasant collective economic organizations of a township (town) may be assumed by peasant collectives in the township (town).

If land owned by peasant collectives of a village has been divided and belongs to two or more agricultural collective economic organizations in the village, ownership of such land may be assumed by peasant collectives in the respective agricultural collective economic organizations.

Article 9   Land owned by collectives shall be registered and recorded by people's governments at the county level, which shall, upon verification, issue certificates to affirm the ownership of such land.

State-owned land lawfully used by units under ownership by the whole people or under collective ownership or used by individuals shall be registered and recorded by local people's governments at or above the county level, which shall, upon verification, issue certificates to affirm their right to the use of such land.

Confirmation of the ownership of or the right to the use of forest land or grassland and confirmation of the right to the use of water surface or beaches for aquaculture shall be dealt with in accordance with relevant provisions of the Forestry Law, the Grassland Law and the Fisheries Law respectively.

Article 10   If any change is to be lawfully made in land ownership or in the right to the use of land, the formality of registering such change must be gone through and the certificate changed accordingly.

Article 11 Ownership of land and right to the use of land shall be protected by law. No unit or individual shall infringe upon such ownership and right.

Article 12   Land owned by collectives and state-owned land used by units under ownership by the whole people or under collective ownership may be operated under a contract by collectives or individuals for agricultural, forestry, livestock and fishery production.

Collectives or individuals that contract to operate land shall have the obligation to protect such land and make rational use of it according to the uses provided for by the contract.

The right to operate land under contract shall be protected by law.

Article 13   Disputes concerning ownership of land and the right to the use of land shall be solved through consultation between the parties. If no agreement can be reached through consultation, they shall be decided by the people's government.

Disputes concerning ownership of land and the right to the use of land between units under ownership by the whole people, between units under collective ownership, and between units under ownership by the whole people and units under collective ownership shall be decided by people's governments at or above the county level.

Disputes concerning the right to the use of land between individuals, between individuals and units under ownership by the whole people, or between individuals and units under collective ownership shall be decided by people's governments at the township or county level.

If a party refuses to accept the decision of the relevant people's government, it may file a lawsuit in a people's court within 30 days from the date of receiving notification of the decision.

Before a dispute concerning ownership of land or the right to the use of land is solved, no party may alter the existing condition of the disputed land or destroy anything attached to it.

Chapter III

Utilization and Protection of Land

Article 14   The state shall establish a land survey and statistics system. Land administration departments of people's governments at and above the county level together with departments concerned shall carry out land surveys and prepare statistics thereof.

Article 15   People's governments at all levels shall draw up overall plans for land utilization. The overall plans for land utilization of local people's governments shall be implemented upon approval by people's governments at higher levels.

Article 16   Urban planning shall fit in with the overall plan for land utilization. Within areas covered by urban planning, utilization of land shall be consistent with such urban planning.

In the safety zones of rivers and lakes, utilization of land shall be consistent with a comprehensive plan of development and utilization of rivers and lakes.

Article 17   Development of state-owned barren hills, wastelands and beaches for agricultural, forestry, livestock and fishery production shall be subject to the approval of people's governments at or above the county level; such land may be assigned to be used by the units that develop it.

Article 18   If a piece of land from which minerals have been extracted or soil has been removed can be reclaimed, the land-using unit or individual shall be responsible for reclaiming it and restoring its use.

Article 19   Subject to the approval of a people's government at or above the county level, a land administration department may withdraw the grant of right to the use of state-owned land and cancel the land-use certificate of the land-using unit under any of the following circumstances:

(1) the land-using unit being dissolved or moving away;

(2) the land being set aside without use for two consecutive years without the consent of the original approving authority;

(3) the land being used in a way inconsistent with the approved use; or

(4) public roads, railways, airports, mining areas and so on being abandoned upon due verification and approval.

Article 20   People's governments at all levels shall adopt measures to protect cultivated land, maintain irrigation and drainage installations, improve soil, increase fertility of land, prevent soil from desertification, control soil salinization and soil erosion and prohibit acts allowing land to lie waste and destroying cultivated land.

Economy must be practised in using land for state construction and township (town) and village construction; cultivated land shall not be used when wasteland can serve the purpose; good land shall not be used when poor land is available.

Chapter IV

Use of Land for State Construction

Article 21   When the state needs to requisition land owned by collectives or to use state-owned land for economic, cultural or national defence construction projects and for initiating public works, the matter shall be dealt with in accordance with the provisions of this chapter.

Article 22   Upon approval, construction units may apply for use of land needed for state construction projects which are listed in the state fixed-assets investment plan or which may be built in accordance with state provisions.

Article 23   When land is to be requisitioned for state construction, the construction unit must apply to the land administration department of the local people's governments at or above the county level by presenting a project plan description or other documents of approval issued by the competent authority under the State Council or a local people's government at or above the county level, according to procedures specified for state capital construction. After the application has been examined and approved by the people's government at or above the county level, its land administration department shall reassign the land.

When the state requisitions land for construction, the units whose land is requisitioned should subordinate their wishes to the needs of the state and shall not obstruct the requisition.

Article 24   If land owned by collectives is requisitioned for state construction, the state shall have title to such land, while the unit using the land shall have only the right to its use.

Article 25   Requisition of more than 1,000 *mu* of cultivated land or more than 2,000 *mu* of other types of land for state construction shall be subject to the approval of the State Council.

Requisition of land in the administrative areas of provinces or autonomous regions shall be subject to the approval of the governments of those provinces or regions. Requisition of less than three *mu* of cultivated and less than ten *mu* of other types of land shall be subject to the approval of people's governments at the county level. The limits of approval authority of people's governments of municipalities under provinces and of autonomous prefectures shall be decided by the standing committees of people's congresses of the respective provinces and autonomous regions.

Requisition of land within the administrative areas of municipalities directly under the Central Government shall be subject to the approval of the people's governments of those municipalities. The limits of approval authority of the people's governments of districts and counties under centrally administered municipalities shall be decided by the standing committees of the people's congresses of such municipalities.

Article 26   Application for the land needed in a single construction project shall be submitted for approval according to the overall design; such application shall not be broken up into parts. Requisition of land for a project which is being constructed in stages shall be conducted stage by stage but not long before it is used. Application for land needed for the construction of railways, public roads, oil or water pipelines and so on shall be presented for approval section by section and the procedures for land requisition shall be completed accordingly.

Article 27   Units using requisitioned land for state construction shall pay land compensation. The compensation for requisition of cultivated land shall be three to six times the average annual output value of the requisitioned land for the three years preceding such requisition. Provinces, autonomous regions, and municipalities directly under the Central Government shall stipulate standards of compensation for requisition of other types of land with reference to the standard of compensation for requisition of cultivated land.

Standards of compensation for attachments and young crops on the requisitioned land shall be stipulated by provinces, autonomous regions, and municipalities directly under the Central Government.

Units using requisitioned vegetable plots in city suburbs shall pay for a development and construction fund for new vegetable plots in accordance with relevant provisions of the state.

Article 28   In addition to payment of compensation when requisitioning land for state construction, the land-using units shall also pay for resettlement subsidies.

Resettlement subsidies for requisition of cultivated land shall be calculated according to the agricultural population needing to be resettled. The agricultural population needing to be resettled shall be calculated by dividing the amount of requisitioned cultivated land by the average amount of original cultivated land per person of the unit being requisitioned. The standard resettlement subsidy to be divided among members of the agricultural population needing resettlement shall be two to three times the average annual output value of each *mu* of the requisitioned cultivated land for the three years preceding such requisition. However, the highest resettlement subsidy for each *mu* of requisitioned cultivated land shall not exceed ten times its average annual output value for the three years preceding such requisition. Provinces, autonomous regions, and municipalities directly under the Central Government shall stipulate respective standards for resettlement subsidies for requisition of other types of land with reference to the standard resettlement subsidy for cultivated land.

Article 29 If land compensation and resettlement subsidies paid in accordance with Articles 27 and 28 of this Law are still insufficient to maintain the original living standard of the peasants needing resettlement, the resettlement subsidy may be increased upon approval of people's governments of provinces, autonomous regions, or municipalities directly under the Central Government. However, the total land compensation and resettlement subsidy shall not exceed 20 times the average yearly output value of the requisitioned land for the three years preceding such requisition.

Article 30 All kinds of compensation and resettlement subsidies paid for requisitioned land on account of state construction, except for the compensation for individually owned attachments or young crops on the requisitioned land which shall be paid to such individuals, shall be used by the units being requisitioned to develop production, to provide employment for the extra labour force due to requisition of the land and as living subsidies for people who cannot be employed; such funds shall not be used for other purposes and shall not be appropriated by any unit or individual.

Article 31 Land administration departments of local people's governments at or above the county level shall coordinate the units being requisitioned, units using requisitioned land and other units concerned to help resettle the extra labour force due to requisition of land for state construction by developing agricultural and sideline production and setting up township (town) or village enterprises. If there are still people who cannot be resettled, the qualified persons among them may be given work in the units using the requisitioned land or other units under collective ownership or ownership by the whole people and the corresponding resettlement subsidy shall be transferred to the units which absorb such a labour force.

If all the land of a unit is requisitioned, members originally registered in agricultural households may change their status to non-agricultural households upon approval of people's governments of provinces, autonomous regions, or municipalities directly under the Central Government. People's governments at or above the county level may consult with the relevant township (town) or village to decide upon the settlement of the original collective-owned property and the compensation and resettlement subsidies received, which shall be used for organizing production and as living subsidies for those who cannot be employed, but shall not be distributed privately.

Article 32 The compensation standard for requisition of land and the means of resettling people relocated due to construction of large or medium-sized water conservancy or hydroelectric projects shall be stipulated separately by the State Council.

Article 33 Storage sites for materials, transportation routes and other temporary installations of construction projects shall be situated within the limits of the requisitioned land as far as possible. When additional land for temporary use is truly necessary, the construction units may apply to the agencies authorizing the use of land for projects, specifying the amount of land and the time limit for such temporary use, and shall sign temporary land-use agreements with collective agricultural economic organizations upon such applications, being approved. Construction units shall pay compensation each year during the time limit based on the average annual output value of such land for the preceding three years. No permanent structures shall be erected on such land for temporary use. Construction units shall restore the production conditions of such land and return it promptly after the period for temporary use expires.

Requisition of land for the temporary uses of erecting lines above-ground, laying pipelines underground, building other underground projects, carrying out geological prospecting and so on shall be subject to the approval of local people's governments at the county level, and compensation shall be paid in accordance with the provisions of the preceding paragraph.

Construction units shall ask for approval from local people's governments at the county level if land surveys are needed for choosing construction sites and shall pay proper compensation for any losses caused.

Article 34 For the purpose of state construction, state-owned barren hills, wasteland and state-owned land presently used by other units shall be allocated after approval has been granted in accordance with due procedures and limits of approval authority over land requisition for state construction. The state-owned barren hills and wasteland shall be allocated without charge. Construction units which require state-owned land currently used by other units shall pay proper compensation to those units if losses are caused by the requisition and shall be responsible for moving such units if necessary.

Article 35 Requisition of land for construction by urban units under collective ownership shall be dealt with in accordance with the provisions in this chapter.

Article 36 When land owned by collectives is needed by an enterprise under ownership by the whole people or an enterprise under ownership by collectives in cities and a collective agricultural economic organization, for setting up a jointly operated enterprise under joint investment, application thereof must be submitted to the land administration department of a local people's government at or above the county level by presenting a project plan description or other documents of approval issued by the competent authority under the State Council or a local people's government at or above the county level in accordance with procedures specified for state capital construction. The people's government at or above the county level shall approve the application within the limits of authority for approval of land requisitions for state construction. The land approved for such use may be requisitioned in accordance with the provisions for land requisitions for state construction, or the right to the use of such land may be offered by a collective agricultural economic organization as a condition for agreement on joint operation.

Chapter V

Use of Land for Township (Town) and Village Construction

Article 37   Plans for township (town) and village construction shall be made in accordance with the principles of rational distribution and economical use of land and shall be put into practice upon approval of people's governments at the county level. Plans for township (town) or village construction within planned areas in cities shall be put into practice upon approval of municipal people's governments.

Rural residence construction, township (town) and village enterprise construction, township (town) and village public works and public welfare construction and so on shall be conducted in accordance with construction plans of the township (town) and village concerned.

Article 38   Rural residents shall use original house sites and idle lots in villages to build residences. If cultivated land needs to be used, the matter shall be subject to the examination and verification of people's governments at the township level and the approval of people's governments at the county level. Use of original house sites, idle lots and other land in villages shall be subject to approval of people's governments at the township level.

The land that rural residents use to build residences shall not exceed the standards set by provinces, autonomous regions, and municipalities directly under the Central Government.

Approval for other house sites shall not be granted to those who have sold or leased their houses.

Article 39   A township (town) or village enterprise that needs land for construction must apply to the land administration department of a people's government at the county level by presenting a project plan description or other documents of approval issued by a local government at or above the county level; the application shall be subject to the approval of a local people's government at or above the county level within the limits of approval authority granted by the relevant province, autonomous region, or municipality directly under the Central Government.

Land required for construction by township (town) and village enterprises must be strictly controlled. Provinces, autonomous regions, and municipalities directly under the Central Government may stipulate respective land use standards after taking into consideration the various trades and operational scope of township (town) and village enterprises.

Township (town) enterprises which use land owned by village peasant collectives for construction shall make proper compensation to the units which provide land for such use and shall properly arrange the production and livelihood of peasants concerned in accordance with respective provisions of their province, autonomous region, or municipality directly under the Central Government.

Article 40 Land required by townships (towns) and villages for public works and public welfare construction shall be subject to the examination and verification of people's governments at the township level and the approval of people's governments at the county level.

Article 41 When non-agricultural households in cities or towns need to use land owned by collectives to build residences, they must obtain the approval of people's governments at the county level. The size of land for such use shall not exceed the standards set by provinces, autonomous regions, and municipalities directly under the Central Government, and compensation and resettlement subsidies shall be paid with reference to the standards provided for land requisition for state construction.

Article 42 Local people's governments at various levels may set controlling indices for use of land in township (town) and village construction and submit such indices to people's governments at the next higher level for approval and implementation.

Chapter VI

Legal Liability

Article 43 Units under ownership by the whole people and urban units under collective ownership that unlawfully encroach upon land without approval or with fraudulently obtained approval shall be ordered to return such land and demolish, within a definite period of time, any structures or other installations newly erected thereon, or such structures or installations shall be confiscated and fines shall be imposed concurrently.

Disciplinary sanctions shall be adopted against those who bear the main responsibility in their respective units for such unlawful encroachment, either by the units to which they belong or by offices at a higher level.

If the amount of land occupied exceeds the approved amount, the excessive portion shall be handled as in the case of unlawful encroachment of land.

Article 44   Township (town) and village enterprises which unlawfully encroach upon land without approval or with fraudulently obtained approval shall be ordered to return such land and demolish, within a definite period of time, any structures or other installations newly erected thereon, or such structures or installations shall be confiscated and fines may be imposed concurrently.

If the amount of land occupied exceeds the approved amount, the excessive portion shall be handled as in the case of unlawful encroachment of land.

Article 45   Rural residents who unlawfully encroach upon land to build residences without approval or with fraudulently obtained approval shall be ordered to return such land and demolish, within a definite period of time, the houses newly built on such land, or such newly built houses shall be confiscated.

Article 46   Residents in non-agricultural households in cities or towns who unlawfully encroach upon land to build residences without approval or with fraudulently obtained approval shall be ordered to return such land and demolish, within a definite period of time, the houses newly built on such land, or such newly built houses shall be confiscated.

State functionaries who, by abusing authority, unlawfully encroach upon land to build residences without approval or with fraudulently obtained approval shall be ordered to return such land and demolish, within a definite period of time, the houses newly built on such land, or such houses shall be confiscated and disciplinary sanctions shall be imposed upon such functionaries either by the units to which they belong or by offices at a higher level.

Article 47   Anyone who unlawfully transfers land through sale, lease or other means shall have his unlawful proceeds confiscated and shall be ordered to demolish, within a definite period of time, any structures or other installations newly erected on such land, or such structures or installations shall be confiscated and the party concerned may be fined. Disciplinary sanctions shall be adopted against the person who bears the main responsibility either by the unit to which he belongs or by an office at a higher level.

Article 48   If units or individuals without authority to approve requisition or use of land unlawfully approve occupation of land, or if they unlawfully approve occupation of land by overstepping their authority of approval, the documents of such approval shall be void and disciplinary sanctions shall be adopted against those who bear the main responsibility in such units or other individuals who have unlawfully approved occupation of land, either by the units to which they belong or by offices at a higher level. Those who take bribes shall be investigated for criminal responsibility in accordance with relevant provisions of the Criminal Law. Land occupied through unlawful approval shall be handled as in the case of unlawful encroachment of land.

Article 49   Units at higher levels or other units that unlawfully seize land compensation and resettlement subsidies paid to the units whose land has been requisitioned shall be ordered to return such funds and make compensation, and they may be fined concurrently. Disciplinary sanctions shall be adopted against those who bear the main responsibility either by the units to which they belong or by offices at a higher level. Unlawful seizures by individuals shall be handled as in the case of graft.

Article 50   Whoever makes temporary use of land in accordance with Article 33 of this Law and fails to return the land after the term for such use expires and whoever refuses to surrender land after the right to the use of it has been withdrawn in accordance with Article 19 of this Law shall be ordered to return the land and shall be fined concurrently.

Article 51   Whoever in developing land causes soil desertification, soil salinization or soil erosion shall be ordered to make rectification within a definite period of time and may be fined concurrently.

Article 52   Administrative sanctions under this Law shall be decided by land administration departments of local people's governments at or above the county level; administrative sanctions under Article 45 of this Law may be decided by people's governments at the township level. If the party concerned refuses to accept the administrative sanctions, it may file suit in a people's court within 30 days after receiving notification of the decision regarding such sanctions. If the party neither files suit nor complies with the decision within that period, the sanction-imposing office shall apply to the people's court for compulsory enforcement.

Article 53   The land administration department of a local people's government at or above the county level shall order anyone who has infringed upon others' ownership of land and right to the use of land to stop the infringement and pay compensation for the losses caused. If a party refuses to accept the order, it may file suit in a people's court within 30 days after receiving notification of the order. The party infringed on may also file suit directly in the people's court.

Article 54   During the course of changing ownership of land or the right to its use or solving disputes concerning ownership of land or the right to its use, anyone who offers or takes bribes, extorts money, commits embezzlement or theft of state or collective property, or incites the masses to disorderly conduct or obstruction of state construction, if his acts constitute a crime, shall be investigated for criminal responsibility in accordance with relevant provisions of the Criminal Law.

Chapter VII

Supplementary Provisions

Article 55 Administrative procedures for the land used by Chinese-foreign equity joint ventures, Chinese-foreign contractual joint ventures and foreign-capital enterprises shall be stipulated separately by the State Council.

Article 56 The land administration department under the State Council shall formulate rules for implementation of this Law, which shall be put into force after being submitted to and approved by the State Council.

The standing committees of the people's congresses of provinces, autonomous regions, and municipalities directly under the Central Government shall formulate measures for implementation of this Law.

Article 57 This Law shall go into effect on January 1, 1987. On the same day, the Regulations on the Administration of Land Used by Villages and Towns for House Building, promulgated on February 13, 1982, and the Regulations on the Requisition of Land for State Construction, promulgated on May 14, 1982, by the State Council, shall be invalidated.

Regulations of the People's Republic of China on Administrative Penalties for Public Security

*(Adopted at the 17th Meeting of the Standing Committee of the Sixth
National People's Congress, promulgated by Order No. 43
of the President of the People's Republic of China on
September 5, 1986, and effective as of January 1, 1987)*

Contents

Chapter   I

General Provisions

Article 1   These Regulations are formulated for the purpose of strengthening the administration of public security, maintaining social order and public safety, protecting the lawful rights of citizens and guaranteeing the smooth progress of the socialist modernization.

Article 2   Whoever disturbs social order, endangers public safety, infringes upon a citizen's rights of the person or encroaches upon public or private property, if such an act constitutes a crime according to the Criminal Law of the People's Republic of China, shall be investigated for criminal responsibility; if such an act is not serious enough for criminal punishment but should be given administrative penalties for public security, penalties shall be given according to these Regulations.

Article 3   These Regulations shall apply to acts violating the administration of public security within the territory of the People's Republic of China, except when otherwise stipulated by law.

These Regulations shall also apply to acts violating the administration of public security aboard ships or airborne vehicles of the People's Republic of China.

Article 4   In dealing with those who violate the administration of public security, public security organs shall adhere to the principle of combining education with punishment.

Article 5   Acts caused by civil disputes which violate the administration of public security, such as brawling and damaging or destroying another person's property, if the adverse effects are minor, may be handled by public security organs through mediation.

Chapter   II

Types and Application of Penalties

Article 6   Penalties for acts violating the administration of public security are divided into three types as follows:

(1) warning;

(2) fine, ranging from a minimum of one yuan to a maximum of two hundred yuan. In cases where Articles 30, 31 and 32 in these Regulations stipulate otherwise, such provisions shall be observed; or

(3) detention, ranging from a minimum of one day to a maximum of fifteen days.

Article 7   Property obtained and contraband seized through acts violating the administration of public security shall be returned to the owner or confiscated according to relevant provisions. Instruments belonging to the offender used in acts violating the administration of public security may be confiscated according to relevant provisions. Detailed measures shall be stipulated separately by the Ministry of Public Security.

Article 8   When losses or injuries are caused by acts violating the administration of public security, the offender shall compensate for the loss or bear the medical expenses; if the offender is not an able person or is a person of limited ability, unable to compensate for the loss or bear the medical expenses, his guardian shall make the compensation or bear the medical expenses according to law.

Article 9   Acts violating the administration of public security committed by a person between fourteen and eighteen years of age shall be given relatively light penalties; acts violating the administration of public security committed by a person under fourteen shall be exempted from penalties, but a reprimand may be given and his guardian shall be instructed to subject the offender to strict discipline.

Article 10   A mentally disordered person who violates the administration of public security at a time when he is unable to account for or to control his own conduct shall not be penalized, but his guardian shall be instructed to keep a strict guard on him and subject him to medical treatment. An intermittently insane person who violates the administration of public security while in normal mental condition shall be punished.

Article 11   A deaf-mute or blind person who violates the administration of public security owing to his physiological defects shall not be penalized.

Article 12   An intoxicated person who violates the administration of public security shall be penalized.

An intoxicated person who may cause danger to himself or who threatens the safety of others owing to his drunken state shall be restrained until he returns to a sober state.

Article 13   If a person commits two or more acts violating the administration of public security, rulings shall be made separately but executed concurrently.

Article 14   When acts violating the administration of public security are committed jointly by two or more persons, they shall be penalized separately according to the seriousness of each person's case.

Whoever instigates, coerces or induces others to violate the administration of public security shall be penalized according to the seriousness of the act he instigates, coerces or induces.

Article 15   For acts violating the administration of public security committed by government offices, organizations, enterprises or institutions, penalties shall be given to the persons directly responsible; if the acts are committed at the order of persons in charge of units, such persons shall be penalized at the same time.

Article 16   Penalties for acts violating the administration of public security shall be mitigated or exempted under any of the following circumstances:

(1) the adverse effects are extremely minor;

(2) when those responsible voluntarily admit their mistakes and correct them in time;

(3) when those responsible were coerced or induced by others.

Article 17   Heavier penalties shall be given for acts violating the administration of public security under any of the following circumstances:

(1) when acts have caused relatively serious consequences;

(2) when those responsible coerce or induce others or instigate persons under the age of eighteen to violate the administration of public security;

(3) when those responsible take revenge on the informants or witnesses;

(4) when those responsible have been repeatedly punished and refuse to amend.

Article 18   Acts violating the administration of public security shall not be penalized if they have not been discovered by the public security organs within six months.

The period of time mentioned in the paragraph above shall be counted from the day the acts violating the administration of public security are committed or from the day the acts stopped if they are continuous or continuing acts.

Chapter   III

Acts Violating the Administration
of Public Security and Penalties

Article 19   Whoever commits one of the following acts disturbing public order, if it is not serious enough for criminal punishment, shall be detained for a maximum of fifteen days, fined a maximum of two hundred yuan or given a warning:

(1) disturbing the public order of government offices, organizations, enterprises or institutions, making it impossible for the work, productive or business operations, medical care, teaching or scientific research to go on smoothly but not having caused serious losses.

(2) disturbing the public order of stations, wharves, civil airports, markets, bazaars, parks, theatres, entertainment centres, sports grounds, exhibition halls or other public places;

(3) disturbing the public order of buses, trolleybuses, trains, ships and other public transit vehicles;

(4) gang-fighting, instigating quarrels, taking liberties with women or other indecent behaviour;

(5) spreading disruptive rumours and inciting disturbances;

(6) making false reports of dangerous situations and fomenting chaos;

(7) refusing or obstructing state personnel who are carrying out their functions according to law, without resorting to violence and threat.

Article 20   Whoever commits one of the following acts impairing public security shall be detained for a maximum of fifteen days, fined a maximum of two hundred yuan or given a warning:

(1) carrying or keeping firearms or ammunition, or committing other acts in violation of firearms control regulations, but not serious enough for criminal punishment;

(2) making, storing, transporting or using dangerous objects, in violation of regulations concerning the control of dangerous objects such as explosives, deadly poisons, combustibles and radioactive elements, but not having caused serious consequences;

(3) illegally manufacturing, selling or carrying daggers, knives with three edges, switchblades or other types of controlled knives;

(4) running hotels, restaurants, theatres, entertainment centres, sports grounds, exhibition halls or other public places for mass gatherings in violation of safety provisions and refusing to improve after notification by the public security organs;

(5) organizing mass gatherings, exhibitions, fairs, or other public activities in the fields of culture, entertainment, or sports without appropriate safety precautions and refusing to improve after notification by the public security organs;

(6) violating safety regulations concerning ferry boats and ferries and refusing to improve after notification by the public security organs;

(7) rushing to board a ferry despite dissuasion, causing the ferry boat to be overloaded or forcing the pilot to navigate under dangerous conditions in violation of safety regulations, when circumstances are not serious enough for criminal punishment;

(8) digging holes, placing obstacles, damaging, destroying or removing markers on railways, highways, navigation routes or dams which may affect safe traffic and transportation, when circumstances are not serious enough for criminal punishment.

Article 21 Whoever commits one of the following acts impairing public security shall be fined a maximum of two hundred yuan or given a warning:

(1) establishing or using a civilian shooting range not in accordance with safety regulations;

(2) installing or using electrified wire-nettings without approval, or not in accordance with safety regulations, without having caused grave consequences;

(3) when setting up a construction site in a place where vehicles and pedestrians pass, installing no covers, signs or fences for pits, wells, ridges and holes, or intentionally damaging, destroying, or removing covers, signs and fences.

Article 22 Whoever commits one of the following acts infringing upon a citizen's rights of the person, but not serious enough for criminal punishment, shall be detained for a maximum of fifteen days, fined a maximum of two hundred yuan or given a warning:

(1) striking another person, causing slight injury;

(2) illegally limiting others' personal freedom or illegally breaking into others' houses;

(3) openly insulting other persons or fabricating stories to slander other persons;

(4) maltreating family members, when the victims thereof ask for disposition;

(5) threatening others' safety or disturbing others' normal lives by writing letters of intimidation or by other methods;

(6) coercing or inveigling a person under the age of eighteen to give frightening or cruel performances, ruining the person's physical and mental health;

(7) hiding, destroying, discarding or illegally opening another person's postal articles or telegrams.

Article 23   Whoever commits one of the following acts encroaching upon public or private property, but not serious enough for criminal punishment, shall be detained for a maximum of fifteen days, given a warning or fined simply or concurrently a maximum of two hundred yuan:

(1) stealing, swindling or seizing a small amount of public or private property;

(2) starting a riot to seize state-owned, collective-owned and private property;

(3) extorting or demanding with menace public or private property;

(4) intentionally damaging public or private property.

Article 24   Whoever commits one of the following acts impairing the administration of social order shall be detained for a maximum of fifteen days, fined a maximum of two hundred yuan or given a warning:

(1) knowingly buying stolen goods;

(2) illegally dealing in train tickets, ship tickets, admission tickets for theatrical performances or sports games or other tickets or certificates, when circumstances are not serious enough for criminal punishment;

(3) taking opium or injecting morphine and other drugs in violation of the government's prohibition;

(4) disturbing public order or swindling money by way of feudal superstition, when circumstances are not serious enough for criminal punishment;

(5) driving others' motor vehicles without permission.

Article 25   Whoever commits one of the following acts, from item one to item three, impairing the administration of social order, shall be fined a maximum of two hundred yuan or given a warning; anyone committing acts covered in items four through seven shall be fined a maximum of fifty yuan or given a warning:

(1) hiding, not reporting, and not handing in to the state cultural relics discovered underground, in internal waters, in territorial waters or other places;

(2) accepting orders to engrave official seals in violation of administrative provisions, but not having caused serious consequences;

(3) deliberately defacing and damaging cultural relics, scenic spots or historic relics, under protection of the state, and damaging or destroying sculptures in public places, when circumstances are not serious enough for criminal punishment;

(4) deliberately damaging, destroying or removing without approval

street nameplates or traffic markers;

(5) deliberately damaging or destroying street lamps, postboxes, public telephone booths or other public facilities, when circumstances are not serious enough for criminal punishment;

(6) damaging lawns, flowers, shrubs and trees in violation of relevant regulations;

(7) operating acoustic equipment in cities and towns at too high a volume in violation of the relevant regulations, disturbing the neighbouring residents' work or rest, and refusing to stop such acts.

Article 26 Whoever commits one of the following acts, from item one to item four, violating fire control shall be detained for a maximum of ten days, fined a maximum of one hundred yuan or given a warning; anyone committing acts in items five to eight shall be fined a maximum of one hundred yuan or given a warning:

(1) smoking and using open fire in places where there are combustibles and explosive devices, in violation of the prohibitions;

(2) deliberately blocking the passage of fire engines or fire boats, or disturbing order at the scene of a fire, when circumstances are not serious enough for criminal punishment;

(3) refusing to follow the instructions of the commander at the scene of a fire and hindering fire fighting and rescue work;

(4) causing fire by negligence, but not having caused serious damage or injury;

(5) instigating or coercing others to work at risk of causing fire in violation of safety measures against fire, but not having resulted in serious consequences;

(6) occupying fire prevention belts, putting up shelters, building houses, digging trenches or building walls blocking the passage of fire engines in violation of the safety measures against fire;

· (7) burying, enclosing or damaging and destroying fire-fighting facilities such as fire hydrants, water pumps, water towers, cisterns, or using such instruments and equipment for other purposes, and refusing to correct such acts after being informed by the public security organs;

(8) being in serious potential danger of fire, but refusing to take corrective measures after notification by the public security organs.

Article 27 Whoever commits one of the following acts, from item one to item six, in violation of traffic regulations shall be detained for a maximum of fifteen days, fined a maximum of two hundred yuan or given a warning; anyone committing acts in items seven to eleven shall be fined a maximum of fifty yuan or given a warning:

(1) misappropriating, borrowing or lending vehicle licence plates or a driver's licence;

(2) driving a motor vehicle without a licence or in an intoxicated condition, or lending a vehicle to a person who drives without a driving

licence;

(3) blocking traffic by rallying or demonstrating in cities, violating relevant regulations in disregard of police directions;

(4) deliberately intercepting or boarding vehicles by force or impeding the normal operation of vehicles in disregard of dissuasion;

(5) deliberately passing through an area when passage is forbidden in express terms by public security organs at or above the county level, in disregard of dissuasion;

(6) violating traffic regulations so as to cause traffic accidents, when circumstances are not serious enough for criminal punishment;

(7) driving motor vehicles not examined or sanctioned by traffic administration organs;

(8) driving motor vehicles with parts not up to safety requirements;

(9) driving motor vehicles after drinking alcoholic liquor;

(10) instigating or coercing drivers to violate traffic regulations;

(11) blocking traffic by putting up shelters, building houses, setting up stalls, piling up goods or conducting other operations without approval of the appropriate department.

Article 28   Whoever commits one of the following acts in violation of traffic regulations shall be fined a maximum of five yuan or given a warning:

(1) driving a motor vehicle in violation of stipulations concerning loading and speed or in violation of directions indicated by traffic signs and signals;

(2) breaking of traffic regulations by non-motorized vehicle users or pedestrians;

(3) parking vehicles in places where parking is forbidden in express terms by traffic administration organs;

(4) illegally installing or using special sirens or signal light equipment in motor vehicles.

Article 29   Whoever commits one of the following acts, from item one to item three, in violation of residence control or administration of resident cards shall be fined a maximum of fifty yuan or given a warning; whoever commits an act in item four or item five shall be fined a maximum of one hundred yuan or fined:

(1) failing to register for residence or apply for a resident card according to regulations, in disregard of the notice of the public security organs;

(2) faking a residence registration or assuming another person's residence registration or resident card;

(3) deliberately altering a residence certificate;

(4) failing to register hotel guests according to regulations;

(5) failing to report and register lodgers according to regulations in letting a house or bed to another person.

Article 30   Prostitution, whoring, pandering or housing prostitution or whoring with a prostitute is strictly forbidden. Whoever breaks the above ban shall be detained for a maximum of fifteen days, given a warning, made to sign a statement of repentance or given re-education through labour according to regulations, and may be concurrently fined a maximum of five thousand yuan. Criminal responsibility shall be investigated if the actions constitute a crime.

Whoring with a girl under the age of fourteen shall be dealt with as rape according to the provisions of Article 139 of the Criminal Law.

Article 31 Planting opium poppy and other raw narcotics in violation of government decrees is strictly forbidden. Whoever violates the above decree shall be detained for a maximum of fifteen days and may be fined simply or concurrently a maximum of three thousand yuan, in addition to having his opium poppy and other narcotic plants rooted out; criminal responsibility shall be investigated if the actions constitute a crime.

Article 32 The following acts are strictly forbidden:

(1) gambling or facilitating gambling;

(2) making, duplicating, selling, lending or distributing pornographic books, pictures, videotapes or other pornographic objects.

Whoever commits one of the above acts shall be detained for a maximum of fifteen days, fined simply or concurrently a maximum of three thousand yuan or given re-education through labour according to regulations. Criminal responsibility shall be investigated if the actions constitute a crime.

Chapter IV

Ruling and Enforcement

Article 33 Penalties for acts violating the administration of public security shall be ruled on by the city or county public security bureaus or sub-bureaus or public security organs equivalent to the county level.

Warnings and fines of a maximum of fifty yuan can be ruled on by local police stations; in rural areas where there is no local police station, the people's government of a township or town can be entrusted with the ruling.

Article 34 Warnings and fines of a maximum of fifty yuan involving persons who violate the administration of public security, or fines exceeding fifty yuan with no objections from the offenders, may be imposed on the spot by the public security officials.

Other penalties for persons who violate the administration of public security shall follow the following procedures:

(1) Summons. A summoning warrant shall be issued by a public security organ when it is necessary to summon an offender. A person discovered

committing an offense may be summoned verbally. Whoever refuses to be summoned or avoids summons without good reasons shall be summoned compulsorily.

(2) Interrogation. Whoever violates the administration of public security should honestly answer to the interrogation by public security organs. A written record of the interrogation should be made. After checking the record and finding no mistake, the person interrogated shall sign or seal the written statement, and the interrogator shall also sign the same document.

(3) Obtaining evidence. Active support and cooperation shall be rendered by the departments and citizens concerned to the public security organs in the course of obtaining evidence. Honest statements shall be given by witnesses during the inquiry, and written statements shall be made, which shall be signed or sealed by the witnesses after checking and finding no error.

(4) Ruling. A ruling shall be made according to relevant provisions of these Regulations if the facts of violating the administration of public security are obvious and evidence is confirmed after interrogation and investigation.

A written ruling on the punishment should be made and declared to the offender immediately. Three copies of such a ruling shall be made and distributed to the offender himself, his work unit and the local police station of his permanent abode. The enforcement of the ruling shall be assisted by his work unit and the local police station.

(5) After being summoned to the public security organ, the offender should be interrogated and investigated promptly. The time of interrogation and investigation shall not exceed twenty-four hours in complicated cases subject to detainment according to these Regulations.

Article 35   Whoever shall be detained should receive the penalty in a specified detention house over a specified time. Compulsory detainment shall be used against one who resists enforcement of the punishment.

During the time of detention the detainee's food costs shall be paid by himself.

Article 36   A fine shall be paid by the offender on the spot to the public security officials or paid to the appointed public security organs within five days after receiving the notice of fine or written ruling. Failure to pay a fine in time without good cause shall be punished by an addition of one to five yuan per day. Whoever refuses to pay a fine shall be detained for a maximum of fifteen days and shall still be subject to the fine.

Receipt for payment of a fine shall be given to the offender by the public security organ or officials as soon as the fine is received.

The entire fine shall be delivered to the state treasury.

Article 37   A receipt shall be given to the offender after the penalty of confiscation is enforced by the ruling organs. All the property confiscated shall be delivered to the state treasury. Property stolen, robbed, swindled, or extorted, with the exception of contraband, shall be returned according to law to the original owners, to be located within six months.

Article 38   Whoever is required by a ruling to make reparations for loss or to bear medical cost shall deliver the cost to the organ making the ruling for transmission within five days after receiving the written ruling. Payments by instalments may be accepted if the amount is large. In case the offender denies responsibility, the organs making the ruling shall notify his work unit to deduct the reparations from his salary or retain his property to be converted into payment.

Article 39   If an offender or victim protests the ruling of the public security organ or the people's governments of townships or towns, he may petition the public security organs at the next higher level within five days after receiving the notice, and the public security organs at the next higher level shall make a new ruling within five days after receiving the petition. Whoever protests the ruling of the public security organ at the next higher level may file suit with the local people's court within five days after the notice.

Article 40   The original ruling shall continue to be executed during the time a petition or suit against the penalty for violating the administration of public security is taking place.

In case a guarantor can be found or bail has been paid according to regulations by the detainee or his family, the original ruling can be suspended temporarily during the time a petition or suit is taking place. When the ruling is revoked or starts to be enforced, the bail shall be returned according to regulations.

Article 41   In implementing these Regulations, the public security officials should strictly abide by laws and disciplines and impartially implement the provisions, allowing no favouritism or fraudulent practices. It is forbidden to beat or abuse, mistreat or insult the offender. An administrative disciplinary sanction shall be incurred against those who break the above mentioned provision. If such actions constitute a crime, criminal responsibility shall be investigated.

Article 42   The public security organs shall admit their mistakes to those who are punished by mistake and return fines and confiscated property; in case the legal rights and interests of those who are so punished have been infringed upon, the loss shall be compensated for.

Chapter V

Supplementary Provisions

Article 43   In numerical phrases containing the words "for a minimum of," "for a maximum of" or "within" used in these Regulations, the indicated numbers are understood to be included in the time limit.

Article 44   The enforcement measures for dealing with acts violating traffic regulations shall be formulated separately by the State Council.

Article 45   These Regulations shall go into effect on January 1, 1987. On the same day, the Regulations of the People's Republic of China Concerning Administrative Penalties for Public Security, promulgated on October 22, 1957, shall be invalidated.

Regulations of the People's Republic of China Concerning Diplomatic Privileges and Immunities

(Adopted at the 17th Meeting of the Standing Committee of the Sixth
National People's Congress, promulgated by Order No. 44
of the President of the People's Republic of China
and effective as of September 5, 1986)

Article 1   The present Regulations are formulated for the purpose of defining the diplomatic privileges and immunities of the diplomatic missions in China and their members and facilitating the efficient performance of the functions of the diplomatic missions in China as representing States.

Article 2   The members of the diplomatic staff of a mission shall in principle be of the nationality of the sending State. They may be appointed from among persons of Chinese or third-state nationality only with the consent of the competent Chinese authorities, which may be withdrawn at any time by the said authorities.

Article 3   The mission and its head shall have the right to use the flag and emblem of the sending State on the premises of the mission and on the means of transport of the head of the mission.

Article 4   The premises of the mission shall be inviolable. Chinese government functionaries may enter them only with the consent of the head of the mission or another member of the mission authorized by him. The Chinese authorities concerned shall take appropriate measures to protect the premises of the mission against any intrusion or damage.

The premises of the mission, their furnishings and other property thereon and the means of transport of the mission shall be immune from search, requisition, attachment or execution.

Article 5   The premises of the mission shall be exempt from dues and taxes, other than such as represent payment for specific services rendered.

The fees and charges levied by the mission in the course of its official duties shall be exempt from all dues and taxes.

Article 6   The archives and documents of the mission shall be inviolable.

Article 7   The members of the mission shall enjoy freedom of movement and travel within Chinese territory except for areas the entry into which is prohibited or restricted by the regulations of the Chinese Government.

Article 8   The mission may for official purposes communicate freely with the Government and the other missions and consulates of the sending State. In so doing, it may employ all appropriate means, including diplomatic couriers, diplomatic bag, and messages in code or cipher.

Article 9   The mission may install and use a wireless transmitter-receiver for the purpose of communication only with the consent of the Chinese Government. The import of the above-mentioned equipment shall be subject to the relevant procedure as specified by the Chinese Government.

Article 10   The official correspondence of the mission shall be inviolable.

The diplomatic bag shall not be opened or detained.

The diplomatic bag may contain only diplomatic papers or articles intended for official use and must be sealed and bear visible external marks of its contents.

Article 11   The diplomatic courier shall be provided with a courier certificate issued by the competent authorities of the sending State. He shall enjoy personal inviolability and shall not be liable to arrest or detention.

Diplomatic couriers *ad hoc* shall be provided with certificates of courier *ad hoc* issued by the competent authorities of the sending State, and shall enjoy the same immunities as the diplomatic courier while charged with the carrying of the diplomatic bag.

A diplomatic bag may be entrusted to the captain of a commercial aircraft. He shall be provided with an official document issued by the consigner state indicating the number of packages constituting the bag, but he shall not be regarded as a diplomatic courier. The mission shall send its members to receive the diplomatic bag from the captain of the aircraft or deliver it to him.

Article 12   The person of a diplomatic agent shall be inviolable. He shall not be liable to arrest or detention. The Chinese authorities concerned shall take appropriate measures to prevent any attack on his personal freedom and dignity.

Article 13   The residence of a diplomatic agent shall enjoy inviolability and protection.

His papers, correspondence and, except as provided in Article 14, his property, shall be inviolable.

Article 14   A diplomatic agent shall enjoy immunity from criminal jurisdiction.

He shall also enjoy immunity from civil and administrative jurisdiction, except in the case of:

(1) an action relating to succession in which he is involved as a private person;

(2) an action relating to any professional or commercial activity con-

ducted by him in China outside his official functions in violation of paragraph 3 of Article 25.

No measures of execution shall be taken in respect of a diplomatic agent except in cases coming under the preceding paragraphs of this Article, where the measures of execution do not constitute any violations of his person and residence.

A diplomatic agent is not obliged to give evidence as a witness.

Article 15   The immunity from jurisdiction of diplomatic agents and of persons enjoying immunity under Article 20 may be waived through explicit expression by the Government of the sending State.

The initiation of proceedings by a diplomatic agent or by a person enjoying immunity from jurisdiction under Article 20 shall preclude him from invoking immunity from jurisdiction in respect of any counter-claim directly connected with the claim.

Waiver of immunity from civil or administrative jurisdiction shall not imply waiver of immunity in respect of the execution of the judgment, for which a separate and explicit waiver shall be necessary.

Article 16   A diplomatic agent shall be exempt from all dues and taxes, except:

(1) dues and taxes of a kind which are normally incorporated in the price of goods or services;

(2) estate, succession or inheritance duties, except for the movable property in China of a deceased diplomatic agent;

(3) dues and taxes on private income having its source in China;

(4) charges levied for specific services rendered.

Article 17   Diplomatic agents shall be exempt from all personal and public services as well as military obligations.

Article 18   Imported articles for the official use of the mission and those for the personal use of a diplomatic agent shall, in accordance with the relevant regulations of the Chinese Government, be exempt from customs duties and all other related dues and taxes.

The personal baggage of a diplomatic agent shall be exempt from inspection, unless the competent Chinese authorities have serious grounds for presuming that it contains articles not covered by the exemptions specified in the previous paragraph, or articles the import or export of which is prohibited by Chinese laws and government regulations or controlled by the quarantine law and regulations. Such inspection shall be conducted in the presence of the diplomatic agent or of his authorized representative.

Article 19   The diplomatic missions and their members may bring and import firearms and bullets into China for their personal use, subject to the approval of the Chinese government and to its relevant regulations.

Article 20   The spouse and under-age children of a diplomatic agent forming part of his household shall, if they are not nationals of China, enjoy the privileges and immunities specified in Articles 12 to 18.

The members of the administrative and technical staff of the mission, together with their spouses and under-age children forming part of their respective households, shall, if they are not nationals of and permanently resident in China, enjoy the privileges and immunities specified in Articles 12 to 17. However, the immunity from civil and administrative jurisdiction shall be confined to acts performed in the course of official duties. The members of the administrative and technical staff shall also enjoy the privilege of exemption from dues and taxes specified in paragraph one of Article 18 in respect of articles intended for their establishment which are imported within six months of the time of installation.

The members of the service staff of the mission who are not nationals of and permanently resident in China shall enjoy immunity in respect of acts performed in the course of official duties and exemption from income tax on the emoluments they receive by reason of their employment. They shall enjoy the privilege of exemption from dues and taxes as specified in paragraph one of Article 18 of the present Regulations in respect of articles intended for their establishment which are imported within six months of the time of installation.

The private attendants of members of the mission shall, if they are not nationals of and permanently resident in China, be exempt from income tax on the emoluments they receive by reason of their employment.

Article 21 Diplomatic agents who are nationals of China or foreigners having obtained permanent residence in China shall enjoy immunity from jurisdiction and inviolability only in respect of acts performed in the course of official duties.

Article 22 The following persons shall enjoy immunity and inviolability necessary for their transit through or sojourn in China:

(1) a diplomatic agent stationed in a third State who passes through China together with his spouse and underage children forming part of his household;

(2) a visiting foreign official who has obtained a diplomatic visa from China or who holds a diplomatic passport of a State with which China has an agreement on the mutual exemption of visas;

(3) other visiting foreigners to whom the Chinese Government has granted the privileges and immunities specified in the present Article.

The provisions of Articles 10 and 11 shall apply, *mutatis mutandis*, to a diplomatic courier of a third state passing through China and his accompanying diplomatic bag.

Article 23 Visiting heads of State or government, foreign ministers and other officials of comparable status from foreign States shall enjoy the privileges and immunities specified in the present Regulations.

Article 24 Representatives of foreign States coming to China to attend international conferences sponsored by the United Nations or its specialized agencies, visiting officials and experts of the United Nations and its specialized agencies, and offices of the United Nations and its specialized agencies in China and their personnel shall enjoy such treatment as specified in the relevant international conventions to which China has acceded and agreements which China has concluded with the international organizations concerned.

Article 25   Persons enjoying diplomatic privileges and immunities under the present Regulations shall:

(1) respect Chinese laws and regulations;

(2) not interfere in the internal affairs of China;

(3) not practise for personal profit any professional or commercial activity on Chinese territory;

(4) not use the premises of the mission and the residence of the members of the staff of the mission for purposes incompatible with the functions of the mission.

Article 26   In case the diplomatic privileges and immunities accorded by a foreign State to the Chinese mission and its members in that State and to visiting Chinese personnel concerned are fewer than those China would give under the present Regulations to the mission of that State and its members in China and its visiting personnel concerned, the Chinese Government may accord them such diplomatic privileges and immunities as appropriate on a reciprocal basis.

Article 27   Where there are other provisions in international treaties to which China is a contracting or acceding party, the provisions of those treaties shall prevail, with the exception of those provisions on which China has expressed reservations.

Where there are other provisions in agreements on diplomatic privileges and immunities between China and other countries, the provisions of those agreements shall prevail.

Article 28   For the purpose of the present Regulations, the following expressions shall have the meanings hereunder assigned to them:

(1) the "head of the mission" is the ambassador, minister, chargé d'affaires or other person of equivalent rank charged by the sending State with the duty of acting in that capacity;

(2) the "members of the mission" are the head of the mission and the members of the staff of the mission;

(3) the "members of the staff of the mission" are the members of the diplomatic staff, of the administrative and technical staff and of the service staff of the mission;

(4) the "members of the diplomatic staff of the mission" are the members of the staff of the mission having diplomatic rank;

(5) a "diplomatic agent" is the head of the mission or a member of the

diplomatic staff of the mission;

(6) the "members of the administrative and technical staff of the mission" are the members of the staff of the mission engaged in the administrative and technical work of the mission;

(7) the "members of the service staff of the mission" are the members of the staff of the mission in the domestic service of the mission;

(8) a "private attendant" is a person in the private employment of a member of the mission;

(9) the "premises of the mission" are the buildings and the land ancillary thereto used for the purposes of the mission and the residence of the head of the mission.

Article 29   The present Regulations shall enter into force on the date of their promulgation.

Law of the People's Republic of China on Enterprise Bankruptcy

(For Trial Implementation)

*(Adopted at the 18th Meeting of the Standing Committee of the Sixth
National People's Congress and promulgated by Order No. 45 of the
President of the People's Republic of China on December 2,
1986, for trial implementation three full months after the
Law on Industrial Enterprises with Ownership
by the Whole People comes into effect)*

Contents

Chapter I

General Provisions

Article 1   This Law is formulated in order to suit the development of a planned socialist commodity economy and the needs of the reform of the economic structure, to promote the autonomous operation of enterprises owned by the whole people, to strengthen the economic responsibility system and democratic management, to improve the state of operations, to increase economic efficiency and to protect the lawful rights and interests of creditors and debtors.

Article 2   This Law applies to enterprises owned by the whole people.

Article 3   Enterprises which, owing to poor operations and management that result in serious losses, are unable to repay debts that are due shall be declared bankrupt in accordance with the provisions of this Law.

Enterprises for which creditors file for bankruptcy shall not be declared bankrupt under any of the following circumstances:

(1) public utility enterprises and enterprises that have an important relationship to the national economy and the people's livelihood, for which the relevant government departments grant subsidies or adopt other measures to assist the repayment of debts;

(2) enterprises that have obtained guarantees for the repayment of debts within six months from the date of the application for bankruptcy.

With respect to enterprises for which creditors file for bankruptcy, bankruptcy proceedings shall be suspended if the enterprise's superior departments in charge have applied for reorganization and if the enterprise and its creditors have reached a settlement agreement through consultation.

Article 4   The state through various means shall arrange for the appropriate reemployment of the staff and workers of bankrupt enterprises and shall guarantee their basic living needs prior to reemployment; specific measures shall be separately stipulated by the State Council.

Article 5   Bankruptcy cases shall be under the jurisdiction of the people's courts in the location of the debtor.

Article 6   Where this Law has not stipulated the procedures for bankruptcy cases, the legal provisions for civil procedures shall apply.

Chapter II

The Submission and Acceptance of Bankruptcy Applications

Article 7   Where the debtor is unable to repay debts that are due, the creditors may file to declare the debtor bankrupt.

When the creditor is submitting the bankruptcy application, it should provide relevant evidence relating to the amount of the claim, whether or not it is secured with property, and to the inability of the debtor to repay debts that are due.

Article 8   The debtor, upon the agreement of the superior departments in charge, may apply for the declaration of bankruptcy.

When the debtor is submitting the bankruptcy application, it shall explain the circumstances of the enterprise's losses and deliver relevant accounting statements, a detailed list of debts and a detailed list of claims.

Article 9   After the people's court has accepted a bankruptcy case, it shall notify the debtor within ten days and make a public announcement. Within ten days after receiving the detailed list of debts delivered by the debtor, the people's court shall notify known creditors. The public announcement and notice shall stipulate the date of the first convening of the creditors' meeting.

Creditors who have been notified shall, within one month after receiving the notice, and creditors who have not been notified shall, within three months after the date of the public announcement, report their claims to the people's court and explain the amount of the claims, as well as whether or not they are secured with property, and also deliver relevant materials of proof. Creditors who do not report their claims during these periods shall be deemed to have automatically abandoned their claims.

The people's court shall register separately claims that are secured with property and claims that are not secured with property.

Article 10   Where creditors have made a bankruptcy application, the debtor shall, within 15 days after receiving the notice of the people's court, deliver to the people's court the relevant materials described in the second paragraph of Article 8 of this Law.

If the debtor is a guarantor for another unit, it shall, within five days after receiving the notice of the people's court, in turn notify the relevant parties.

Article 11   After the people's court has accepted a bankruptcy case, other civil enforcement proceedings against the property of the debtor must be suspended.

Article 12   After the people's court has accepted a bankruptcy case, payment by the debtor to only some of the creditors is null and void, with the exception of payments required for the normal production and operations of the debtor.

Chapter   III

Creditors' Meetings

Article 13   All creditors are members of the creditors' meeting. Members of the creditors' meeting enjoy the right to vote, with the exception of creditors with claims secured with property who have not abandoned their priority right to be repaid. Guarantors of the debtor, after having repaid debts on behalf of the debtor, may be deemed creditors and enjoy the right to vote.

The chairman of the creditors meeting is designated by the people's court from among the creditors with the right to vote.

The legal representative of the debtor must attend the creditors' meetings and answer the creditors inquiries.

Article 14   The first creditors' meeting is called by the people's court and shall be convened within 15 days after the expiration of the period for reporting claims. Subsequent creditors' meetings are convened at such times as the people's court or the chairman of the meeting deems necessary, and may also be convened on the request of the liquidation committee or of creditors whose claims comprise more than one fourth of the total amount of claims not secured with property.

Article 15   The functions and powers of the creditors' meeting are:

(1) to examine materials of proof relating to the claims, and to confirm the amount of such claims and whether or not the claims are secured with property;

(2) to discuss and adopt a draft settlement agreement; and

(3) to discuss and adopt a plan for the disposition and distribution of bankruptcy property.

Article 16   Resolutions of the creditors meeting must be adopted by a majority of creditors with the right to vote present at the meeting; the amount of their claims must comprise more than half the total amount of claims not secured with property; however, with respect to a resolution adopting a draft settlement agreement, such amount must comprise more than two thirds the total amount of claims not secured with property.

Resolutions of the creditors' meeting shall have binding force on all the creditors.

Creditors who consider the resolutions of the creditors' meeting to be contrary to the provisions of law may, within seven days after the creditors' meeting has made such resolutions, apply to the people's court for judgment.

Chapter   IV

Settlement and Reorganization

Article 17   With respect to an enterprise for which the creditors apply for bankruptcy, the superior departments in charge of the enterprise that is the subject of the bankruptcy application may, within three months after the people's court has accepted the case, apply to carry out reorganization of the enterprise; the period of reorganization shall not exceed two years.

Article 18   After an application for reorganization is submitted, the enterprise shall propose a draft settlement agreement to the creditors' meeting.

The settlement agreement shall stipulate the period in which the enterprise shall repay the debts.

Article 19   After the enterprise and creditors' meeting have reached a settlement agreement which has been recognized by the people's court, the people's court shall make a public announcement and suspend the bankruptcy proceedings. The settlement agreement shall have legal effect from the date of the public announcement.

Article 20   The reorganization of the enterprise shall be supervised by its superior departments in charge.

The reorganization plan of the enterprise shall be discussed by a congress of the staff and workers of the enterprise. The circumstances of the reorganization of the enterprise shall be reported to the congress of the staff and workers of the enterprise and its opinion shall be heeded.

The circumstances of the reorganization of the enterprise shall be periodically reported to the creditors' meeting.

Article 21   During the period of reorganization, an enterprise in any of the following circumstances shall, upon judgment of the people's court, terminate reorganization and declare its bankruptcy:

(1) not implementing the settlement agreement;

(2) continued worsening of its financial condition, for which reason the creditors' meeting has applied for the termination of reorganization; and

(3) committing any of the acts listed in Article 35 of this Law and seriously harming the interests of creditors.

Article 22   With respect to an enterprise that has undergone reorganization and is able to repay debts in accordance with the settlement agreement, the people's court shall terminate the bankruptcy proceedings for such an enterprise, and also make a public announcement thereof.

With respect to an enterprise that, on the expiration of the period of reorganization, is unable to repay debts in accordance with the settlement agreement, the people's court shall declare the enterprise bankrupt, and shall re-register the claims in accordance with the provisions of Article 9 of this Law.

Chapter V

Bankruptcy Declarations and Bankruptcy Liquidations

Article 23   In any of the following circumstances, after the judgment of the people's court, an enterprise shall be declared bankrupt:

(1) if, in accordance with the provisions of Article 3 of this Law, it should be declared bankrupt;

(2) if reorganization has been terminated in accordance with the provisions of Article 21 of this Law; and

(3) if, upon the expiration of the period of reorganization, it is unable to repay debts in accordance with the settlement agreement.

Article 24   The people's court shall, within 15 days after the date the enterprise is declared bankrupt, establish a liquidation team to take over the bankrupt enterprise. The liquidation team shall be responsible for the keeping, putting into order, appraisal, disposition and distribution of the bankruptcy property. The liquidation team may carry out necessary civil actions in accordance with the law.

The members of the liquidation team shall be designated by the people's court from among the superior departments in charge, government finance departments, and other relevant departments and professional personnel. The liquidation team may hire necessary work personnel.

The liquidation team is responsible to, and shall report on its work to, the people's court.

Article 25   No unit or individual may illegally dispose of the property, account books, documents, materials, seals, etc., of a bankrupt enterprise.

The debtors of a bankrupt enterprise and persons holding the property of a bankrupt enterprise can repay debts or deliver property only to the liquidation team.

Article 26   The liquidation team may decide to terminate or to continue to perform the contracts that have not yet been performed by the bankrupt enterprise.

If the liquidation team decides to terminate a contract, and the other party to the contract suffers harm as the result of the termination of the contract, the amount of compensation for the harm constitutes a bankruptcy claim.

Article 27   Before the legal representative of the bankrupt enterprise handles the procedures for transfer to the liquidation team, he shall be responsible for the keeping of the property, account books, documents, materials, seals, etc., of such enterprise.

Before the conclusion of the bankruptcy proceedings, the legal representative of the bankrupt enterprise shall carry out work according to the requirements of the people's court or the liquidation team, and may not leave his position without authorization.

Article 28   Bankruptcy property comprises the following property:

(1) all property that the bankrupt enterprise operated and managed at the time bankruptcy was declared;

(2) property obtained by the bankrupt enterprise during the period from the declaration of bankruptcy until the conclusion of the bankruptcy proceedings; and

(3) other property rights that the bankrupt enterprise should exercise.

Property that already constitutes security collateral is not bankruptcy property; the portion of the value of the security collateral exceeding the amount of the debt that it secures is bankruptcy property.

Article 29   Property in the bankrupt enterprise that belongs to other persons shall be retrieved by the persons with the right to such property through the means of the liquidation team.

Article 30   Claims not secured with property and claims secured with property for which the priority right to receive repayment has been abandoned, which were established before bankruptcy was declared, are bankruptcy claims.

The expenses of creditors for participating in the bankruptcy proceedings may not constitute bankruptcy claims.

Article 31 Claims that are not due when bankruptcy is declared shall be deemed to be claims that have already become due; however, the interest that is not yet due shall be deducted.

Article 32 With respect to claims secured with property that are established before bankruptcy is declared, the creditors enjoy the right to receive repayment with priority with respect to such security.

With respect to claims that are secured with property whose amount exceeds the value of the security collateral, the part that is not repaid constitutes a bankruptcy claim, and will be repaid in accordance with the bankruptcy proceedings.

Article 33 Creditors who owe debts to the bankrupt enterprise may offset them before the bankruptcy liquidation.

Article 34 Priority shall be given to saving the following bankruptcy expenses from the bankruptcy property:

(1) the expenses needed for the management, sale and distribution of the bankruptcy property, including the expenses of hiring work personnel;

(2) the litigation expenses of the bankruptcy case; and

(3) other expenses paid in the course of bankruptcy proceedings for the common interest of the creditors.

With respect to enterprises whose bankruptcy property is insufficient to cover bankruptcy expenses, the people's court should declare termination of bankruptcy proceedings.

Article 35 During the period from six months before the people's court accepts the bankruptcy case until the date that bankruptcy is declared, the following actions of a bankrupt enterprise are null and void:

(1) concealment, secret distributions or transfers of property without compensation;

(2) sale of property at abnormally depressed prices;

(3) securing with property claims that originally were not secured with property;

(4) early repayment of claims that are not yet due; and

(5) abandonment of the enterprise's own claims.

With respect to bankrupt enterprises which have committed acts listed in the previous paragraphs, the liquidation team has the right to apply to the people's court to recover the property, which shall be added to the bankruptcy property.

Article 36 Complete sets of equipment in the bankruptcy property shall be sold as a whole, and that which cannot be sold as a whole may be sold in parts.

Article 37 The distribution plan for the bankruptcy property shall be proposed by the liquidation team, adopted by the creditors' meeting and submitted to the people's court for judgment before implementation.

After the prior deduction of bankruptcy expenses from the bankruptcy property, repayment shall be made in the following order:

(1) wages of staff and workers and labour insurance expenses that are owed by the bankrupt enterprise;

(2) taxes that are owed by the bankrupt enterprise; and

(3) bankruptcy claims.

Where the bankruptcy property is insufficient to repay all the repayment needs within a single order of priority, it shall be distributed on a pro-rata basis.

Article 38 Upon the completion of the distribution of the bankruptcy property, the liquidation team shall apply to the people's court for the conclusion of the bankruptcy proceedings. After the termination of bankruptcy proceedings, claims that have not been repaid shall no longer be repaid.

Article 39 After the conclusion of the bankruptcy proceedings, the liquidation team shall handle the procedures for the cancellation of registration at the original registration authorities of the bankrupt enterprise.

Article 40 With respect to bankrupt enterprises that are discovered within one year after the date of the conclusion of the bankruptcy proceedings to have committed any of the acts listed in Article 35 of this Law, the people's court shall recover the property and order repayment in accordance with Article 37 of this Law.

Article 41 With respect to bankrupt enterprises that have committed any of the acts listed in Article 35 of this Law, the legal representative and the directly responsible personnel of the bankrupt enterprise shall be subject to administrative sanctions; where the acts of the legal representative and the directly responsible personnel of the bankrupt enterprise constitute crimes, criminal responsibility shall be investigated in accordance with the law.

Article 42 After an enterprise is declared bankrupt, the government supervisory departments and audit departments are responsible for pinpointing the responsibility for the bankruptcy of the enterprise.

Where the legal representative of the bankrupt enterprise bears the major responsibility for the bankruptcy of the enterprise, administrative sanctions shall be applied.

Where the superior departments in charge of the bankrupt enterprise bear the major responsibility for the bankruptcy of the enterprise, administrative sanctions shall be applied to the leaders of such superior departments in charge.

With respect to the legal representative of the bankrupt enterprise and the leaders of superior departments in charge of the bankrupt enterprise who, owing to neglect of duty, caused the bankruptcy of the enterprise, resulting in the major loss of state property, criminal responsibility shall be investigated in accordance with Article 187 of the Criminal Law of the People's Republic of China.

Chapter VI

Supplementary Provisions

Article 43   This Law is to be implemented on a trial basis three full months after the Law on Industrial Enterprises with Ownership by the Whole People comes into effect, and the specific plans and steps for the trial implementation shall be stipulated by the State Council.

Frontier Health and Quarantine Law of the People's Republic of China

(Adopted at the 18th Meeting of the Standing Committee of the Sixth National People's Congress, promulgated by Order No. 46 of the President of the People's Republic of China on December 2, 1986, and effective as of May 1, 1987)

Contents

Chapter I

General Provisions

Article 1 This Law is formulated in order to prevent infectious diseases from spreading into or out of the country, to carry out frontier health and quarantine inspection and to protect human health.

Article 2 Frontier health and quarantine offices shall be set up at international seaports, airports and ports of entry at land frontiers and boundary rivers (hereinafter referred to as "frontier ports") of the People's Republic of China. These offices shall carry out the quarantining and monitoring of infectious diseases, and health inspection in accordance with the provisions of this Law.

Health administration departments under the State Council shall be in charge of frontier health and quarantine work throughout the country.

Article 3 Infectious diseases specified in this Law shall include quarantinable infectious diseases and infectious diseases to be monitered.

Quarantinable infectious diseases shall include plague, cholera, yellow fever and other infectious diseases determined and announced by the State

Council.

Infectious diseases to be monitored shall be determined and announced by health administration departments under the State Council.

Article 4   Persons, conveyances and transport equipment, as well as articles such as baggage, goods and postal parcels that may transmit quarantinable infectious diseases, shall undergo quarantine inspection upon entering or exiting the country. No entry or exit shall be allowed without the permission of a frontier health and quarantine office. Specific measures for implementation of this Law shall be stipulated in detailed regulations.

Article 5   On discovering a quarantinable infectious disease or a disease suspected to be quarantinable, a frontier health and quarantine office shall, in addition to taking necessary measures, immediately notify the local health administration department; at the same time, it shall make a report to the health administration department under the State Council by the most expeditious means possible, within 24 hours at the latest. Post and telecommunications departments shall give priority to transmissions of reports of epidemic diseases.

Messages exchanged between the People's Republic of China and foreign countries on the epidemic situation of infectious diseases shall be handled by the health administration department under the State Council in conjunction with other departments concerned.

Article 6   When a quarantinable infectious disease is prevalent abroad or within China, the State Council may order relevant sections of the border to be blockaded or adopt other emergency measures.

Chapter   II

Quarantine Inspection

Article 7   Persons and conveyances on entering the country shall be subject to quarantine inspection at designated places at the first frontier port of their arrival. Except for harbour pilots, no person shall be allowed to embark on or disembark from any means of transport and no articles such as baggage, goods or postal parcels shall be loaded or unloaded without the health and quarantine inspector's permission. Specific measures for the implementation of this Law shall be stipulated in detailed regulations.

Article 8   Persons and conveyances exiting the country shall be subject to quarantine inspection at the last frontier port of departure.

Article 9   When foreign ships or airborne vehicles anchor or land at places other than frontier ports in China, the persons in charge of the ships or airborne vehicles must report immediately to the nearest frontier health and quarantine office or to the local health administration department.

Except in cases of emergency, no person shall be allowed to embark on or disembark from the ship or airborne vehicle, and no articles such as baggage, goods and postal parcels shall be loaded or unloaded without the permission of a frontier health and quarantine office or the local health administration department.

Article 10 When a quarantinable infectious disease, a disease suspected to be quarantinable or a death due to an unidentified cause other than accidental harm is discovered at a frontier port, the relevant department at the frontier port and the person in charge of the conveyance must report immediately to the frontier health and quarantine office and apply for provisional quarantine inspection.

Article 11 According to the results of an inspection made by quarantine doctors, the frontier health and quarantine office shall sign and issue a quarantine certificate for entry or exit to a conveyance either uncontaminated by any quarantinable infectious disease or already given decontamination treatment.

Article 12 A person having a quarantinable infectious disease shall be placed in isolation by the frontier health and quarantine office for a period determined by the results of the medical examination, while a person suspected of having a quarantinable infectious disease shall be kept for inspection for a period determined by the incubation period of such disease.

The corpse of anyone who died from a quarantinable infectious disease must be cremated at a nearby place.

Article 13 Any conveyance subject to entry quarantine inspection shall be disinfected, deratted, treated with insecticides or given other sanitation measures when found to be in any of the following conditions:

(1) having come from an area where a quarantinable infectious disease is epidemic;

(2) being contaminated by a quarantinable infectious disease; or

(3) revealing the presence of rodents which affect human health or insects which are carriers of disease.

Apart from exceptional cases, when the person in charge of the foreign conveyance refuses to allow sanitation measures to be taken, the conveyance shall be allowed to leave the frontier of the People's Republic of China without delay under the supervision of the frontier health and quarantine office.

Article 14 A frontier health and quarantine office shall conduct sanitation inspections and disinfect, derat, treat with insecticides or apply other sanitation measures to articles such as baggage, goods and postal parcels that come from an epidemic area and are contaminated by a quarantinable infectious disease or may act as a vehicle of a quarantinable infectious disease.

A consignor or an agent for the transportation of a corpse or human remains into or out of the country must declare the matter to a frontier health and quarantine office; transport thereof, in either direction across the border, shall not be allowed until sanitary inspection proves satisfactory and an entry or exit permit is given.

Chapter III

Monitoring of Infectious Diseases

Article 15 Frontier health and quarantine offices shall monitor persons on entry or exit for quarantinable infectious diseases and shall take necessary preventive and control measures.

Article 16 Frontier health and quarantine offices shall be authorized to require persons on entry or exit to complete a health declaration form and produce certificates of vaccination against certain infectious diseases, a health certificate or other relevant documents.

Article 17 For persons who suffer from infectious diseases to be monitored, who come from areas in foreign countries where infectious diseases to be monitored are epidemic or who have close contact with patients suffering from infectious diseases to be monitored, the frontier health and quarantine offices shall, according to each case, issue them medical convenience cards, keep them for inspection or take other preventive or control measures, while promptly notifying the local health administration department about such cases. Medical services at all places shall give priority in consultation and treatment to persons possessing medical convenience cards.

Chapter IV

Health Supervision

Article 18 Frontier health and quarantine offices shall, in accordance with state health standards, exercise health supervision over the sanitary conditions at frontier ports and the sanitary conditions of conveyances on entry or exit at frontier ports. They shall:

(1) supervise and direct concerned personnel on the prevention and elimination of rodents and insects that carry diseases;

(2) inspect and test food and drinking water and facilities for their storage, supply and delivery;

(3) supervise the health of employees engaged in the supply of food and drinking water and check their health certificates; and

(4) supervise and inspect the disposal of garbage, waste matter, sewage, excrement and ballast water.

Article 19 Frontier health and quarantine offices shall have frontier port health supervisors, who shall carry out the tasks assigned by the frontier health and quarantine offices.

In performing their duties, frontier port health supervisors shall be authorized to conduct health supervision and give technical guidance regarding frontier ports and conveyances on entry or exit; to give advice for improvement wherever sanitary conditions are unsatisfactory and factors exist that may spread infectious diseases; and to coordinate departments concerned to take necessary measures and apply sanitary treatment.

Chapter V

Legal Liability

Article 20 A frontier health and quarantine office may warn or fine, according to the circumstances, any unit or individual that has violated the provisions of this Law by committing any of the following acts:

(1) evading quarantine inspection or withholding the truth in reports to the frontier health and quarantine office;

(2) embarking on or disembarking from conveyances upon entry, or loading or unloading articles such as baggage, goods or postal parcels, without the permission of a frontier health and quarantine office and refusing to listen to the office's advice against such acts.

All fines thus collected shall be turned over to the state treasury.

Article 21 If a concerned party refuses to obey a decision on a fine made by a frontier health and quarantine office, he may, within 15 days after receiving notice of the fine, file a lawsuit in a local people's court. The frontier health and quarantine office may apply to the people's court for mandatory enforcement of a decision if the concerned party neither files a lawsuit nor obeys the decision within the 15-day term.

Article 22 If a quarantinable infectious disease is caused to spread or is in great danger of being spread as a result of a violation of the provisions of this Law, criminal responsibility shall be investigated in accordance with Article 178 of the Criminal Law of the People's Republic of China.

Article 23 The personnel of frontier health and quarantine offices must enforce this Law impartially, perform duties faithfully and promptly conduct quarantine inspection on conveyances and persons upon entry or exit. Those who violate the law or are derelict in their duties shall be given disciplinary sanctions; where circumstances are serious enough to constitute a crime, criminal responsibility shall be investigated in accordance with the law.

Chapter   VI

Supplementary Provisions

Article 24   Where the provisions of this Law differ from those of international treaties on health and quarantine that China has concluded or joined, the provisions of such international treaties shall prevail, with the exception of the treaty clauses on which the People's Republic of China has declared reservations.

Article 25   In cases of temporary contact between frontier defence units of the People's Republic of China and those of a neighbouring country, of a temporary visit at a designated place on the frontier by residents of the border areas of the two countries and of entry or exit of conveyances and persons of the two sides, quarantine inspection shall be conducted in line with the agreements between China and the other country or, in the absence of such an agreement, in accordance with the relevant regulations of the Chinese Government.

Article 26   Frontier health and quarantine offices shall charge for health and quarantine services according to state regulations.

Article 27   The health administration department under the State Council shall, in accordance with this Law, formulate rules for its implementation, which shall go into effect after being submitted to and approved by the State Council.

Article 28   This Law shall go into effect on May 1, 1987. On the same day, the Frontier Health and Quarantine Regulations of the People's Republic of China promulgated on December 23, 1957, shall be invalidated.

Postal Law of the People's Republic of China

(Adopted at 18th Meeting of the Standing Committee of the National People's Congress, promulgated by Order No. 47 of the President of the People's Republic of China on December 2, 1986, and effective as of January 1, 1987)

Contents

Chapter I

General Provisions

Article 1   This Law is formulated in accordance with the Constitution of the People's Republic of China, with a view to protecting freedom and privacy of correspondence, ensuring normal progress of postal work, and promoting development of postal services, so as to suit the needs of socialist construction and the livelihood of the people.

Article 2   The competent department of postal services under the State Council shall administer postal services throughout the country.

The competent department of postal services under the State Council shall set up regional administrative organs of postal services as required to administer postal services of each region.

Article 3   The postal enterprises attached to the competent department of postal services under the State Council are public enterprises, owned by the whole people, that operate postal businesses.

According to stipulations of the competent department of postal services under the State Council, postal enterprises shall establish branch offices that operate postal businesses.

Article 4   Freedom and privacy of correspondence shall be protected by law. No organization or individual shall infringe upon the freedom and privacy of correspondence of other persons for any reason, except when the inspection of correspondence in accordance with legal procedures by the public security organ, the state security organ or the procuratorial organ is necessary for the state's safety or the investigation of criminal offence.

Article 5   Postal materials handed in or posted, remittances made and savings deposited by users shall be protected by law, and shall not be inspected and withheld by any organization or individual except as otherwise provided by law.

Article 6   Postal enterprises shall provide users with fast, accurate, safe and convenient postal services.

Postal enterprises and postal staff shall not provide information to any organization or individual about users' dealings with postal services except as otherwise provided for by law.

Article 7   Postal materials and remittances shall be owned by senders and remitters before they are delivered to recipients and remittees.

Article 8   Posting and delivery services of mail and other articles with characteristics of mail shall be exclusively operated by postal enterprises, except as otherwise provided by the State Council.

Postal enterprises may, according to needs, entrust other units or individuals as agents to run businesses exclusively operated by postal enterprises. The provisions on postal personnel specified in this Law shall apply to agents when they handle postal businesses.

Article 9   No unit or individual shall produce false copies or make fraudulent use of special postal marks, postal uniforms and special postal articles.

Chapter   II

Establishment of Postal Enterprises and Postal Facilities

Article 10   Standards for establishment of postal enterprises and their branch offices shall be formulated by the competent department of postal services under the State Council.

Article 11   Postal enterprises shall establish branch offices, postal kiosks, newspaper and periodical stands, mailboxes, etc., in places convenient to the masses, or provide mobile services.

Residents' mailboxes for receiving letters and newspapers shall be installed in residential buildings in cities.

Places shall be provided for handling postal business in larger railway stations, airports, ports and guest houses.

Chapter III

Classification of Postal Businesses and Postal Rates

Article 12   Postal enterprises operate the following businesses:

(1) posting and delivery of domestic and international postal materials;

(2) distributing domestic newspapers and periodicals;

(3) postal savings and postal remittances; and

(4) other suitable businesses stipulated by the competent department of postal services under the State Council.

Article 13   Postal enterprises and their branch offices shall not arbitrarily close down postal businesses that must be handled according to the stipulations made by the competent department of postal services under the State Council and the regional administrative organ of postal services.

Owing to force majeure or special reasons, if postal enterprises and their branch offices need to close down temporarily or restrict the handling of some postal businesses, they must obtain approval of the competent department of postal services under the State Council or of regional postal administrative organs.

Article 14   Postal enterprises shall strengthen distribution work of newspapers and periodicals. If publishing units entrust postal enterprises with distribution of newspapers and periodicals, they must make distribution contracts with postal enterprises.

Article 15   The basic postal rates of postal services shall be set by the competent department in charge of pricing under the State Council and shall be reported to the State Council for approval. Non-basic postal rates shall be formulated by the competent department of postal services under the State Council.

Article 16   The payment of postage on various postal materials shall be indicated by postage certificates or by postmarks showing postage paid.

Article 17   Postage stamps, stamped envelopes, stamped postcards, stamped aerogrammes and other postage certificates shall be issued by the competent department of postal services under the State Council, and no unit or individual shall be allowed to produce false copies.

The administrative measures on making facsimiles of stamp patterns shall be formulated by the competent department of postal services under the State Council.

Article 18   Postage certificates sold shall not be cashed in postal enterprises or their branch offices.

Postage certificates to be withdrawn from circulation shall be announced to the public, and sales will be stopped one month in advance by the competent department of postal services under the State Council. Holders of such postage certificates may exchange them for valid postage certificates at postal enterprises and their branch offices within six months from the date of the announcement.

Article 19   The following postage certificates shall not be used:

(1) those which the competent department of postal services under the State Council has announced as withdrawn from usage;

(2) those that have been postmarked or cancelled;

(3) those that are contaminated, incomplete or illegible due to fading or discolouring; and

(4) stamp patterns cut from stamped envelopes, stamped postcards and stamped aerogrammes.

Chapter IV

Posting and Delivery of Postal Materials

Article 20   In handing in or posting postal materials, users must abide by the provisions formulated by the relevant competent department under the State Council on articles forbidden to post or deliver and articles to be posted or delivered in limited amounts.

Article 21   The contents of postal materials, other than letters, to be handed in or posted by users, shall be checked on the spot by postal enterprises or branch offices, and if such examination is refused, the postal material shall not be accepted and posted.

Mail handed in or posted by users must be in line with the stipulations concerning the content allowed to be posted; postal enterprises and their branch offices have the right to request users to take out the contents for examination, when necessary.

Article 22   Postal enterprises and their branch offices shall deliver postal materials within the time limits laid down by the competent department of postal services under the State Council.

Article 23   Undeliverable postal materials shall be returned to the senders.

Mail that is both undeliverable and unreturnable, and unclaimed within the time limit stipulated by the competent department of postal services under the State Council, shall be destroyed on the authority of regional administrative organs of postal services.

Incoming international postal articles that are undeliverable and unreturnable, and unclaimed within the time limit stipulated by the competent department of postal offices under the State Council, shall be handled by the Customs in accordance with the law.

Disposal measures for other undeliverable and unreturnable postal materials shall be formulated by the competent department of postal services under the State Council.

Article 24   The remittees of postal remittances shall cash the postal remittances with valid documents at postal enterprises or branch offices within two months of receiving notice of a postal remittance. Remittances unclaimed when the time period expires shall be returned to the remitters by postal enterprises or branch offices. Returned remittances which are unclaimed for a period of ten months, counting from the date of delivering the return-remittance notice to the remitter, shall be turned over to the state treasury.

Article 25   In posting and delivering postal materials, postal codes shall be adopted gradually, and specific pertinent measures shall be formulated by the competent department of postal services under the State Council.

Chapter V

Transportation, Customs Examination and Quarantine Inspection of Postal Materials

Article 26   Transportation units operating railways, highways, waterways and airlines shall all have the responsibility of carrying and transporting postal materials, and shall ensure priority to transporting postal materials at preferential freight charges.

Article 27   When postal enterprises transfer postal materials in railway stations, airports and ports, transportation units concerned shall make coordinated arrangement of space and in-and-out passageways for loading and unloading postal materials.

Article 28   Ships with special postal marks, postal vans and postal staff shall be given priority in entering and departing ports and crossing on ferries. Postal vehicles with special postal marks which need to pass through a lane closed to traffic or to stop in no-parking sections of the road shall be verified and approved by the competent department concerned for passing or parking.

Article 29   When transported by sea, postal materials shall not be included in arrangements for sharing common sea losses.

Article 30 Postal enterprises shall not post or deliver international postal articles that are not examined and allowed to pass by the Customs. The Customs shall supervise the entry and exit, opening, sealing and dispatching of international mailbags. Postal enterprises shall inform the Customs of their business hours in advance, and the Customs shall promptly send officials to supervise on-the-spot checking and examination.

Article 31 Postal materials that are subject to health and quarantine inspections or animal and plant quarantine inspections according to law shall be sorted out and quarantined under the charge of quarantine offices; no transportation and delivery shall be conducted by postal enterprises without a permit from a quarantine office.

Chapter VI

Compensation for Losses

Article 32 Users may present receipts and inquire, within one year counting from the date of the posting or remitting, about vouchered postal materials and remittances which they handed in for posting or remitting at the postal enterprises or their branch offices that took in the postal materials or accepted the remittances. Postal enterprises or branch offices shall inform inquirers of the results of inquiry within the time limit set by the competent department of postal services under the State Council.

If no result is found within the time limit for responding to the inquiry, postal enterprises shall make compensation first or take remedial measures. Within a year counting from the date of making such compensation, if it is ascertained that the circumstance for which the compensation was made conforms with either item (2) or item (3) of Article 34 of this Law, the postal enterprises shall have the right to recall the compensation.

Article 33 For loss, damage, destruction or missing contents of vouchered postal materials, postal enterprises shall make compensation or take remedial measures according to the following stipulations:

(1) For registered mail, compensation shall be made according to standard amounts formulated by the competent department of postal services under the State Council.

(2) For insured postal materials which are lost or totally damaged or destroyed, compensation shall be made according to the insurance coverage. For missing contents or partial damage or destruction of insured postal materials, compensation shall be made according to the actual losses of the postal materials, based on the ratio between the insurance coverage and the whole value of the postal materials.

(3) For uninsured postal parcels, compensation shall be made according to the actual damage due to loss of such postal parcels, but the maximum compensation shall not exceed the amount formulated by the competent department of postal services under the State Council.

(4) For other types of vouchered postal materials, compensation shall be made or remedial measures taken according to the measures provided for by the competent department of postal services under the State Council.

Article 34　Postal enterprises shall not be held liable for compensation if one of the following situations occurs:

(1) losses of ordinary postal materials;

(2) losses of vouchered postal materials caused by the user or due to some characteristic of the posted articles per se;

(3) losses of vouchered postal materials, other than postal remittances and insured postal materials, caused by force majeure; and

(4) users failing to inquire about or demand compensation at the end of one year, counting from the date of handing in or posting the vouchered postal materials or making the remittance.

Article 35　If disputes over compensation for losses occur between users and postal enterprises, users may request the competent department of postal services at higher levels to settle; users who refuse to accept the settlement thereof may file lawsuits with the people's court; users may also file lawsuits with the people's court directly.

Chapter VII

Penalty Provisions

Article 36　Persons who infringe upon the citizens' right to freedom of correspondence by concealing, destroying, discarding or illegally opening mail of another person, where circumstances are serious, shall be investigated for criminal liability according to the provisions of Article 149 of the Criminal Law of the People's Republic of China; those whose acts are not serious enough for criminal punishment shall be punished according to the provisions of Article 22 of Regulations of the People's Republic of China on Administrative Penalties for Public Security.

Article 37　Postal personnel who without permission open or conceal, destroy or discard postal materials shall be investigated for criminal liability in accordance with Paragraph 1 in Article 191 of the Criminal Law of the People's Republic of China.

Those who commit the crime specified in the preceding provision and also steal property therein shall be given a heavier punishment for the crime of embezzlement in accordance with Paragraph 2 in Article 191 of the

Criminal Law of the People's Republic of China.

Article 38   Persons who intentionally damage or destroy public postal facilities such as mailboxes, where such acts are not serious enough for criminal punishment, shall be punished in accordance with the provisions of Article 25 of Regulations of the People's Republic of China on Administrative Penalties for Public Security; where circumstances are serious, such persons shall be investigated for criminal liability in accordance with the provisions of Article 156 of the Criminal Law of the People's Republic of China.

Article 39   Postal personnel who refuse to handle postal business which should be handled according to law or who intentionally delay the delivery of postal materials shall be given administrative disciplinary sanction. Postal personnel who are derelict in their duties and bring about great loss to public property and the interests of the state and the people shall be investigated for criminal liability in accordance with the provisions of Article 187 of the Criminal Law of the People's Republic of China.

Article 40   Persons who, in violation of provisions of Article 8 of this Law, handle the business of posting and delivering mail or articles with characteristics of mail shall be ordered by industrial and commercial administrative authorities to return the mail and other articles and the postal fees they have obtained from the senders, and a fine shall be imposed on them.

Parties concerned who refuse to obey the decision of punishment may bring suit to the people's court within 15 days of receiving the penalty notice. If parties concerned neither bring suit to the people's court nor implement the decision before the time limit expires, the industrial and commercial administrative authorities shall apply to the people's court for mandatory enforcement.

Chapter   VIII

Supplementary Provisions

Article 41   The meanings of the following terms used in this Law are:

(1) postal materials: referring to mail, printed matter, postal parcels, money orders, newspapers, periodicals, etc., posted and delivered by postal enterprises.

(2) mail: referring to letters and postcards.

(3) ordinary postal materials: referring to the postal materials that postal enterprises and their branch offices do not issue receipts for upon acceptance and posting, and do not request recipients to sign for on delivery.

(4) vouchered postal materials: referring to postal materials such as

registered mail, postal parcels, insured postal materials, etc., that the postal enterprises and their branch offices issue receipts for upon acceptance and posting, and for which recipients are requested to sign on delivery.

(5) international postal articles: referring to printed matter and postal parcels posted and delivered between users of the People's Republic of China and users of foreign countries or regions.

(6) special postal articles: referring to postal date-marks, postal tongs for lead sealing and postal bags.

Article 42   If provisions of this Law contravene those of the international treaties concerning international postal affairs which the People's Republic of China has concluded or to which China is a party, the provisions of the international treaties concerned shall prevail, with the exception of the treaty clauses on which the People's Republic of China has declared reservations.

Article 43   The competent department of postal services under the State Council shall, in accordance with this Law, formulate rules for its implementation, which shall go into effect after being submitted to and approved by the State Council.

Article 44   This Law shall go into effect on January 1, 1987.

Decision of the Standing Committee of the National People's Congress Regarding the Revision of the Electoral Law of the National People's Congress and Local People's Congresses of the People's Republic of China

(Adopted at the 18th Meeting of the Standing Committee
of the Sixth National People's Congress
on December 2, 1986)

The 18th Meeting of the Standing Committee of the Sixth National People's Congress has decided, in accordance with the Constitution, the basic principles of the electoral law and the practical experience of conducting elections in the past few years, to make the following amendments and supplements to the Electoral Law of the National People's Congress and Local People's Congresses of the People's Republic of China:

1. A new paragraph shall be added to Article 6 as the second paragraph: "Citizens of the People's Republic of China who reside abroad but who are in China during the election of deputies to people's congresses below the county level may take part in such elections conducted in their ancestral home towns or place of residence before they went abroad."

2. The provision of the second paragraph of Article 7, "The election committees of townships, nationality townships, and towns shall be under the leadership of the people's governments of townships, nationality townships, and towns," shall be amended as: "The election committees of townships, nationality townships, and towns shall be under the leadership of the election committees of cities not divided into districts, municipal districts, counties and autonomous counties."

A new paragraph shall be added as the third paragraph: "The standing committees of the people's congresses of provinces, autonomous regions, municipalities directly under the Central Government, cities divided into districts, and autonomous prefectures shall direct the work of electing deputies to the people's congresses below the county level in their administrative areas."

3. The second paragraph of Article 13 shall be amended as: "The number of deputies to the National People's Congress shall not exceed 3,000. The allocation of the number of deputies shall be decided by the Standing Committee of the National People's Congress in accordance with existing conditions."

4. The second paragraph of Article 16 shall be amended as: "Where the total population of a minority nationality in such an area exceeds 30 percent of the total local population, the number of people represented by each deputy of that minority nationality shall be equal to the number of people represented by each of the other deputies to the local people's congress."

A new paragraph shall be added as the fourth paragraph: "Where the total population of a minority nationality in such an area accounts for not less than 15 percent and not more than 30 percent of the total local population, the number of people represented by each deputy of that minority nationality may be appropriately smaller than the number of people represented by each of the other deputies to the local people's congress, but the number of deputies of that minority nationality shall not exceed 30 percent of the total number of deputies."

5. Article 22 shall be amended as: "The number of deputies to the people's congresses in cities not divided into districts, municipal districts, counties, autonomous counties, townships, nationality townships, and towns shall be allocated to the electoral districts, and elections shall be held in the electoral districts. The zoning of electoral districts may be decided according to the voters' residence or on the basis of production units, institutions and work units."

6. The first paragraph of Article 23 shall be amended as: "The registration of voters shall be conducted on the basis of electoral districts, and the voters' qualifications, confirmed through registration, shall have long-term validity. Prior to each election, voters who have reached the age of 18 since the last registration of voters, or who have had their political rights restored after a period of deprivation of political rights has expired, shall be registered. Voters who have moved out of the electoral districts where they originally registered shall be included in the roll of voters in the electoral districts to which they have newly moved; those who are deceased or have been deprived of political rights according to law shall be removed from the roll."

7. The provision in Article 25, "If the appellant is not satisfied with the decision, he may bring suit in the people's court. The judgment of the

people's court shall be final," shall be amended as: "If the appellant is not satisfied with the decision, he may bring suit in the people's court at least five days prior to the date of election, and the people's court shall make a judgment before the date of election. The judgment of the people's court shall be final."

8. The second paragraph of Article 26 shall be amended as: "Political parties and people's organizations may either jointly or separately recommend candidates for deputies. A joint group of at least ten voters or deputies may also recommend candidates. Those who submit recommendations shall inform the election committee or the presidium of the congress of their candidates' backgrounds."

9. The second paragraph of Article 27 shall be amended as: "The number of candidates for deputies to be directly elected by the voters shall be from one third to 100 percent greater than the number of deputies to be elected; the number of candidates for deputies to be elected by various local people's congresses to the people's congresses at the next higher level shall be from 20 to 50 percent greater than the number of deputies to be elected."

10. Article 28 shall be amended as: "Candidates for deputies to the people's congresses to be directly elected by the voters shall be nominated by the voters in the various electoral districts and by the various political parties and people's organizations. The election committee shall collect and publish, 20 days prior to the date of election, the list of nominees for deputies for repeated deliberation, discussion and consultation by voter groups in the respective electoral districts and shall decide, in accordance with the opinion of the majority of voters, upon a formal list of candidates to be made public five days prior to the date of election.

"When a local people's congress at or above the county level is to elect deputies to a people's congress at the next higher level, the presidium of the lower people's congress shall refer the list of nominees proposed by the various political parties, people's organizations and deputies to all the deputies for repeated deliberation, discussion and consultation and shall decide upon a formal list of candidates in accordance with the opinion of the majority of deputies."

11. Article 30 shall be amended as: "The election committee or the presidium of the people's congress shall brief voters or deputies on the candidates for deputies. Political parties, people's organizations, voters and deputies that have nominated candidates for deputies may brief voters on those candidates at group meetings of voters or deputies. However, such briefings must stop on the day of election."

12. Article 35 shall be amended as: "A voter who is absent from his electoral district during the time of an election may, with the approval of

the election committee and by written authorization, entrust another voter with a proxy vote. A voter shall not stand proxy for more than three persons."

13. The first paragraph of Article 38 shall be amended as two paragraphs, which shall be the first and the second paragraphs:

"In a direct election of deputies to the people's congresses, the election shall be valid if more than half of all the voters in an electoral district cast their votes. Candidates for deputies shall be elected only if they have obtained more than half of the votes cast by the voters that take part in the election.

"When a local people's congress at or above the county level is to elect deputies to a people's congress at the next higher level, candidates for deputies shall be elected only if they have obtained more than half of the votes of all the deputies."

14. A new paragraph shall be added to Article 40 as the third paragraph: "Specific procedures for recalling deputies shall be stipulated by the standing committees of the people's congresses of provinces, autonomous regions, and municipalities directly under the Central Government."

15. Article 41 shall be deleted, and a new article shall be added as Article 41: "Deputies to the National People's Congress and deputies to the people's congresses of provinces, autonomous regions, municipalities directly under the Central Government, cities divided into districts, and autonomous prefectures may submit their resignations to the standing committee of the people's congress that elected them."

16. A new paragraph shall be added to Article 42 as the fourth paragraph: "When by-elections are conducted to fill the vacant posts of deputies, the number of candidates may be greater than the number of deputies to be elected, or it may be equal to the number of deputies to be elected. The procedures and methods of conducting by-elections shall be stipulated by the standing committees of the people's congresses of provinces, autonomous regions, and municipalities directly under the Central Government."

In addition, in accordance with the Constitution and this Decision, appropriate adjustments and revisions shall be made to the wording of some of the clauses and order of some of the articles.

The Electoral Law of the National People's Congress and Local People's Congresses of the People's Republic of China shall be appropriately revised according to this Decision and promulgated anew.

Appendix:

The Election Law of the National People's Congress and Local People's Congresses of the People's Republic of China

*(Adopted at the Second Session of the Fifth National People's Congress
on July 1, 1979; revised for the first time in accordance with the
Resolution on the Revision of Certain Provisions in the Electoral Law
of the National People's Congress and Local People's Congresses of
the People's Republic of China, adopted at the Fifth Session of the
Fifth National People's Congress on December 10, 1982; revised for
the second time in accordance with the Decision on the Revision of
the Electoral Law of the National People's Congress and Local
People's Congresses of the People's Republic of China, adopted
at the 18th Meeting of the Standing Committee of the Sixth
National People's Congress on December 2, 1986)*

Contents

Chapter I

General Provisions

Article 1   The Electoral Law of the National People's Congress and

Local People's Congresses is formulated in accordance with the Constitution of the People's Republic of China.

Article 2   Deputies to the National People's Congress and to the people's congresses of provinces, autonomous regions, municipalities directly under the Central Government, cities divided into districts, and autonomous prefectures shall be elected by the people's congresses at the next lower level.

Deputies to the people's congresses of cities not divided into districts, municipal districts, counties, autonomous counties, townships, nationality townships, and towns shall be elected directly by their constituencies.

Article 3   All citizens of the People's Republic of China who have reached the age of 18 shall have the right to vote and stand for election, regardless of ethnic status, race, sex, occupation, family background, religious belief, education, property status or length of residence.

Persons who have been deprived of political rights according to the law shall not have the right to vote and stand for election.

Article 4   Each voter shall have the right to vote only once in an election.

Article 5   Elections shall be conducted separately in the People's Liberation Army, and the procedures for such elections shall be formulated separately.

Article 6   The National People's Congress and the local people's congresses in areas with a relatively large number of returned overseas Chinese shall have an appropriate number of deputies who are returned overseas Chinese.

Citizens of the People's Republic of China who reside abroad but who are in China during the election of deputies to people's congresses below the county level may take part in such elections conducted in their ancestral home town or place of domicile before they went abroad.

Article 7   The Standing Committee of the National People's Congress shall conduct the election of deputies to the National People's Congress. The standing committees of the people's congresses of provinces, autonomous regions, municipalities directly under the Central Government, cities divided into districts, and autonomous prefectures shall conduct the election of deputies to the people's congresses at the corresponding levels.

In cities divided into districts, municipal districts, counties, autonomous counties, townships, nationality townships, and towns, election committees shall be established to conduct the election of deputies to the people's congresses at the corresponding levels. The election committees of cities not divided into districts, municipal districts, counties and autonomous counties shall be under the leadership of the standing committees of the people's congresses at the corresponding levels. The election committees of townships, nationality townships, and towns shall be under the leadership of the election committees of cities not divided into districts, municipal districts, counties and autonomous counties.

The standing committees of the people's congresses of provinces, autonomous regions, municipalities directly under the Central Government, cities divided into districts, and autonomous prefectures shall direct the work of electing deputies to the people's congresses below the county level in their administrative areas.

Article 8   Election funds for the National People's Congress and the local people's congresses at various levels shall be disbursed by the State Treasury.

Chapter II

Number of Deputies to the Local People's Congresses at Various Levels

Article 9   The number of deputies to the local people's congresses at various levels shall be independently decided by the standing committees of the people's congresses of the provinces, autonomous regions, or municipalities directly under the Central Government, in accordance with the principle of facilitating the convening of meetings and discussion and solution of problems as well as ensuring appropriate representation of all nationalities, all localities and people of all circles; the number of deputies so decided shall be reported to the Standing Committee of the National People's Congress for the record.

Article 10   The number of deputies to the people's congresses of autonomous prefectures, counties and autonomous counties shall be allocated by the standing committees of the people's congresses at the corresponding levels, in accordance with the principle that the number of people represented by each rural deputy shall be four times the number of people represented by each town deputy. Townships, nationality townships, and towns with exceptionally small populations shall have at least one deputy in the people's congresses of their respective counties and autonomous counties.

In the administrative areas of counties or autonomous counties which have towns with exceptionally large populations, or have enterprises and institutions not under the leadership of the people's governments at or below the county level whose workers and staff account for a relatively large portion of the county's total population, the ratio between the number of people represented by a rural deputy and the number of people represented by a town deputy or a deputy of an enterprise or institution may, upon a decision made by the standing committee of the people's congress of the province, autonomous region, or municipality directly under the Central Government, be smaller than four to one, even to the extent of one to one.

Article 11   In municipalities directly under the Central Government, cities and municipal districts, the number of people represented by a rural deputy shall be greater than the number of people represented by an urban deputy.

Article 12   The number of deputies to the people's congresses of provinces or autonomous regions shall be allocated by the standing committees of the people's congresses at the corresponding levels, in accordance with the principle that the number of people represented by each rural deputy shall be five times the number of people represented by each urban deputy.

Chapter   III

Number of Deputies to
the National People's Congress

Article 13   Deputies to the National People's Congress shall be elected by the people's congresses of the provinces, autonomous regions, and municipalities directly under the Central Government and by the People's Liberation Army.

The number of deputies to the National People's Congress shall not exceed 3,000. The allocation of the number of deputies shall be decided by the Standing Committee of the National People's Congress in accordance with existing conditions.

Article 14   The number of deputies to the National People's Congress to be elected by the provinces, autonomous regions, and municipalities directly under the Central Government shall be allocated by the Standing Committee of the National People's Congress in accordance with the principle that the number of people represented by each rural deputy shall be eight times the number of people represented by each urban deputy.

Article 15   The number of deputies to the National People's Congress to be elected by minority nationalities shall be allocated by the Standing Committee of the National People's Congress, in light of the population and distribution of each minority nationality, to the people's congresses of the various provinces, autonomous regions, and municipalities directly under the Central Government, which shall elect them accordingly. Nationalities with exceptionally small populations shall each have at least one deputy.

Chapter IV

Elections Among Minority Nationalities

Article 16 In areas where minority nationalities live in concentrated communities, each minority nationality shall have its deputy or deputies sit in the local people's congress.

Where the total population of a minority nationality in such an area exceeds 30 percent of the total local population, the number of people represented by each deputy of that minority nationality shall be equal to the number of people represented by each of the other deputies to the local people's congress.

Where the total population of a minority nationality in such an area is less than 15 percent of the total local population, the number of people represented by each deputy of that minority nationality may be appropriately smaller, but shall not be less than half the number of people represented by each of the other deputies to the local people's congress. In autonomous counties where the population of the minority nationality practising regional autonomy is exceptionally small, the number of people represented by each deputy of this minority nationality may, upon a decision made by the standing committee of the people's congress of the province or autonomous region, be less than half the number of people represented by each of the other deputies. Other nationalities with exceptionally small populations shall each have at least one deputy.

Where the total population of a minority nationality in such an area accounts for not less than 15 percent and not more than 30 percent of the total local population, the number of people represented by each deputy of that minority nationality may be appropriately smaller than the number of people represented by each of the other deputies to the local people's congress, but the number of deputies of that minority nationality shall not exceed 30 percent of the total number of deputies.

Article 17 In autonomous regions, autonomous prefectures and autonomous counties, and in townships, nationality townships, and towns where a certain minority nationality lives in a concentrated community, the provisions of Article 16 of this Law shall apply to the election to the local people's congresses of deputies of other minority nationalities and the Han nationality also living in concentrated communities in such areas.

Article 18 With respect to minority nationalities living in scattered groups, the number of people represented by each of their deputies to the local people's congresses may be less than the number of people represented by each of the other deputies to such congresses.

In autonomous regions, autonomous prefectures and autonomous counties, and in townships, nationality townships, and towns where a certain minority nationality lives in a concentrated community, the provisions of the preceding paragraph shall apply to the election to the local people's congresses of deputies of other minority nationalities and the Han nationality living in scattered groups in such areas.

Article 19 In cities not divided into districts, municipal districts, counties, townships, nationality townships, and towns where various minority nationalities live in concentrated communities, the minority nationality electorates may vote separately or jointly in the election of deputies to the local people's congress, depending on the relations between the nationalities and their residential situation in such areas.

In autonomous counties and in townships, nationality townships, and towns where a certain minority nationality lives in a concentrated community, the provisions of the preceding paragraph shall apply to the election to the respective people's congresses of deputies of other minority nationalities and the Han nationality living in such areas.

Article 20 The electoral documents, roll of voters, voter registration cards, list of candidates for deputies, deputies' election certificates and election committee seals made or published by autonomous regions, autonomous prefectures and autonomous counties shall be in the written languages commonly used in the locality.

Article 21 Other matters concerning elections among minority nationalities shall be handled with reference to the provisions of the relevant articles of this Law.

Chapter V

Zoning of Electoral Districts

Article 22 The number of deputies to the people's congresses in cities not divided into districts, municipal districts, counties, autonomous counties, townships, nationality townships, and towns shall be allocated to the electoral districts, and elections shall be held in the electoral districts. The zoning of electoral districts may be decided according to the voters' residence or on the basis of production units, institutions and work units.

Chapter VI

Registration of Voters

Article 23   The registration of voters shall be conducted on the basis of electoral districts, and the voters' qualifications, confirmed through registration, shall have long-term validity. Prior to each election, voters who have reached the age of 18 since the last registration of voters or who have had their political rights restored after a period of deprivation of political rights has expired, shall be registered. Voters who have moved out of the electoral districts where they originally registered shall be included in the roll of voters in the electoral districts to which they have newly moved; those who are deceased or have been deprived of political rights according to law shall be removed from the roll.

Citizens who suffer from mental illness and are incapable of exercising their electoral rights shall, upon determination by the election committee, not be included in the roll of voters.

Article 24   The roll of voters shall be made public 30 days prior to the date of election, and voter registration cards shall be issued.

Article 25   Anyone who has an objection to the roll of voters may appeal to the election committee. The election committee shall make a decision on the appeal within three days. If the appellant is not satisfied with the decision, he may bring suit in the people's court at least five days prior to the date of election, and the people's court shall make a judgment before the date of election. The judgment of the people's court shall be final.

Chapter VII

Nomination of Candidates for Deputies

Article 26   Candidates for deputies to the national and local people's congresses shall be nominated on the basis of electoral districts or electoral units.

Political parties and people's organizations may either jointly or separately recommend candidates for deputies. A joint group of at least ten voters or deputies may also recommend candidates. Those who submit recommendations shall inform the election committee or the presidium of the congress of their candidates' backgrounds.

Article 27   The number of candidates for deputies to the national and local people's congresses shall be greater than the number of deputies to be elected.

The number of candidates for deputies to be directly elected by the voters shall be from one third to 100 percent greater than the number of deputies to be elected; the number of candidates for deputies to be elected by various local people's congresses to the people's congresses at the next higher level shall be 20 to 50 percent greater than the number of deputies to be elected.

Article 28   Candidates for deputies to the people's congresses to be directly elected by the voters shall be nominated by the voters in the various electoral districts and by the various political parties and people's organizations. The election committee shall collect and publish, 20 days prior to the date of election, the list of nominees for deputies for repeated deliberation, discussion and consultation by voter groups in the respective electoral districts and shall decide, in accordance with the opinion of the majority of voters, upon a formal list of candidates to be made public five days prior to the date of election.

When a local people's congress at or above the county level is to elect deputies to a people's congress at the next higher level, the presidium of the lower people's congress shall refer the list of nominees proposed by the various political parties, people's organizations and deputies to all the deputies for repeated deliberation, discussion and consultation and shall decide upon a formal list of candidates in accordance with the opinion of the majority of deputies.

Article. 29   When a local people's congress at or above the county level is to elect deputies to the people's congress at the next higher level, the nominees for deputies shall not be limited to the current deputies to the lower people's congress.

Article 30   The election committee or the presidium of the people's congress shall brief. voters or deputies on the candidates for deputies. Political parties, people's organizations, voters and deputies that have nominated candidates for deputies may brief voters on those candidates at group meetings of voters or deputies. However, such briefings must stop on the day of election.

Chapter   VIII

Election Procedure

Article 31   Where the deputies to a people's congress are to be elected directly by the voters, the election shall be conducted at polling centres in the various electoral districts or at election meetings. The polling centres or election meetings shall be presided over by the election committee.

Article 32   Where a local people's congress at or above the county level is to elect deputies to the people's congress at the next higher level, the election shall be presided over by the presidium of the lower people's congress.

Article 33   The election of deputies to the national and local people's congresses shall be by secret ballot.

If a voter is illiterate or handicapped and is therefore unable to write his ballot, he may entrust another person to write it for him.

Article 34   A voter may vote for or against a candidate for deputy and may vote instead for any other voter or abstain.

Article 35   A voter who is absent from his electoral district during the time of an election may, with the approval of the election committee and by written authorization, entrust another voter with a proxy vote. A voter shall not stand proxy for more than three persons.

Article 36   When balloting has been concluded, scrutinizers and vote counters elected by the voters or deputies and members of the election committee or members of the presidium of the people's congress shall check the number of people who voted against the number of votes cast and make a record of it; the record shall be signed by the scrutinizers.

Article 37   An election shall be null and void if the number of votes cast is greater than the number of people who voted, and it shall be valid if the number of votes cast is less than the number of people who voted.

A ballot shall be null and void if more candidates are voted for than the number of deputies to be elected, and it shall be valid if fewer candidates are voted for than the number of deputies to be elected.

Article 38   In a direct election of deputies to the people's congresses, the election shall be valid if more than half of all the voters in an electoral district cast their votes. Candidates for deputies shall be elected only if they have obtained more than half of the votes cast by the voters that take part in the election.

When a local people's congress at or above the county level is to elect deputies to a people's congress at the next higher level, candidates for deputies shall be elected only if they have obtained more than half of the votes of all the deputies.

When the number of candidates for deputies who have obtained more than half of the votes exceeds the number of deputies to be elected, those who have obtained the most votes shall be elected. If the number of votes for some candidates is tied, making it impossible to determine who is elected, another balloting shall be conducted between those candidates to resolve the tie.

If the number of elected deputies who have obtained more than half of the votes is less than the number of deputies to be elected, another election shall be held among the candidates for deputies who failed to be elected to make up the difference. Those who obtain the most votes shall be elected; however, to be elected they must obtain no less than one third of the votes cast.

Article 39   The election committee or the presidium of the people's congress shall determine, in accordance with this Law, whether or not the result of an election is valid and shall announce it accordingly.

Chapter IX

Supervision, Recall and By-Elections Held to Fill Vacancies

Article 40   All deputies to the national and local people's congresses shall be subject to the supervision of the voters and the electoral units which elect them. Both the voters and the electoral units shall have the right to recall the deputies they elect.

The recall of a deputy directly elected by the voters shall be approved by a majority vote of all the voters in the electoral district from which the deputy was elected; the recall of a deputy elected by a people's congress shall be approved by a majority vote of all the deputies of that people's congress or by a majority vote of all its standing committee members when the people's congress is not in session. A deputy to be recalled may attend the above-mentioned meetings to state his views or submit a written statement of his views. The resolution of a recall shall be reported to the standing committee of the people's congress at the next higher level for the record.

Specific procedures for recalling deputies shall be stipulated by the standing committees of the people's congresses of provinces, autonomous regions, and municipalities directly under the Central Government.

Article 41   Deputies to the National People's Congress and deputies to the people's congresses of provinces, autonomous regions, municipalities directly under the Central Government, cities divided into districts, and autonomous prefectures may submit their resignations to the standing committee of the people's congress that elected them.

Article 42   If a deputy's post becomes vacant for some reason during his term of office, the electoral district or electoral unit which elected him shall hold a by-election to fill the vacancy.

If a deputy to a local people's congress at any level is transferred or moves out of his administrative area during his term of office, he is automatically disqualified as deputy and a by-election shall be held to fill the vacancy.

When the local people's congresses at or above the county level are not in session, their standing committees may conduct by-elections to fill vacancies left by deputies to the people's congresses at the next higher level.

When by-elections are conducted to fill the vacant posts of deputies, the number of candidates may be greater than the number of deputies to be elected, or it may equal the number of deputies to be elected. The procedures and methods of conducting by-elections shall be stipulated by the standing committees of the people's congresses of provinces, autonomous regions, and municipalities directly under the Central Government.

Chapter X

Sanctions Against Disruption of Elections

Article 43 In order to ensure that the voters and deputies freely exercise their right to vote and stand for election, administrative or criminal sanctions shall, in accordance with the law, be taken against persons who commit any of the following illegal acts:

(1) use of violence, threat, deception, bribery or other illegal means to disrupt an election or interfere with a voter or deputy in the free exercise of his right to vote and stand for election;

(2) forgery of electoral documents, falsification of vote tallies or other illegal acts; and

(3) suppression of or retaliation against anyone who incriminates or informs against a person committing illegal acts in an election or who demands the recall of a deputy.

Chapter XI

Supplementary Provisions

Article 44 The standing committees of the people's congresses of the provinces, autonomous regions, and municipalities directly under the Central Government may formulate rules for the implementation of elections in accordance with this Law and submit them to the Standing Committee of the National People's Congress for the record.

Decision of the Standing Committee of the National People's Congress Regarding the Revision of the Organic Law of the Local People's Congresses and Local People's Governments of the People's Republic of China

(Adopted at the 18th Meeting of the Standing Committee of the Sixth National People's Congress and promulgated by Order No. 49 of the President of the People's Republic of China on December 2, 1986)

The 18th Meeting of the Standing Committee of the Sixth National People's Congress has decided, in accordance with the Constitution, the basic principles of the Organic Law of the Local People's Congresses and Local People's Governments and the practical experience of the past few years, to make the following amendments and supplements to the Organic Law of the Local People's Congresses and Local People's Governments of the People's Republic of China:

1. Article 6 shall be changed into Article 7, with a new paragraph added as the second paragraph: "The people's congresses of cities where provincial and autonomous regional people's governments are located and the people's congresses of relatively large cities, with the approval of the State Council, may, in light of the specific conditions and actual needs of their respective cities, formulate local regulations, which must not contravene the Constitution, the law, administrative rules and regulations, and the local regulations of their respective provinces and autonomous regions; they shall report such local regulations to the standing committees of the people's congresses of their respective provinces and autonomous regions for approval before implementation, and for submission to the Standing Committee of the National People's Congress and the State Council for the record."

Article 27 shall be changed into Article 38, with the second paragraph amended as: "The standing committees of the people's congresses of cities where the provincial and autonomous regional people's governments are located and the standing committees of the people's congresses of relatively large cities, with the approval of the State Council, may, when their respective people's congresses are not in session, formulate local regulations in accordance with the specific conditions and actual needs of their respective cities, provided that these regulations do not contravene the Constitution, the law, administrative rules and regulations and the local regulations of the respective provinces and autonomous regions; they shall submit such local regulations to the standing committees of the people's congresses of the respective provinces and autonomous regions for approval before implementation and for submission to the Standing Committee of the National People's Congress and the State Council for the record."

2. Article 7 shall be changed into Article 8, with Item 3 amended as: "to discuss and decide on major issues in political, economic, educational, scientific, cultural, public health, and civil and nationality affairs in their respective administrative areas."

Item 5 shall be amended as: "to elect governors and deputy governors, chairmen and vice-chairmen of autonomous regions, mayors and deputy mayors, prefects and deputy prefects, and heads and deputy heads of counties and districts."

Items 6 and 7 shall be combined as Item 6 and amended as: "to elect the presidents of the people's courts and the chief procurators of the people's procuratorates at the corresponding levels; the election of the chief procurator of a people's procuratorate shall be reported to the chief procurator of the people's procuratorate at the next higher level, who shall submit it to the standing committee of the people's congress at that same level for approval."

Item 12 shall be changed into Item 10 and amended as: "to alter or annul inappropriate resolutions of the standing committees of the people's congresses at the corresponding levels."

Item 16 shall be changed into Item 15 and amended as: "to safeguard women's rights as endowed by the Constitution and the law, such as equality with men, equal pay for equal work and freedom of marriage."

3. Article 8 shall be changed into Article 9, with a new item added as Item 4: "to examine and approve the budgets of their respective administrative areas as well as the reports on the implementation of the budgets."

Item 11 shall be changed into Item 12 and amended as: "to safeguard women's rights as endowed by the Constitution and the law, such as equality with men, equal pay for equal work and freedom of marriage."

4. Article 13 shall be added as follows: "A preliminary meeting shall be held for each session of a local people's congress at or above the county level to elect the presidium and secretary-general of that session, adopt the agenda for the session and decide on other preparations.

"The preliminary meeting shall be presided over by the standing committee of the people's congress. The preliminary meeting for the first session of a people's congress shall be presided over by the standing committee of the preceding people's congress at the corresponding level.

"When a local people's congress at or above the county level meets, its session shall be conducted by the presidium.

"When a local people's congress at or above the county level meets, it shall propose a number of deputy secretaries-general; the choice of deputy secretaries-general shall be decided by the presidium."

5. The second paragraph of Article 10 shall be changed into Article 14 and amended as: "When the people's congress of a township, nationality township, or town holds a session, it shall elect a presidium, which shall preside over the session and be responsible for convening the next session of that people's congress."

6. Article 15 shall be added as follows: "The first session of each local people's congress at any level shall be convened, within two months after the election of its deputies, by the standing committee of the preceding people's congress at the corresponding level or by the presidium of the preceding session of the people's congress of the township, nationality township, or town."

7. Article 13 shall be changed into three articles, Articles 25, 27 and 45, which shall read:

a. "Article 25 The people's congresses of provinces, autonomous regions, municipalities directly under the Central Government, autonomous prefectures, and cities divided into districts may, where necessary, establish special committees such as legislative (political and law) committees, finance and economic committees, and education, science, culture and public health committees. The special committees shall work under the direction of the respective people's congresses; when the people's congresses are not in session, they shall work under the direction of the standing committees of the people's congresses.

"Nominations for the chairman, vice-chairmen and members of a special committee shall be made by the presidium from among the deputies and approved by the people's congress. When the people's congress is not in session, its standing committee may appoint additional individual vice-chairmen and some members of the special committees through nomination by its council of chairmen and approval by a meeting of the standing committee.

"The special committees shall discuss, examine and draw up relevant bills and draft resolutions under the direction of the people's congresses and their standing committees at the corresponding levels; they shall make investigations and studies of and put forward proposals on matters related to those committees and within the scope of functions and powers of the respective people's congresses and their standing committees."

b. "Article 27 The credentials committee established at the first session of each people's congress of a township, nationality township, and town shall exercise its functions and powers until the term of office of that people's congress expires."

c. "Article 45 The standing committee of each local people's congress at or above the county level shall establish a credentials committee.

"Nominations for the chairman, vice-chairmen and members of a credentials committee shall be made by the council of chairmen of the standing committee from among the members of the standing committee and adopted at a meeting of the standing committee."

Article 26 shall be added as follows: "A local people's congress at or above the county level and its standing committee may appoint committees of inquiry into specific questions."

8. Article 14 shall be changed into two articles, Articles 17 and 18, which shall read:

a. "Article 17   When a local people's congress holds its sessions, its presidium, standing committee and special committees and the people's government at the corresponding level may submit bills and proposals to that people's congress within the scope of its functions and powers. The presidium shall decide to refer such bills and proposals to a session of the people's congress for deliberation, or to simultaneously refer them to relevant special committees for deliberation and reports before the presidium decides, upon examination of such reports, to submit them to the people's congress for a vote.

"Ten or more deputies to a local people's congress at or above the county level, or five or more deputies to the people's congress of a township, nationality township or town, may jointly submit a bill or proposal to the people's congress at the corresponding level within the scope of its functions and powers. The presidium shall decide whether to place the bill or proposal on the agenda of the people's congress or to first refer it to a relevant special committee for deliberation and a recommendation on whether to place it on the agenda before the presidium makes such a decision.

"Deliberation shall be terminated on a bill or proposal submitted to a people's congress if the party that submitted the bill or proposal requests its withdrawal before it has been referred to the congress for a vote."

b. "Article 18   Suggestions, criticisms and complaints on any aspect of work put forward by deputies to a local people's congress at or above the county level to that people's congress and its standing committee shall be referred by the administrative office of the standing committee to the departments and organizations concerned for consideration, disposition and reply.

"Suggestions, criticisms and complaints on any aspect of work put forward by deputies to the people's congress of a township, nationality township, or town to that people's congress shall be referred by its presidium to the departments and organizations concerned for consideration, disposition and reply."

Article 41 shall be added as follows: "A local people's government at or above the county level or a special committee of the people's congress at the corresponding level may submit bills and proposals to its standing committee within its scope of functions and powers. The council of chairmen shall decide to refer them to a meeting of the standing committee for deliberation or to first refer them to relevant special committees for deliberation and reports before submitting them to a meeting of the standing committee for deliberation.

"Five or more standing committee members of the people's congress of a province, autonomous region, municipality directly under the Central Government, autonomous prefecture or city divided into districts, or three or more standing committee members of a people's congress at the county level, may jointly submit a bill or proposal to its standing committee within its scope of functions and powers. The council of chairmen shall decide whether to refer the bill or proposal to a meeting of the standing committee for deliberation or to first refer it to a relevant special committee for deliberation and a report before deciding on whether to submit it to a meeting of the standing committee for deliberation."

9. Article 16 shall be changed into Article 20, with the first paragraph divided into two paragraphs, which shall read:

"Members of the standing committees of local people's congresses at and above the county level, governors and deputy governors, chairmen and vice-chairmen of autonomous regions, mayors and deputy mayors, prefects and deputy prefects, heads and deputy heads of counties, districts, townships and towns, presidents of people's courts and chief procurators of people's procuratorates at and above the county level shall be nominated by the presidium of the people's congress at the corresponding level or jointly nominated by a minimum of ten deputies.

"In elections for chairmen and secretaries-general of the standing committees of local people's congresses, governors, chairmen of autonomous regions, mayors, prefects, heads of counties, districts, townships and towns, presidents of people's courts and chief procurators of people's procuratorates, there shall generally be one more candidate for each vacancy, and the election method of having more candidates than vacancies shall be adopted. If only one candidate is nominated, the election method of having the same number of candidates as vacancies may be adopted. In elections for vice-chairmen of the standing committees of the people's congresses, deputy governors, vice-chairmen of autonomous regions, deputy mayors, deputy prefects, and deputy heads of counties, districts, townships and towns, there shall be one to three more candidates than the number of vacancies for each post; for members of the standing committees of the people's congresses, there shall be one tenth to one fifth more candidates than vacancies. The election method here used shall be that of having more candidates than vacancies. If the number of candidates nominated exceeds the guidelines mentioned above, the presidium of the relevant people's congress shall submit the entire list of candidates to all the deputies for consideration and discussion, and the official list of candidates shall be determined according to the majority opinion of the deputies."

A new paragraph shall be added as the fourth paragraph: "When by-elections are held by the local people's congresses at various levels for chairmen, vice-chairmen, secretaries-general and members of their standing committees, governors, deputy governors, chairmen and vice-chairmen of autonomous regions, mayors, deputy mayors, prefects, deputy prefects, heads and deputy heads of counties, districts, townships and towns, presidents of people's courts and chief procurators of people's procuratorates, the number of candidates may exceed or equal the number of vacancies, and the election procedures and methods shall be decided by the people's congresses at the corresponding levels."

10. Article 21 shall be added as follows: "When a local people's congress at or above the county level is in session, its presidium, its standing committee, or a joint group of at least one tenth of its deputies may submit a proposal to remove from office members of its standing committee or leading personnel of the people's government, the president of the people's court or the chief procurator of the people's procuratorate at the corresponding level; the presidium shall refer such proposals to the congress for deliberation.

"When the people's congress of a township, nationality township, or town is in session, its presidium or a joint group of at least one fifth of its deputies may submit a proposal to remove from office the head or deputy heads of the township or town; the presidium shall refer such proposals to the congress for deliberation."

11. Article 22 shall be added as follows: "A leading functionary of a local people's government at any level, a standing committee member of a local people's congress at or above the county level, the president of a people's court or the chief procurator of a people's procuratorate may submit his resignation to the people's congress at the corresponding level, which shall decide whether or not to accept the resignation; if the people's congress is not in session, such resignations may be submitted to its standing committee, which shall decide whether or not to accept the resignations. If the standing committee decides to accept a resignation, it shall report it to its people's congress for the record. A resignation of the chief procurator of a people's procuratorate must be reported to the chief procurator of the people's procuratorate at the next higher level, who shall refer it to the standing committee of the people's congress at the corresponding level for approval."

12. Article 17 shall be changed into Article 16 and amended as: "Members of local people's governments at various levels, the presidents of the people's courts and the chief procurators of the people's procuratorates

shall attend sessions of the people's congresses at the corresponding levels as nonvoting delegates; responsible persons of government agencies and people's organizations concerned may, by decision of the presidiums, attend sessions of the people's congresses at the corresponding levels as nonvoting delegates."

13. Article 18 shall be changed into two articles, Articles 23 and 24, which shall read:

a. "Article 23 When a local people's congress at any level is in session, a joint group of at least ten of its deputies may address questions to the people's government or any of its departments, the people's court or the people's procuratorate at the corresponding level. The presidium shall decide to refer such questions to the organ addressed, which must responsibly answer the questions at the session."

b. Article 24 "When a local people's congress at any level examines a bill or proposal, its deputies may address questions to the local state organs concerned, which shall send their personnel to the congress to give explanations."

Article 42 shall be added as follows: "A joint group of five or more standing committee members of the people's congress of a province, autonomous region, municipality directly under the Central Government, autonomous prefecture or city divided into districts, or a joint group of three or more standing committee members of a people's congress at the county level may, when the standing committee is in session, address questions to the people's government, people's court or people's procuratorate at the corresponding level. The council of chairmen shall decide whether to refer them to the organ addressed for a reply."

14. Article 28 shall be added as follows: "The term of office of the deputies to a local people's congress at any level shall begin with the first session of that people's congress and shall expire at the first session of the succeeding people's congress at the same level."

Article 37 shall be added as follows: "The standing committee of a local people's congress at or above the county level shall have the same term of office as that people's congress and shall exercise its functions and powers until a new standing committee is elected by the succeeding people's congress at the same level."

15. Article 29 shall be added as follows: "Deputies to local people's congresses at various levels and members of their standing committees may not be held legally liable for their speeches and voting at sessions of the people's congresses or meetings of their standing committees."

Article 19 shall be changed into Article 30 and amended as: "No deputy to a local people's congress at or above the county level may be arrested or placed on criminal trial without the consent of the presidium of that people's congress or, when the people's congress is not in session, without the consent of its standing committee. If a deputy is caught in the act of crime and detained, the public security organ executing the detention shall immediately report the matter to the presidium or the standing committee of that people's congress."

16. Article 24 shall be changed into Article 3 and amended as: "The organs of self-government of autonomous regions, autonomous prefectures and autonomous counties shall, in addition to exercising the functions and powers specified in this Law, exercise the power of autonomy within the limits of their authority as prescribed by the Constitution, the Law on Regional National Autonomy and other laws."

17. Article 26 shall be changed into Article 36, with the first paragraph divided into two paragraphs, which shall read:

"The standing committee of a people's congress of a province, autonomous region, municipality directly under the Central Government, autonomous prefecture, or city divided into districts shall be composed of a chairman, vice-chairmen, a secretary-general and members to be elected by the people's congress from among its deputies.

"The standing committee of a people's congress of a county, autonomous county, city not divided into districts, or municipal district shall be composed of a chairman, vice-chairmen and members to be elected by the people's congress from among its deputies."

The third paragraph of Article 29 shall be changed into Article 43 and amended as: "The chairman, vice-chairmen and secretary-general of the standing committee of the people's congress of a province, autonomous region, municipality directly under the Central Government, autonomous prefecture, or city divided into districts shall constitute its council of chairmen; the chairman and vice-chairmen of the standing committee of the people's congress of a county, autonomous county, city not divided into districts, or municipal district shall constitute its council of chairmen. The council of chairmen shall handle the important day-to-day work of its standing committee."

18. Article 28 shall be changed into Article 39, with three paragraphs added as Items (1), (8) and (12) as follows:

a. "(1) to ensure the observance and execution, in its administrative area, of the Constitution, the law, administrative rules and regulations, and the resolutions of the people's congresses and their standing committees at higher levels."

b. "(8) to annul inappropriate decisions and orders of the people's government at the corresponding level."

c. "(12) to decide, when its people's congress is not in session, on the removal from office of individual deputy governors, vice-chairmen of the autonomous region, deputy mayors, deputy prefects, and deputy heads of the county or district; to decide on the removal from office of personnel it has appointed among other members of the people's government, vice-presidents, chief judges and associate chief judges of divisions, members of the judicial committees and judges of the people's courts, deputy chief procurators, members of the procuratorial committees and procurators of the people's procuratorates, presidents of intermediate people's courts and chief procurators of people's branch procuratorates, all at the corresponding level."

Item (3) shall be changed into Item (4) and amended as: "to discuss and decide on major issues in political, economic, educational, scientific, cultural, public health, and civil and nationality affairs in its administrative area."

Item (7) shall be changed into Item (9) and amended as: "to decide, when its people's congress is not in session, on the appointment or removal of individual deputy governors, vice-chairmen of the autonomous region, deputy mayors, deputy prefects and deputy heads of the county or district; when, for any reason, the governor, chairman of the autonomous region, mayor, prefect, or head of the county or district, president of the people's court or chief procurator of the people's procuratorate is unable to perform his duties, to choose a person from among the deputy heads of the people's government, people's court or people's procuratorate at the corresponding level to act on his behalf; the choice of an acting chief procurator must be reported to the people's procuratorate and the standing committee of the people's congress at the next higher level for the record."

Item (8) shall be changed into Item (10) and amended as: "to decide, upon nomination by the governor, chairman of the autonomous region, mayor, prefect, or head of the county or district, on the appointment or removal of the secretary-general and the department and bureau directors, commission chairmen and section chiefs of the people's government at the corresponding level and to report such decisions to the people's government at the next higher level for the record."

Item (9) shall be changed into Item (11) and amended as: "to appoint or remove, in accordance with the provisions of the Organic Law of the People's Courts and the Organic Law of the People's Procuratorates, vice-presidents, chief judges and associate chief judges of divisions, members of the judicial committees and judges of the people's courts, to appoint or remove deputy chief procurators, members of the procuratorial committees and procurators of the people's procuratorates, and to approve the appointment or removal of the chief procurators of the people's procuratorates at the next lower level; the standing committee of the people's congress of a province, autonomous region, or municipality directly under the Central Government shall, upon nomination by its council of chairmen, decide on the appointment or removal of presidents of intermediate people's courts established in prefectures of provinces and autonomous regions or in municipalities directly under the Central Government and, upon nomination by the chief procurator of the people's procuratorate of a province, autonomous region or municipality directly under the Central Government, decide on the appointment or removal of chief procurators of people's branch procuratorates."

19. Article 44 shall be added as follows: "In the event that the chairman of a standing committee is unable to work owing to feeble health or that his office falls vacant, the standing committee shall select one of the vice-chairmen to act on behalf of the chairman until he recovers his health or a new chairman is elected by the people's congress."

20. Article 33 shall be changed into Article 49 and amended as:

"The people's government of a province, autonomous region, municipality directly under the Central Government, autonomous prefecture or city divided into districts shall be respectively composed of the governor and deputy governors, the chairman and vice-chairmen of the autonomous region, the mayor and deputy mayors, or the prefect and deputy prefects, and additionally the secretary-general, department directors, bureau directors and commission chairmen.

"The people's government of a county, autonomous county, city not divided into districts, or municipal district shall be respectively composed of the head and deputy heads of the county, the mayor and deputy mayors, or the head and deputy heads of the district, and additionally the bureau directors and section chiefs.

"The people's government of a township or nationality township shall have a township head and deputy heads. The head of a nationality township shall be a citizen of the minority nationality that establishes the nationality township. The people's government of a town shall have a town head and deputy heads."

21. Article 35 shall be changed into Article 51, with Item (5) amended as: "to implement the plan for national economic and social development and the budget, and conduct administrative work concerning the economy, education, science, culture, public health, physical culture, urban and rural development, finance, civil affairs, public security, nationality affairs, judicial administration, supervision and family planning within its administrative area."

Item (8) shall be amended as: "to safeguard the rights of minority nationalities and respect their folkways and customs, assist those areas where minority nationalities live in concentrated communities within its sphere of jurisdiction to exercise regional autonomy in accordance with the Constitution and the law and assist the various minority nationalities in their political, economic and cultural development."

Item (9) shall be amended as: "to safeguard women's rights as endowed by the Constitution and the law, such as equality with men, equal pay for equal work and freedom of marriage."

22. Article 36 shall be changed into Article 52, with Items (2) and (3) deleted and Item (4) changed into Item (2) and amended as: "to implement the plan for economic and social development and the budget of its administrative area and conduct administrative work concerning the economy, education, science, culture, public health, physical culture, finance, civil affairs, public security, judicial administration and family planning in its administrative area."

Item (8) shall be changed into Item (6) and amended as: "to safeguard women's rights as endowed by the Constitution and the law, such as equality with men, equal pay for equal work and freedom of marriage."

23. Article 54 shall be added as follows: "Meetings of a local people's government at or above the county level shall consist of plenary meetings and executive meetings. The plenary meetings shall be attended by all the members of that people's government. The executive meetings of the people's government of a province, autonomous region, municipality directly under the Central Government, autonomous prefecture, or city divided into districts shall be attended, respectively, by the governor and deputy governors, chairman and vice-chairmen of the autonomous region, mayor and deputy mayors or prefect and deputy prefects, and additionally the secretary-general. The executive meetings of the people's government of a county, autonomous county, city not divided into districts, or municipal district shall be attended, respectively, by the head and deputy heads of the county, mayor and deputy mayors or head and deputy heads of the district. The governor, chairman of the autonomous region, mayor, prefect, or head of the county or district shall convene and preside over the plenary meetings and executive meetings of the people's government at the corresponding level. Important issues in government work must be discussed and decided at the executive meetings or plenary meeting of the respective government."

24. Article 38 shall be changed into Article 55, with a new paragraph added as the second paragraph, which shall read: "Auditing bodies shall be established by local people's governments at or above the county level. Local auditing bodies at various levels shall independently exercise their power of supervision through auditing in accordance with the law and shall be responsible to the people's governments at the corresponding levels and to the auditing body at the next higher level."

25. Article 42 shall be changed into Article 59, with the first paragraph amended as: "When necessary and with the approval of the State Council, the people's government of a province or autonomous region may establish certain agencies."

26. Chapter Five, "Supplementary Provisions," shall be added as follows: "Article 60 The people's congresses of provinces, autonomous regions, and municipalities directly under the Central Government and their stand-

ing committees may, in accordance with this Law and the actual situations, formulate specific provisions concerning problems that occur in the course of implementing this Law."

In addition, in accordance with the Constitution and this Decision, appropriate adjustments and revisions shall be made to the wording of some of the clauses and the order of some of the articles, paragraphs and items.

The Organic Law of the Local People's Congresses and Local People's Governments of the People's Republic of China shall be revised according to this Decision and promulgated anew.

The second paragraph of Article 35 of the Organic Law of the People's Courts of the People's Republic of China and the first paragraph of Article 22 of the Organic Law of the People's Procuratorates of the People's Republic of China shall be revised according to No. 18 of this Decision.

Annexe:

1. In accordance with this Decision, the second paragraph of Article 35 of the Organic Law of the People's Courts of the People's Republic of China, which reads, "The presidents of the intermediate people's courts established in prefectures of provinces or in municipalities directly under the Central Government shall be elected by the people's congresses of the provinces and municipalities directly under the Central Government, and their vice-presidents, chief judges and associate chief judges of divisions, and judges shall be appointed and removed by the standing committees of the people's congresses of the provinces and municipalities directly under the Central Government" shall be amended as: "The presidents, vice-presidents, chief judges and associate chief judges of divisions, and judges of the intermediate people's courts established in prefectures of provinces or autonomous regions, or in municipalities directly under the Central Government, shall be appointed and removed by the standing committees of the people's congresses of the respective provinces, autonomous regions or municipalities directly under the Central Government."

2. In accordance with this Decision, the first paragraph of Article 22 of the Organic Law of the People's Procuratorates of the People's Republic of China, which reads, "The chief procurators of the people's procuratorates of provinces, autonomous regions, and municipalities directly under the Central Government and their branches shall be elected and removed by the people's congresses of the respective provinces, autonomous regions, or municipalities directly under the Central Government; their deputy chief procurators, members of procuratorial committees and procurators shall be appointed and removed by the standing committees of the people's congresses at corresponding levels upon the recommendation of the chief procurators of the provinces, autonomous regions, and municipalities directly under the

Central Government," shall be amended as: "The chief procurators of the people's procuratorates of provinces, autonomous regions, and municipalities directly under the Central Government shall be elected and removed by the people's congresses of the respective provinces, autonomous regions, or municipalities directly under the Central Government. Their deputy chief procurators, members of procuratorial committees and procurators, and the chief procurators, deputy chief procurators, members of the procuratorial committees and procurators of the people's branch procuratorates shall be appointed and removed by the standing committees of the people's congresses at the corresponding levels, upon recommendation by the chief procurators of the people's procuratorates of the respective provinces, autonomous regions, or municipalities directly under the Central Government."

Appendix:

The Organic Law of the Local People's Congresses and Local People's Governments of the People's Republic of China

(Adopted at the Second Session of the Fifth National People's Congress on July 1, 1979;

Amended for the first time in accordance with the Resolution of the Fifth Session of the Fifth National People's Congress Revising Certain Provisions of the Organic Law of the Local People's Congresses and Local People's Governments of the People's Republic of China, adopted on December 10, 1982;

Amended for the second time in accordance with the Decision of the 18th Meeting of the Standing Committee of the Sixth National People's Congress Regarding the Revision of the Organic Law of the Local People's Congresses and Local People's Governments of the People's Republic of China, adopted on December 2, 1986)

Contents

Chapter I

General Provisions

Article 1 People's congresses and people's governments shall be established in provinces, autonomous regions, municipalities directly under the Central Government, autonomous prefectures, counties, autonomous counties, cities, municipal districts, townships, nationality townships, and towns.

Article 2 Standing committees shall be established by local people's congresses at and above the county level.

Article 3 The organs of self-government of autonomous regions, autonomous prefectures and autonomous counties shall, in addition to exercising the functions and powers specified in this Law, exercise the power of autonomy within the limits of their authority as prescribed by the Constitution, the Law on Regional National Autonomy and other laws.

Chapter II

Local People's Congresses at Various Levels

Article 4 Local people's congresses at various levels shall be local organs of state power.

Article 5 Deputies to the people's congresses of provinces, autonomous regions, municipalities directly under the Central Government, autonomous prefectures and cities divided into districts shall be elected by the people's congresses at the next lower level; deputies to the people's congresses of counties, autonomous counties, cities not divided into districts, municipal districts, townships, nationality townships, and towns shall be elected directly by their constituencies.

The number of deputies to the local people's congresses at various levels and the manner of their election shall be prescribed by the electoral law. There shall be an appropriate number of deputies elected from the minority nationalities in each administrative area.

Article 6 The term of office of the people's congresses of provinces, autonomous regions, municipalities directly under the Central Government, autonomous prefectures, and cities divided into districts shall be five years.

The term of office of the people's congresses of counties, autonomous counties, cities not divided into districts, municipal districts, townships, nationality townships, and towns shall be three years.

Article 7   The people's congresses of provinces, autonomous regions, and municipalities directly under the Central Government may, in light of the specific conditions and actual needs of their respective administrative areas, formulate and promulgate local regulations, which must not contravene the Constitution, the law and administrative rules and regulations; they shall report such local regulations to the Standing Committee of the National People's Congress and the State Council for the record.

The people's congresses of cities where provincial and autonomous regional people's governments are located and the people's congresses of relatively large cities, with the approval of the State Council, may, in light of the specific conditions and actual needs of their respective cities, formulate local regulations, which must not contravene the Constitution, the law, administrative rules and regulations, and the local regulations of their respective provinces and autonomous regions; they shall report such local regulations to the standing committees of the people's congresses of the respective provinces and autonomous regions for approval before implementation and for submission to the Standing Committee of the National People's Congress and the State Council for the record.

Article 8   Local people's congresses at and above the county level shall exercise the following functions and powers:

(1) ensure the observance and execution, in their respective administrative areas, of the Constitution, the law, administrative rules and regulations and the resolutions of the people's congresses and their standing committees at higher levels, and ensure the implementation of the state plan and the state budget;

(2) examine and approve the plans for national economic and social development, the budgets of their respective administrative areas and the reports on the implementation of such plans and budgets;

(3) discuss and decide on major issues in political, economic, educational, scientific, cultural, public health, and civil and nationality affairs in their respective administrative areas;

(4) elect the members of their respective standing committees;

(5) elect governors and deputy governors, chairmen and vice-chairmen of autonomous regions, mayors and deputy mayors, prefects and deputy prefects, and heads and deputy heads of counties and districts;

(6) elect the presidents of the people's courts and the chief procurators of the people's procuratorates at the corresponding levels; the election of the chief procurator of a people's procuratorate shall be reported to the chief procurator of the people's procuratorate at the next higher level, who shall submit it to the standing committee of the people's congress at that same

level for approval;

(7) elect deputies to the people's congresses at the next higher level;

(8) hear and examine reports on the work of the standing committees of the people's congresses at the corresponding levels;

(9) hear and examine reports on the work of the people's governments, the people's courts and the people's procuratorates at the corresponding levels;

(10) alter or annul inappropriate resolutions of the standing committees of the people's congresses at the corresponding levels;

(11) annul inappropriate decisions and orders of the people's governments at the corresponding levels;

(12) protect the socialist property owned by the whole people, property owned collectively by working people and citizens' legitimate private property, maintain public order and safeguard citizens' rights of the person and their democratic and other rights;

(13) safeguard the proper decision-making power of rural collective economic organizations;

(14) safeguard the rights of minority nationalities; and

(15) safeguard women's rights as endowed by the Constitution and the law, such as equality with men, equal pay for equal work and freedom of marriage.

Article 9   The people's congresses of townships, nationality townships, and towns shall exercise the following functions and powers:

(1) ensure the observance and execution, in their respective administrative areas, of the Constitution, the law, administrative rules and regulations, and the resolutions of the people's congresses and their standing committees at higher levels;

(2) adopt and promulgate resolutions within the scope of their functions and powers;

(3) decide, in accordance with state plans, on plans for the development of the economy, cultural affairs and public services in their respective administrative areas;

(4) examine and approve the budgets of their respective administrative areas as well as the reports on the implementation of the budgets;

(5) decide on plans for civil affairs in their respective administrative areas;

(6) elect heads and deputy heads of townships and towns;

(7) hear and examine reports on the work of the people's governments of townships, nationality townships, and towns;

(8) annul inappropriate decisions and orders of the people's governments of townships, nationality townships, and towns;

(9) protect the socialist property owned by the whole people, property owned collectively by working people and citizens' legitimate private prop-

erty, maintain public order and safeguard citizens' rights of the person and their democratic and other rights;

(10) safeguard the proper decision-making power of rural collective economic organizations;

(11) safeguard the rights of minority nationalities; and

(12) safeguard women's rights as endowed by the Constitution and the law, such as equality with men, equal pay for equal work and freedom of marriage.

In exercising their functions and powers, the people's congresses of townships, nationality townships, and towns in which minority nationalities live in concentrated communities shall adopt specific measures appropriate to the characteristics of the nationalities concerned.

Article 10 Local people's congresses at various levels shall have the power to remove from office members of the people's governments at the corresponding levels. Local people's congresses at or above the county level shall have the power to remove from office members of their standing committees and the presidents of the people's courts and the chief procurators of the people's procuratorates elected by those standing committees. The removal of the chief procurator of a people's procuratorate shall be reported to the chief procurator of the people's procuratorate at the next higher level, who shall submit the matter to the standing committee of the people's congress at that same level for approval.

Article 11 Local people's congresses at various levels shall meet in session at least once a year.

A session of a local people's congress may be convened at any time upon the proposal of one fifth of its deputies.

Article 12 Sessions of local people's congresses at or above the county level shall be convened by their standing committees.

Article 13 A preliminary meeting shall be held for each session of a local people's congress at or above the county level to elect the presidium and secretary-general of that session, adopt the agenda for the session and decide on other preparations.

The preliminary meeting shall be presided over by the standing committee of the people's congress. The preliminary meeting for the first session of a people's congress shall be presided over by the standing committee of the preceding people's congress at the corresponding level.

When a local people's congress at or above the county level meets, its session shall be conducted by the presidium.

When a local people's congress at or above the county level meets, it shall propose a number of deputy secretaries-general; the choice of deputy secretaries-general shall be decided by the presidium.

Article 14 When the people's congress of a township, nationality township, or town holds a session, it shall elect a presidium, which shall preside over the session and be responsible for convening the next session of that people's congress.

Article 15   The first session of each local people's congress at any level shall be convened, within two months after the election of its deputies, by the standing committee of the preceding people's congress at the corresponding level or by the presidium of the preceding session of the people's congress of the township, nationality township, or town.

Article 16   Members of local people's governments at various levels, the presidents of the people's courts and the chief procurators of the people's procuratorates shall attend sessions of the people's congresses at the corresponding levels as nonvoting delegates; responsible persons of government agencies and people's organizations concerned may, by decision of the presidiums, attend sessions of the people's congresses at the corresponding levels as nonvoting delegates.

Article 17   When a local people's congress holds its sessions, its presidium, standing committee and special committees and the people's government at the corresponding level may submit bills and proposals to that people's congress within the scope of its functions and powers. The presidium shall decide to refer such bills and proposals to a session of the people's congress for deliberation, or to simultaneously refer them to relevant special committees for deliberation and reports before the presidium decides, upon examination of such reports, to submit them to the people's congress for a vote.

Ten or more deputies to a local people's congress at or above the county level or five or more deputies to the people's congress of a township, nationality township, or town may jointly submit a bill or proposal to the people's congress at the corresponding level within the scope of its functions and powers. The presidium shall decide whether to place the bill or proposal on the agenda of the people's congress or to first refer it to a relevant special committee for deliberation and a recommendation on whether to place it on the agenda before the presidium makes such a decision.

Deliberation shall be terminated on a bill or proposal submitted to a people's congress if the party that submitted the bill or proposal requests its withdrawal before it has been referred to the congress for a vote.

Article 18   Suggestions, criticisms and complaints on any aspect of work put forward by deputies to a local people's congress at or above the county level to that people's congress and its standing committee shall be referred by the administrative office of the standing committee to the departments and organizations concerned for consideration, disposition and reply.

Suggestions, criticisms and complaints on any aspect of work put forward by deputies to the people's congress of a township, nationality township, or town to that people's congress shall be referred by its presidium to the departments and organizations concerned for consideration, disposition and reply.

Article 19   When a local people's congress conducts an election or adopts a resolution, a majority vote of all the deputies shall be required.

Article 20   Members of the standing committees of local people's congresses at and above the county level, governors and deputy governors, chairmen and vice-chairmen of autonomous regions, mayors and deputy mayors, prefects and deputy prefects, heads and deputy heads of counties, districts, townships and towns, presidents of people's courts and chief procurators of people's procuratorates at and above the county level shall be nominated by the presidium of the people's congress at the corresponding level or jointly nominated by a minimum of ten deputies.

In elections for chairmen and secretaries-general of the standing committees of local people's congresses, governors, chairmen of autonomous regions, mayors, prefects, heads of counties, districts, townships and towns, presidents of people's courts and chief procurators of people's procuratorates, there shall generally be one more candidate for each vacancy, and the election method of having more candidates than vacancies shall be adopted. If only one candidate is nominated, the election method of having the same number of candidates as vacancies may be adopted. In elections for vice-chairmen of the standing committees of the people's congresses, deputy governors, vice-chairmen of autonomous regions, deputy mayors, deputy prefects, and deputy heads of counties, districts, townships and towns, there shall be one to three more candidates than the number of vacancies for each post; for members of the standing committees of the people's congresses, there shall be one tenth to one fifth more candidates than vacancies. The election method here used shall be that of having more candidates than vacancies. If the number of candidates nominated exceeds the guidelines mentioned above, the presidium of the relevant people's congress shall submit the entire list of candidates to all the deputies for consideration and discussion, and the official list of candidates shall be determined according to the majority opinion of the deputies.

Elections shall be conducted by secret ballot. The deputies may vote for or against any of the candidates that have been determined, or may instead elect any other deputies or voters or abstain from voting.

When by-elections are held by the local people's congresses at various levels for chairmen, vice-chairmen, secretaries-general and members of their standing committees, governors, deputy governors, chairmen and vice-chairmen of autonomous regions, mayors, deputy mayors, prefects, deputy prefects, heads and deputy heads of counties, districts, townships and towns, presidents of people's courts, and chief procurators of people's procuratorates, the number of candidates may exceed or equal the number of vacancies, and the election procedures and methods shall be decided by the people's congresses at the corresponding levels.

Article 21 When a local people's congress at or above the county level is in session, its presidium, its standing committee, or a joint group of at least one tenth of its deputies may submit a proposal to remove from office members of its standing committee or leading personnel of the people's government, the president of the people's court or the chief procurator of the people's procuratorate at the corresponding level; the presidium shall refer such proposals to the congress for deliberation.

When the people's congress of a township, nationality township, or town is in session, its presidium or a joint group of at least one fifth of its deputies may submit a proposal to remove from office the head or deputy heads of the township or town; the presidium shall refer such proposals to the congress for deliberation.

Article 22 A leading functionary of a local people's government at any level, a standing committee member of a local people's congress at or above the county level, the president of a people's court or the chief procurator of a people's procuratorate may submit his resignation to the people's congress at the corresponding level, which shall decide whether or not to accept the resignation; if the people's congress is not in session, such resignations may be submitted to its standing committee, which shall decide whether or not to accept the resignations. If the standing committee decides to accept a resignation, it shall report it to its people's congress for the record. A resignation of the chief procurator of a people's procuratorate must be reported to the chief procurator of the people's procuratorate at the next higher level, who shall refer it to the standing committee of the people's congress at the corresponding level for approval.

Article 23 When a local people's congress at any level is in session, a joint group of at least ten of its deputies may address questions to the people's government or any of its departments, the people's court or the people's procuratorate at the corresponding level. The presidium shall decide to refer such questions to the organ addressed, which must responsibly answer the questions at the session.

Article 24 When a local people's congress at any level examines a bill or proposal, its deputies may address questions to the local state organs concerned, which shall send their personnel to the congress to give explanations.

Article 25 The people's congresses of provinces, autonomous regions, municipalities directly under the Central Government, autonomous prefectures, and cities divided into districts may, where necessary, establish special committees such as legislative (political and law) committees, finance and economic committees, and education, science, culture and public health committees. The special committees shall work under the direction of the respective people's congresses; when the people's congresses are not in session, they shall work under the direction of the standing committees of the people's congresses.

Nominations for the chairman, vice-chairmen and members of a special committee shall be made by the presidium from among the deputies and approved by the people's congress. When the people's congress is not in session, its standing committee may appoint additional individual vice-chairmen and some members of the special committees through nomination by its council of chairmen and approval by a meeting of the standing committee.

The special committees shall discuss, examine and draw up relevant bills and draft resolutions under the direction of the people's congresses and their standing committees at the corresponding levels; they shall make investigations and studies of and put forward proposals on matters related to those committees and within the scope of the functions and powers of the respective people's congresses and their standing committees.

Article 26   A local people's congress at or above the county level and its standing committee may appoint committees of inquiry into specific questions.

Article 27   The credentials committee established at the first session of each people's congress of a township, nationality township, and town shall exercise its functions and powers until the term of office of that people's congress expires.

Article 28   The term of office of the deputies to a local people's congress at any level shall begin with the first session of that people's congress and shall expire at the first session of the succeeding people's congress at the same level.

Article 29   Deputies to local people's congresses at various levels and members of their standing committees may not be legally liable for their speeches and voting at sessions of the people's congresses or meetings of their standing committees.

Article 30   No deputy to a local people's congress at or above the county level may be arrested or placed on criminal trial without the consent of the presidium of that people's congress or, when the people's congress is not in session, without the consent of its standing committee. If a deputy is caught in the act of crime and detained, the public security organ executing the detention shall immediately report the matter to the presidium or the standing committee of that people's congress.

Article 31   When deputies to local people's congresses at various levels attend people's congress sessions or perform their duties as deputies, the state shall, as necessary, provide them with round-trip travelling expenses and requisite material facilities or subsidies.

Article 32   Deputies to local people's congresses at various levels shall maintain close contact with the units that elected them or with their constituencies; publicize laws and policies; assist the people's governments at the corresponding levels in their work; and relay the opinions and demands of the masses to the people's congresses, their standing committees and the people's governments.

Deputies to the people's congresses of provinces, autonomous regions, municipalities directly under the Central Government, autonomous prefectures, and cities divided into districts may attend, as nonvoting delegates, sessions of the people's congresses of the units which elected them.

Deputies to the people's congresses of counties, autonomous counties, cities not divided into districts, municipal districts, townships, nationality townships, and towns shall apportion among themselves the task of maintaining contact with their constituencies; in residential areas or production units with three or more deputies, a deputies group may be set up to help promote the work of the people's government at the corresponding level.

Article 33   Deputies to the people's congresses of provinces, autonomous regions, municipalities directly under the Central Government, autonomous prefectures, and cities divided into districts shall be subject to supervision by the units which elected them; deputies to the people's congresses of counties, autonomous counties, cities not divided into districts, municipal districts, townships, nationality townships, and towns shall be subject to supervision by their constituencies.

Electoral units and voters shall have the power to recall and replace at any time the deputies they elect to a local people's congress at any level. The recall and replacement of a deputy shall require a majority vote of all the deputies of the unit which elected him or of all the voters in his electoral district.

Article 34   In the event that a deputy to a local people's congress is unable to perform his duties as deputy for any reason, the unit which elected him or the voters in the electoral district shall hold a by-election to replace him.

Chapter III

The Standing Committees of Local People's Congresses at and Above the County Level

Article 35   Standing committees shall be established by the people's congresses of provinces, autonomous regions, municipalities directly under the Central Government, autonomous prefectures, counties, autonomous counties, cities and municipal districts.

The standing committee of a local people's congress at or above the county level shall be a permanent organ of that people's congress and shall be responsible to and report on its work to it.

Article 36 The standing committee of the people's congress of a province, autonomous region, municipality directly under the Central Government, autonomous prefecture, or city divided into districts shall be composed of a chairman, vice-chairmen, a secretary-general and members to be elected by the people's congress from among its deputies.

The standing committee of a people's congress of a county, autonomous county, city not divided into districts, or municipal district shall be composed of a chairman, vice-chairmen and members to be elected by the people's congress from among its deputies.

No one on the standing committee may hold office in an administrative, judicial or procuratorial organ of the state; if a member assumes any of the above-mentioned offices, he must resign from his post on the standing committee.

The number of members on the various standing committees shall be as follows:

(1) 35 to 65 members for those of provinces, autonomous regions, and municipalities directly under the Central Government and no more than 85 members for those of provinces with extremely large populations;

(2) 13 to 35 members for those of autonomous prefectures and cities and no more than 45 members for those of cities with extremely large populations;

(3) 11 to 19 members for those of counties, autonomous counties, and municipal districts and no more than 29 members for those of counties or municipal districts with extremely large populations.

Article 37 The standing committee of a local people's congress at or above the county level shall have the same term of office as that people's congress and shall exercise its functions and powers until a new standing committee is elected by the succeeding people's congress at the same level.

Article 38 The standing committees of the people's congresses of provinces, autonomous regions, and municipalities directly under the Central Government may, when their respective people's congresses are not in session, formulate and promulgate local regulations in accordance with the specific conditions and actual needs of their respective administrative areas, provided that these regulations do not contravene the Constitution, the law and administrative rules and regulations; they shall report such local regulations to the Standing Committee of the National People's Congress and the State Council for the record.

The standing committees of the people's congresses of cities where the provincial and autonomous regional people's governments are located and the standing committees of the people's congresses of relatively large cities, with the approval of the State Council, may, when their respective people's congresses are not in session, formulate local regulations in accordance with the specific conditions and actual needs of their respective cities, provided that these regulations do not contravene the Constitution, the law, administrative rules and regulations and the local regulations of the respective provinces and autonomous regions; they shall submit such local regulations to the standing committees of the people's congresses of the respective provinces and autonomous regions for approval before implementation and for submission to the Standing Committee of the National People's Congress and the State Council for the record.

Article 39   The standing committee of a local people's congress at or above the county level shall exercise the following functions and powers:

(1) ensure the observance and execution, in its administrative area, of the Constitution, the law, administrative rules and regulations and the resolutions of the people's congresses and their standing committees at higher levels;

(2) direct or conduct the election of deputies to its people's congress;

(3) convene sessions of its people's congress;

(4) discuss and decide on major issues in political, economic, cultural, educational, scientific, cultural, public health, and civil and nationality affairs in its administrative area;

(5) decide, upon the recommendation of the people's government at the corresponding level, to make partial alterations in the plans for economic and social development and the budgets of its respective administrative area;

(6) supervise the work of the people's government, people's court and people's procuratorate at the corresponding level, maintain contact with the deputies of its people's congress and receive and handle accusations and complaints from the people against the above-mentioned organs and state functionaries;

(7) annul inappropriate resolutions of the people's congress and its standing committee at the next lower level;

(8) annul inappropriate decisions and orders of the people's government at the corresponding level;

(9) decide, when its people's congress is not in session, on the appointment or removal of individual deputy governors, vice-chairmen of the autonomous region, deputy mayors, deputy prefects and deputy heads of the county or district; when, for any reason, the governor, chairman of the autonomous region, mayor, prefect, or head of the county or district, president of the people's court or chief procurator of the people's procuratorate is unable to perform his duties, the standing committee shall choose a person from among the deputy heads of the people's government, people's court or people's procuratorate at the corresponding level to act on his behalf; the choice of an acting chief procurator must be reported to the people's procuratorate and the standing committee of the people's congress

at the next higher level for the record;

(10) decide, upon nomination by the governor, chairman of the autonomous region, mayor, prefect, or head of the county or district, on the appointment or removal of the secretary-general and the department and bureau directors, commission chairmen and section chiefs of the people's government at the corresponding level and report such decisions to the people's government at the next higher level for the record;

(11) appoint or remove, in accordance with the provisions of the Organic Law of the People's Courts and the Organic Law of the People's Procuratorates, vice-presidents, chief judges and associate chief judges of divisions, members of the judicial committees and judges of the people's courts, appoint or remove deputy chief procurators, members of the procuratorial committees and procurators of the people's procuratorates, and approve the appointment or removal of the chief procurators of the people's procuratorates at the next lower level; the standing committee of the people's congress of a province, autonomous region, or municipality directly under the Central Government shall, upon nomination by its council of chairmen, decide on the appointment or removal of presidents of intermediate people's courts established in prefectures of provinces and autonomous regions or in municipalities directly under the Central Government and, upon nomination by the chief procurator of the people's procuratorate of a province, autonomous region or municipality directly under the Central Government, decide on the appointment or removal of chief procurators of people's branch procuratorates.

(12) decide, when its people's congress is not in session, on the removal from office of individual deputy governors, vice-chairmen of the autonomous region, deputy mayors, deputy prefects and deputy heads of the county or district; decide on the removal from office of personnel it has appointed among other members of the people's government, vice-presidents, chief judges and associate chief judges of divisions, members of the judicial committees and judges of the people's courts, deputy chief procurators, members of the procuratorial committees and procurators of the people's procuratorates, presidents of intermediate people's courts and chief procurators of people's branch procuratorates, all at the corresponding level.

(13) conduct a by-election, when its people's congress is not in session, in the event that a post of deputy to the people's congress at the next higher level becomes vacant and recall and replace individual deputies; and

⮞ (14) decide on the conferment of local titles of honour.

Article 40   Meetings of a standing committee shall be convened by its chairman and held at least once every other month.

Resolutions of a standing committee shall be adopted by a majority vote of all its members.

Article 41 A local people's government at or above the county level or a special committee of the people's congress at the corresponding level may submit bills and proposals to its standing committee within its scope of functions and powers. The council of chairmen shall decide to refer them to a meeting of the standing committee for deliberation or to first refer them to relevant special committees for deliberation and reports before submitting them to a meeting of the standing committee for deliberation.

Five or more standing committee members of the people's congress of a province, autonomous region, municipality directly under the Central Government, autonomous prefecture, or city divided into districts or three or more standing committee members of a people's congress at the county level may jointly submit a bill or proposal to its standing committee within its scope of functions and powers. The council of chairmen shall decide whether to refer the bill or proposal to a meeting of the standing committee for deliberation or to first refer it to a relevant special committee for deliberation and a report before deciding on whether to submit it to a meeting of the standing committee for deliberation.

Article 42 A joint group of five or more standing committee members of the people's congress of a province, autonomous region, municipality directly under the Central Government, autonomous prefecture, or city divided into districts or a joint group of three or more standing committee members of a people's congress at the county level may, when the standing committee is in session, address questions to the people's government, people's court or people's procuratorate at the corresponding level. The council of chairmen shall decide whether to refer it to the organ addressed for a reply.

Article 43 The chairman, vice-chairmen and secretary-general of the standing committee of the people's congress of a province, autonomous region, municipality directly under the Central Government, autonomous prefecture, or city divided into districts shall constitute its council of chairmen; the chairman and vice-chairmen of the standing committee of the people's congress of a county, autonomous county, city not divided into districts, or municipal district shall constitute its council of chairmen. The council of chairmen shall handle the important day-to-day work of its standing committee.

Article 44 In the event that the chairman of a standing committee is unable to work owing to feeble health or that his office falls vacant, the standing committee shall select one of the vice-chairmen to act on behalf of the chairman until he recovers his health or a new chairman is elected by the people's congress.

Article 45 The standing committee of each local people's congress at or above the county level shall establish a credentials committee.

Nominations for the chairman, vice-chairmen and members of a credentials committee shall be made by the council of chairmen of the standing committee from among the members of the standing committee and adopted at a meeting of the standing committee.

Article 46   Standing committees may set up administrative offices according to their needs in work.

Chapter   IV

Local People's Governments at Various Levels

Article 47   Local people's governments at various levels shall be the executive organs of the local people's congresses at the corresponding levels; they shall be the local organs of state administration.

Article 48   Local people's governments at various levels shall be responsible to and report on their work to the people's congresses at the corresponding levels and to the state administrative organs at the next higher level. Local people's governments at and above the county level shall be responsible to and report on their work to the standing committees of the people's congresses at the corresponding levels when the congresses are not in session.

The local people's governments at various levels throughout the country shall be state administrative organs under the unified leadership of the State Council and shall be subordinate to it.

Article 49   The people's government of a province, autonomous region, municipality directly under the Central Government, autonomous prefecture, or city divided into districts shall be respectively composed of the governor and deputy governors, the chairman and vice-chairmen of the autonomous region, the ,mayor and deputy mayors, or the prefect and deputy prefects, and additionally the secretary-general, department directors, bureau directors and commission chairmen.

The people's government of a county, autonomous county, city not divided into districts, or municipal district shall be respectively composed of the head and deputy heads of the county, the mayor and deputy mayors, or the head and deputy heads of the district, and additionally the bureau directors and section chiefs.

The people's government of a township or nationality township shall have a township head and deputy heads. The head of a nationality township shall be a citizen of the minority nationality that establishes the nationality township. The people's government of a town shall have a town head and deputy heads.

Article 50   The term of office of the people's governments of provinces, autonomous regions, municipalities directly under the Central Government, autonomous prefectures, and cities divided into districts shall be five years. The term of office of the people's governments of counties, autonomous counties, cities not divided into districts, municipal districts, townships, nationality townships, and towns shall be three years.

Article 51   A local people's government at or above the county level shall exercise the following functions and powers:

(1) implement the resolutions of the people's congress and its standing committee at the corresponding level as well as decisions and orders of state administrative organs at higher levels, formulate administrative measures and issue decisions and orders. The people's government of a province, autonomous region, municipality directly under the Central Government or city where a provincial or autonomous regional people's government is located may draw up regulations in accordance with the law and the State Council's administrative rules and regulations; with the approval of the state council, the people's government of a relatively large city may do the same;

(2) direct the work of its subordinate departments and of the people's governments at lower levels;

(3) alter or annul inappropriate orders and directives of its subordinate departments and inappropriate decisions and orders of the people's governments at lower levels;

(4) appoint or remove personnel in state administrative organs, train them, appraise their performance and award or punish them according to the provisions of the law;

(5) implement the plan for national economic and social development and the budget, and conduct administrative work concerning the economy, education, science, culture, public health, physical culture, urban and rural development, finance, civil affairs, public security, nationality affairs, judicial administration, supervision and family planning within its administrative area;

(6) protect socialist property owned by all the people, property owned collectively by working people and citizens' legitimate private property and maintain public order and safeguard citizens' rights of the person and their democratic and other rights;

(7) safeguard the proper decision-making power of rural collective economic organizations;

(8) safeguard the rights of minority nationalities and respect their folkways and customs, assist those areas where minority nationalities live in concentrated communities within its sphere of jurisdiction to exercise regional autonomy in accordance with the Constitution and the law and assist the various minority nationalities in their political, economic and cultural development;

(9) safeguard women's rights as endowed by the Constitution and the

law, such as equality with men, equal pay for equal work and freedom of marriage; and

(10) handle other matters assigned by state administrative organs at higher levels.

Article 52 The people's government of a township, nationality township, or town shall exercise the following functions and powers:

(1) implement the resolutions of the people's congress at the corresponding level and the decisions and orders of state administrative organs at higher levels and issue decisions and orders;

(2) implement the plan for economic and social development and the budget of its administrative area and conduct administrative work concerning the economy, education, science, culture, public health, physical culture, finance, civil affairs, public security, judicial administration and family planning in its administrative area;

(3) protect socialist property owned by the whole people, property owned collectively by working people and citizens' legitimate private property and maintain public order and safeguard citizens' rights of the person and their democratic and other rights;

(4) safeguard the proper decision-making power of rural collective economic organizations;

(5) safeguard the rights of minority nationalities and respect their folkways and customs;

(6) safeguard women's rights as endowed by the Constitution and the law, such as equality with men, equal pay for equal work and freedom of marriage; and

(7) handle other matters assigned by the people's governments at higher levels.

Article 53 Overall responsibility for the work of local people's governments at various levels shall be assumed respectively by governors, chairmen of autonomous regions, mayors, prefects, and heads of counties, districts, townships and towns.

The governors, chairmen of autonomous regions, mayors, prefects and heads of counties, districts, townships and towns shall direct the work of their local people's governments at the corresponding levels.

Article 54 Meetings of a local people's government at or above the county level shall consist of plenary meetings and executive meetings. The plenary meetings shall be attended by all the members of that people's government. The executive meetings of the people's government of a province, autonomous region, municipality directly under the Central Government, autonomous prefecture, or city divided into districts shall be attended, respectively, by the governor and deputy governors, chairman and vice-chairmen of the autonomous region, mayor and deputy mayors or prefect and deputy prefects, and additionally the secretaries-general. The executive meetings of the people's government of a county, autonomous county, city not divided into districts, or municipal district shall be attended, respectively, by the head and deputy heads of the county, mayor and deputy mayors or head and deputy heads of the district. The governor, chairman of the autonomous region, mayor, prefect, or head of the county or district shall convene and preside over the plenary meetings and executive meetings of the people's government at the corresponding level. Important issues in government work must be discussed and decided at the executive meetings or plenary meetings of the respective government.

Article 55 Local people's governments at various levels shall establish necessary working offices in accordance with work requirements and the principle of compact and efficient organization.

Auditing bodies shall be established by local people's governments at or above the county level. Local auditing bodies at various levels shall independently exercise their power of supervision through auditing in accordance with the law and shall be responsible to the people's governments at the corresponding levels and to the auditing body at the next higher level.

The establishment, increase, reduction or amalgamation of such working offices as departments, bureaus and commissions under people's governments of provinces, autonomous regions, and municipalities directly under the Central Government shall be reported by the respective people's governments to the State Council for approval.

The establishment, increase, reduction or amalgamation of such working offices as bureaus and sections under people's governments of autonomous prefectures, counties, autonomous counties, cities and municipal districts shall be reported by the respective people's governments to the people's governments at the next higher level for approval.

Article 56 Each department, bureau, commission and section shall have a department director, bureau director, commission chairman and section chief, respectively, and may have deputies to those positions when necessary.

A general office shall have a director and, when necessary, deputy directors.

The people's government of a province, autonomous region, municipality directly under the Central Government, autonomous prefecture, or city divided into districts shall have a secretary-general and deputy secretaries-general.

Article 57 The working offices of the people's governments of provinces, autonomous regions, and municipalities directly under the Central Government shall be under the unified leadership of their respective people's governments as well as the leadership or operational guidance of competent departments of the State Council.

The working offices of the people's governments of autonomous prefectures, counties, autonomous counties, cities and municipal districts shall be under the unified leadership of their respective people's governments as well as the leadership or operational guidance of competent departments of the people's governments at higher levels.

Article 58   The people's governments of provinces, autonomous regions, municipalities directly under the Central Government, autonomous prefectures, counties, autonomous counties, cities and municipal districts shall assist in the work of the state organs, enterprises and institutions that are located in their respective administrative areas but not under their jurisdiction, and shall supervise them in the observance and implementation of laws and policies.

Article 59   When necessary and with the approval of the State Council, the people's government of a province or autonomous region may establish certain agencies.

When necessary and with the approval of the people's government of a province, autonomous region, or municipality directly under the Central Government, the people's government of a county or autonomous county may establish district offices as its agencies.

With the approval of the people's government at the next higher level, the people's government of a municipal district or city not divided into districts may establish neighbourhood offices as its agencies.

Chapter   V

Supplementary Provisions

Article 60   The people's congresses of provinces, autonomous regions, and municipalities directly under the Central Government and their standing committees may, in accordance with this Law and the actual situations, formulate specific provisions concerning problems that occur in the course of implementing this Law.

Decision of the Standing Committee of the National People's Congress on Approving the Opening of Nanjing Port on the Yangtze River to Foreign Vessels

(Adopted at the 14th Meeting of the Standing Committee of the Sixth National People's Congress on January 20, 1986)

After considering the proposal put forward by the Central Military Commission for approval of the opening of Nanjing Port to foreign vessels, the 14th Meeting of the Standing Committee of the Sixth National People's Congress has decided to approve the opening of Nanjing Port on the Yangtze River to foreign vessels. The State Council is authorized to grant approval in the future when there is a need to open other ports along the Yangtze River between Nanjing Port and the mouth of the river to foreign vessels.

Decision of the Standing Committee of the National People's Congress on the Time of Election of Deputies to the People's Congresses at County and Township Levels

(Adopted at the 17th Meeting of the Standing Committee of the Sixth National People's Congress on September 5, 1986)

The 17th Meeting of the Standing Committee of the Sixth National People's Congress has decided that, in accordance with the provisions of Article 98 of the Constitution of the People's Republic of China for the term of office of county and township people's congresses, the election of deputies to the next people's congresses at the county and township levels shall be conducted before the end of 1987.